解字与翻译

——叩启中华文化的知识之门

赵 纬 主编

北 京
冶 金 工 业 出 版 社
2018

内 容 提 要

本书介绍了汉译英的一些基本翻译方法，这将有助于读者进一步熟悉与运用英语，从而准确地将我国的文化经典译成英文。书中汉文字例的英译诗、词、曲及文章（节选）有助于读者对汉字字义及其使用的理解和掌握。

本书可供学习中英文翻译的读者阅读与使用，也可供相关专业的大专院校师生参考。

图书在版编目（CIP）数据

解字与翻译：叩启中华文化的知识之门/赵纬主编．—北京：冶金工业出版社，2018.10

ISBN 978-7-5024-7810-0

Ⅰ.①解…　Ⅱ.①赵…　Ⅲ.①英语—翻译—研究—中国　Ⅳ.①H315.9

中国版本图书馆 CIP 数据核字（2018）第 136650 号

出 版 人　谭学余

地　　址　北京市东城区嵩祝院北巷 39 号　邮编　100009　电话　(010)64027926

网　　址　www.cnmip.com.cn　电子信箱　yjcbs@cnmip.com.cn

责任编辑　戈　兰　美术编辑　彭子赫　版式设计　孙跃红

责任校对　石　静　责任印制　李玉山

ISBN 978-7-5024-7810-0

冶金工业出版社出版发行；各地新华书店经销；固安华明印业有限公司印刷

2018 年 10 月第 1 版，2018 年 10 月第 1 次印刷

169mm×239mm；17 印张；332 千字；264 页

76.00 元

冶金工业出版社　投稿电话　(010)64027932　投稿信箱　tougao@cnmip.com.cn

冶金工业出版社营销中心　电话　(010)64044283　传真　(010)64027893

冶金书店　地址　北京市东四西大街 46 号(100010)　电话　(010)65289081(兼传真)

冶金工业出版社天猫旗舰店　yjgycbs.tmall.com

（本书如有印装质量问题，本社营销中心负责退换）

前　　言

现在世界上越来越多的人在学习中文，又有八亿左右的人在使用英文，中文和英文是世界上用得最多的语言。无论是学习中文，还是运用英文，“识字”是第一要件。本书中介绍汉字的构成为普及性内容，目的在于使英语读者能够较为便捷地认识汉字、使用汉字；“译法点滴”中汉译英一些基本翻译方法的介绍将助益于汉语读者进一步熟悉与运用英语：在不超越规矩的前提下发挥其在翻译时的主观能动性，徜徉于汉、英的语言世界，把我国的文化经典译成英文，向世界宏扬中国的古典文化，为建设更加光辉灿烂的世界文化略尽绵薄之力。

书中含有汉文字例的英译诗、词、曲及文章（均为节选）有助于英语读者对汉字字义及其使用的理解和掌握；其上自春秋，下迄现代的部分优秀文学作品及其220多位作者和他们的字字珠玑对引导读者叩启中华文化的知识之门将会有所启迪。

以下是体例方面的几点说明：

（1）第一部分“汉字的构成方式”对汉字的构成作了较为详细的介绍，因此，除象形、会意和部分需解释的形声字外，其他不再对“构成”逐一分析。

（2）例字所对应的英译中，除不对应的情况，其余不做解释。

（3）翻译方法的选择基于汉译英的基本需要及例字译文所显现的技巧。

（4）在形声字中，声旁只有通过繁体才能体现的汉文字例，在简体字旁的括号里一般会给出其繁体形式。

本书第三部分的副主编为张怡老师。张怡老师对本书的编写工作给予了大力支持与帮助，在此表示衷心的感谢。

编　者

2018年4月

目　　录

第一部分　汉字的构成

汉字集象形、语音和语意三者于一体。考虑到字形和字义之间的关联，介绍“汉字的构成”和“以形寓意”的部首偏旁将在一定程度上起到纲举目张的作用。

了解汉字的构成，尤其是对占汉字总数百分之八十以上的形声字来说，不失为认字的一条捷径。

古人归纳出汉字构成的六种方式：指事、象形、形声、会意、转注和假借。

（1）指事字由象征性的符号构成。如“上”字写作“丄”，“下”字写作“丅”。

（2）象形字由描摹实物的形状而构成，其所代表的词即为所像之物。

（3）会意字会合了两字或三字的意义，以组成一个新字的意义。如“信”字，“人言为信”，表示人说的话有信用。

（4）形声字由表示字义的形旁和表明字音的声旁两部分组成[9]。如由形旁的“弓”和声旁的“玄”组成弦；形旁的“木”和声旁的“风”组成“枫”。

（5）转注字由意义上相同或相近的字彼此互相解释而成。如《说文》“老”字的解释是“考也”，“考”字的解释是“老也”。以“考”注“老”，以“老”注“考”，所以叫转注。

（6）假借字就是借用已有的文字表示语言中同音或音近而不同义的词（实际上是在没有专用字的情况下不顾及汉字的形义关系，只把汉字当做标音符号使用[9]）。如“耳”，本意为“耳朵”，假借为表示限止的语气词，相当于“而已”、“罢了”。

除以上六种构成方式外，汉字中还有一种合体字，由两个或两个以上独体字组成。如“轮”由“车”和“仑”两个独体字构成。

“字根”（部首）是构成汉字的最基本单位[9]。尽管汉字形体各不相同，但具有相同字根的汉字意味着其意思来自同一根源。因此，了解部首偏旁的含义，对于了解同一部首所有汉字的含义在一定程度上可以略有所知。

第二部分　独体字部首偏旁

一、二画

力

由“**力**”组合的字，一般与使肌肉张缩的劳作、经营管理的功劳、抵御大灾难的能力有关。例字中除“**男**、**劳**、**幼**、**劣**、**力**”外，其他为形声字，其中“**勇**”为下形上声，余者右形左声。

动（動）

1. 竹喧归浣女，　Din comes from the bamboo forest when the washer-maids homeward go,
莲**动**下渔舟。　The lotuses ***sway*** when a fishing boat sails below.[13]
《山居秋暝》　“A View of the Autumn Evening Near My Mountain Villa”
（唐）王维　（The Tang Dynasty） Wang Wei

2. 万里寒光生积雪，　Cold light comes from the vast stretch of snow white,
三边曙色**动**危旌，　The lofty banners on the three frontiers ***flutter*** high up in the dawning light.[13]
《望蓟门》　“Looking at Jimen in the Distance”
（唐）祖咏　（The Tang Dynasty） Zu Yong

3. 试拂雪衣如雪色，　Hearing of the above-mentioned news he scrubs his armor snow-white,
聊持宝剑**动**星文。　And waves his sword so that the seven stars inlaid on it ***flash*** light.[13]
《老将行》　“Song of an Old General”
（唐）王维　（The Tang Dynasty） Wang Wei

4. 星临万户**动**，　Thousands of the palace doors ***glitter*** under the starlight,
月傍九霄多。　Towering near the moon the palace gets more moonlight.[13]
《春宿左省》　“Staying Overnight at the Left Court in Spring”
（唐）杜甫　（The Tang Dynasty） Du Fu

【译法点滴】 通过上下文语境来确定原文中“字”的意义

翻译的过程主要涉及理解和表达两个阶段。理解是表达的前提，首先要通过对上下文（上下文是一种常见的语境类型）的理解来确定原文中所要翻译的字之意义。任何语言都是在一定的语言环境中进行的，同一个字在不同的上下文中，其翻译的结果就不尽相同，所以脱离语境的翻译都不可能准确无误。

这里通过对以上 4 例中“动”的翻译来说明理解上下文的必要性。

4 例中虽同为一个汉语的“动”，但因其所处之上下文的不同，其译文自然有异。**例 1** 之“动”指“渔舟”在水中晃动，故其译文取“**sway**”（to move from side to side）。**例 2** 之“动”指的是旌旗的飘动、摇动，译文取“**flutter**”（to move lightly and quickly）。**例 3**“聊持宝剑***动***星文”之“动”的译文在于“星文”。“星文”指剑上所嵌之七星文。诗的题目“老将行”说明了此诗的主语是“老将”（“行”是古诗的一种体裁），其整体意思是：老将把昔日的铠甲揩拭得雪亮闪光，而且手持宝剑练起武功。此“动”意在显示出星光闪耀：因其练起武功，所持之剑上下翻飞，剑上所嵌的七星文看起来如星光般一闪一闪的，故译文取“**flash**”（to shine very brightly for a short time）。**例 4** 之“动”译为“**glitter**”。同为星光，“flash”着意于“闪烁”，“glitter”（to shine brightly with little flashes of light）在此则侧重于体现夜空中星光所具有的光照作用。“星临万户***动***”之译文体现出了那种只有在星光映照之下才可闪现出的屋影之错落而产生的动感。

由此可见，没有理解，翻译也就无从谈起。

男：会意字，言男用力于田也。[9]

男儿本自重横行，	***Men*** by nature like to run amok on horses,
天子非常赐颜色。	Moreover the emperor bestows on them special glories. [13]
《燕歌行》	“Song of the Northern Frontiers”
（唐）高适	（The Tang Dynasty） Gao Shi

劳（勞）：会意字，表示火灾烧屋，用力救火的人十分辛苦。[9]

伯仲之间见伊吕，	His talent was as good as that of Yi Yin and Lu Shang,
指挥若定失萧曹。	His calm command outdid that of Xiao He and Cao Can.
运移汉祚终难复，	The fate of the Han Dynasty had ended and he couldn't turn the tide,
志决身歼军务***劳***。	Though his aspiration was resolute, yet in the ***toil*** of the military affairs he died. [13]

《咏怀古迹》	"Cherishing the Memory of Zhuge Liang at the Historical Site"
（唐）杜甫	（The Tang Dynasty） Du Fu

勇

昨夜东风吹血腥，	Last night gust of smell of blood in the east wind came along,
东来橐驼满旧都。	The camels that came from the east crowded Changan.
朔方健儿好身手，	The northern troops commanded by general Ge Shuhan are powerful,
昔何**勇**锐今何愚。	In the past how ***irresistible*** they were but now how dull. [13]
《哀王孙》	"Feeling Sad About a Prince"
（唐）杜甫	（The Tang Dynasty） Du Fu

译文"**Men**"与译文"**toil**"为直译，译文"**irresistible**"为意译。"irresistible"之意为"so strong that it cannot be stopped or resisted"，其意含"勇"，且有"锐"，正确表达出诗文之中"**勇**锐"之意。

【译法点滴】 直译与意译

正确理解并不意味着能够正确表达。表达得正确则需借助一些必要的翻译方法和技巧。这里先介绍两种最基本的翻译手段：直译和意译，其最终的目的都是为了忠实表达原作的思想内容和文体风格。

直译（literal translation），即在译文语言条件许可的情况下，尽可能地保持原文的形式结构、比喻形象和民族文化色彩等，如英语中的"win-win"直译成汉语的"双赢"；汉语的"四书五经"、"一国两制"译为"the Four Books and the Five Classics"、"one country, two systems"。意译（free translation），当原文与译文在表达方式上存在着差异，原文的思想内容或形象无法或不宜采用直译法译出，译者用自己的措辞正确地表达出原文的意思，是谓意译。译文可以不拘泥于原文的形式。英语中的"Love me, love my dog"的汉语译文是"爱屋及乌"；汉语"望子成龙"被译为"long to see one's son succeed in life"。

直译与意译是一个相对的概念，没有截然的划分。无论直译还是意译，都只能根据上下文语境的需要量体裁衣，灵活处理。

功

1. 沙场烽火侵胡月，	To the moon o've Hun's area the beacon fires on the battle-field are soaring,
海畔云山拥蓟城。	Jimen Town is guarded by the seaside mountains into clouds

	towering.
少小虽非投笔吏，	Though, when young, I didn't give up pen for sword as Ban Chao did,
论**功**还欲请长缨。	Yet to serve our country I now beg to go to the frontiers to achieve ***deeds of merit***.[13]
《望蓟门》	"Looking at Jimen in the Distance"
（唐）祖咏	(The Tang Dynasty) Zu Yong
2. 镌**功**勒成告万世，	In order to inscribe his ***feats*** on stone to tell the generations to come,
凿石作鼓隳嵯峨。	He chopped rocks off mountain cliffs to make many a stone drum.[13]
《石鼓歌》	"Song of the Stone Drums"
（唐）韩愈	(The Tang Dynasty) Han Yu

例 1 "功"之译文"**deeds of merit**"为意译。"论**功**还欲请长缨"之意为"论功名我想学终军自愿请缨"。"请长缨"：汉人终军曾向汉武帝请求："愿受长缨，必羁南越王而至阙下。"后被南越王所杀，年仅二十余。本句诗所表达的意思是：作者希望在军中以令人钦佩的行为来实现报国的雄心壮志，此处之"功"并非指具体所建之功绩或成就。

幼：会意字，由"幺（小）"、由"力"会意。[9]

老吾老，以及人之老；***幼***吾***幼***，以及人之***幼***。天下可运于掌。

《孟子》

Respect your own elders and extend such respect to those of others; ***cherish*** your own ***young*** and extend such cherishment to ***those*** of others, and you will find the entire kingdom in your grasp.[24]

"Mencius"

此例中"**幼**"的翻译较为明显地体现出通过理解确定字义之译法的运用：原文中虽同一个"幼"，但通过对上下文的理解，第一个"幼"是动词，其含意为"抚养"、"教育、爱护"，译文"**cherish**"（to love sb/sth very much and want to prodect them or it）即含此意。第二与第三个"幼"是名词"子女"、"小辈"的意思，第二个译为"**young**"，第三个"幼"为避免重复，从原文中的名词转换为译文中的代词"**those**"。

劣：会意字，由"力、少"会意。[9]

1. 将军向宠，性行淑均，晓畅军事，试用于昔日，先帝称之曰"能"，是以众议举宠为督。愚以为营中之事，悉以咨之，必能使行阵和睦，优**劣**得所也。

《前出师表》（汉）诸葛亮

General Xiang Chong, a man of good nature, well versed in tactics, formerly used on probation and considered by the late Emperor as capable, has been recommended by all to be the Military Superintendent. In my humble opinion, he should be consulted on all matters concerning the army, be they great or small. This will surely contribute to the harmony in the army and to putting both the superior and the ***indifferent*** people in their proper places. [12]

"Memorial to the Emperor Before the Northern Expedition" (The Han Dynasty) Zhuge Liang

2. 艺术作品最终成为商品，这是客观规律，无可非议。但在一时盛名之下，往往不够艺术价值的**劣**画也都招摇过市，欺蒙喜爱的收藏者，被市场上来回倒卖，互相欺骗。我早下决心要毁掉所不满意的作品，不愿谬种流传。

《毁画》吴冠中

It is natural and beyond reproach for works of art to end up becoming commodities. The problem is that ***inferior*** paintings of low artistic value, often, under cover of high reputation, openly beguile avid art collectors and people rush for speculative buying and reselling of them, cheating each other. I make up my mind long ago to scrap all of my unsatisfactory paintings so as to prevent the circulation of low-grade products. [15]

"Scrapping My Paintings" Wu Guanzhong

根据对上下文的理解，**例 1** 原文中“优**劣**”所指乃能力不同之人。“优”指“出类拔萃”之人；“劣”与其对应，是普通大众，而非低下之辈，译文“**indifferent**”（not very good）用得贴切。**例 2** 文中所言是“画”，所以，此“劣”是指画的水平（高低）而言，故译文取“**inferior**”（of poor quality）。

力：象形字。“力，筋也。像人筋之形。”[9]

太行，王屋二山，方七百里，高万仞。

北山愚公者，年且九十，面山而居。惩山北之塞出入之迂也，聚室而谋曰：“吾与汝毕**力**平险，指通豫南，达于汉阴，可乎？”杂然相许。

《列子》（战国）

Taihang and Wangwu Mountains are some seven hundred Li around, and hundreds of thousands of feet high.

North of these mountains lived an old man of nearly ninety, who was called the Fool. His house faced these mountains and he found it very inconvenient to have to make a detour each time he went out and came back; so one day he summoned his family to discuss the matter.

"Suppose we ***work*** together to level the mountains?" he suggested. "Then we can open a road southward to the bank of the Han River."

To this they all agreed...[14]

"Lie Zi"(The Warring States Period)

又

"又"构成的字往往与"手"相关。

又：象形字，其本意为"手"。现今所用之"又"，一般是其假借之意"重复或继续"。

只有照片上的童年，至今还留驻下来。当我从箱筐内找到旧作的若干剪报后，便把那一本比我生活过的年代更长久的影集，重又放入书箱里。然后轻轻合上了箱盖。我的童年回忆于是随同影集一起**又**沉入箱底。

《照片上的童年》何为

The only thing that still remained was my photographic childhood. Having found some newspaper clippings of my old writings, I replaced in the suitcase the album that had seen many more winters than I. Then I carefully put back the lid on the suitcase. Memories of my childhood, together with the album sank ***again*** to the bottom of the suitcase.[15]

"The Photographic Record of My Childhood" He Wei

叉：象形字。手指相交错；像手指叉物的形状。[9]

三八年至三九年间，我在香港《大公报》编文艺副刊时，因所登的稿件而与英国新闻审查官起冲突的事，更是屡见不鲜。说是"冲突"，其实，他是主子。在送审的校样上他随便打个红**叉**，我就只好抽掉。可临时补稿不方便，我就索性让"开天窗"，空白着。如果翻阅那一时期的香港《大公报》，天窗是不少的。有一回审查官甚至把半个版面全给枪毙了。

《说起香港》萧乾

From 1938 to 1939, when I was in charge of editing the Art and Literaure Supplement of *The Dagong Bao*, I often got into disputes with British censors (or rather with my masters) over manuscripts. When a British censor put in a red ***cross*** at will, all I could do was withdraw the entire manuscript. Sometimes, being hard pressed to find a replacement for it, I had to leave a blank on the page to show that something had been suppressed by censorship. Take a look at *The Dagong Bao* published in Hong Kong in those days, and you'll find lots of blanks. Once the British censor even had half a page killed[15].

"About Hong Kong" Xiao Qian

取：会意字，由"又"、由"耳"会意。其本意为"捕获"。《周礼》："被捕获的野兽割取左耳。"[9]现今所用之"取"，往往是其引申之意"得到，招致，采取，拿到手里"等。

1. 在这个世界上有三个与我个人存亡牢牢相连的人。那便是我的父亲、母亲还有荷西，如果世界上有他们活着一日，我便不可以死，连神也不能将我***取***去，因为我不肯。

《不死鸟》三毛

Three persons in this world have their fate so closely tied up with my life and death. They are my parents and Hexi. I refuse to die as long as they're alive. Not even a god can ***take*** me away when I say no.[15]

"The Surviving Bird" San Mao

2. 小巷的动人之处就是它无比的悠闲。无论谁，只要你到巷里去踯躅一会，你的心情就会如巷尾不波的古井，那是一种和平的静穆，而不是阴森和肃杀。它闹中***取***静，别有天地，仍是人间。

《巷》柯灵

The charm of the lane lies in its absolute serenity. No matter who you are, if you loiter around in the lane for a while, your mind will become an unruffled as the ancient well at the end of the lane. There you will experience a kind of peaceful calmness rather than gloomy sternness. There ***reigns*** peace and quiet in the midst of noisy bustle.[15]

"The Lane" Ke Ling

此处之"***取***"用"**reigns**"为意译。根据上下文，"闹中***取***静"之意为：虽处于市井之喧嚣，充满小巷的依然是安静平和的气氛。"安静平和"是小巷所特有的氛围。译文中将"静"作为主语，"静"占据着主导地位，此处"取"译为"reign"，用作谓语取其所含的"盛行、显著"之意。

友：会意字，由两个"又（手）"会意，表示相交为友的意思。[9]

择书比择***友***简单得多。不擅辞令，厌恶应酬的人，可以自由自在的徜徉于书林之中，游目四顾，俯拾皆***友***。

《书与人》金圣华

It is much easier to choose a book than a ***friend***. One who is poor at speech and shuns socializing will nevertheless feel like being surrounded by friends while sauntering freely in the midst of books. [15]

"Books and Man" Jin Shenghua

二、三画

囗

由"***囗***"组成的字，大都与围墙、界限有关。例字中除"***国***、***囚***、***回***、***困***"外，其余为形声字：外形内声。

团（團）

新裂绮纨素， Fine, freshly woven silk of Qi
鲜洁如霜雪， Is white as frost or snow;
裁为合欢扇， A piece, embroidered, makes a fan
团团似明月。 As ***round*** as the bright moon. [4]
《怨歌行》 "A Song in Slow Time"
乐府 Yuefu Songs with Regular Five-Syllable Lines

园

会桃李之芳***园***，叙天伦之乐事。

《春夜宴桃李园序》（唐）李白

Gathered in the Peach-Plum ***Garden***, we talk about gladdening things among our dear ones. [12]

"Feast in the Peach-Plum Garden" (The Tang Dynasty) Li Bai

圆

山多石，少土。石苍黑色，多平方，少***圆***。少杂树，多松，生石罅，皆平顶。冰雪，无瀑水，无鸟兽音迹，至日观数里无树，而雪与人膝齐。

《登泰山记》（清）姚鼐

It was in the main a rocky mountain with little earth. The rocks, greenish black, were for the most part square, and ***round*** stones were quite scarce. Bushes were few and pines, grown out of the stone crevices, were many, having all leveled tops. Ice and snow prevailed and no waterfalls could be seen, nor any traces of birds and beasts. Within several *li* around Riguan Arbor no trees were visible, and snow was knee-deep. [12]

"Ascent to Mount Tai" (The Qing Dynasty) Yao Nai

圃

陈康肃公尧咨善射，当世无双，公亦以此自矜。尝射于家***圃***，有卖油翁释担而立，睨之，久而不去。见其发矢十中八九，但微颔之。

《卖油翁》（宋）欧阳修

Sir Chen Yaozi was adept at shooting, unparalleled in the contemporary times. He was therefore proud of it. Once he shot in his ***garden***. An old oil vendor, relieved of his burden, stood by and squinted at the shooting, leaving the place only after a long time. Seeing that Chen could get eight or nine hits out of ten shots, he just nodded his approval.[12]

"The Old Oil Vendor" (The Song Dynasty) Ouyang Xiu

国(國)：会意字，由"口"、由"或"会意。[9] "或"字形像以"戈（武器）"守卫"口（城邑）"。在字的周围加方框，构成"国"。

1. ***国***破山河在，　The ***nation*** has fallen, the land endures;
城春草木深。　Spring trees and grasses flourish in the town.
感时花溅泪，　Troubled by the times—flowers bring tears;
恨别鸟惊心。　Dreading parting—birds startle the soul.[2]
《春望》　"Viewing Spring"
(唐)杜甫　(The Tang Dynasty) Du Fu

2. 他乡生白发，　In the south our hairs have turned white,
旧***国***见青山。　In your ***hometown*** only the green hills will be in your sight.[13]
《贼平后送人北归》　"Seeing Off a Friend Who Returns to the North After the Suppression of the An-Shi Armed Rebellion"
（唐）司空曙　(The Tang Dynasty) Sikong Shu

"旧***国***见青山"中的"国"译为"**hometown**"，在于上一句的"他乡"："家乡（故乡）"对应"他乡"。

囚：会意字，由"人"在"口"中会意[9]。

对景如青鸾舞镜，　Seeing the gloomy scene, I'm sad as gloom phoenix green.
天隔羊车，　From heaven I'm kept far apart
人***囚***凤城。　As if ***imprisoned*** in the phoenix town.
好姻缘辜负了今生，　Could I have a happy marriage with my mate?
痛伤悲雨泪如倾。　I'm so much grieved that tears like rain stream down.

心如醉满杯何日醒？	Drunk with brimming cups, when will wake my heart?
西风传玉漏丁宁。	I hear the water clock of jade stop
恰过半夜，	Dripping in the western breeze drop by drop.
胜似三秋，	Midnight just passed away,
才交四更。	It is colder than autumn late.
	O when will break the day?[5]
《逍遥乐·宫词》	Tune: Joy to Be Free, "Palace Grief"
（元）曾瑞	(The Yuan Dynasty) Zeng Rui

例中"人***囚***风城"为主动形式，但根据对上下文的理解，主语"人"实际上是谓语动词动作"囚"的承受着，故"囚"在译文中为被动形式"I'm...**imprisoned**"。

回：指事字。《段注》："外为大口，内为小口，皆回转之行也。"[9]

1. 少小离乡老大***回***，	To leave very young and to ***return*** very old,
乡音未改鬓毛衰。	With accent unchanged, but hair grown thin.
儿童相见不相识，	They see but know me not,
笑问客从何处来。	the smiling children who inquire:
	"And from where do you come , Honored Guest?"[2]
《回乡偶书》	
	"Impromptu Lines Composed upon Returning to My Native Place"
（唐）贺知章	(The Tang Dynasty) He Zhizhang

2. 人老去西风白发，	I'm growing old, my white hair wafts when west wind blows.
蝶愁来明日黄花。	Tomorrow yellow blooms will sadden butterflies.
回首天涯，	Looking ***back*** to the far-flung skies,
一抹夕阳，	I find the setting sun in bloody dye,
数点寒鸦。	Dotted with a few chilly crows. [5]
《折桂令·九日》	
	Tune: Plucking Laurel Branch, "The Mountain-Climbing Day"
（元）张可久	(The Yuan Dynasty) Zhang Kejiu

困：会意字，由"木"在"口"中会意。

西望夏口，东望武昌，山川相缪，郁乎苍苍，此非孟德之***困***于周郎者乎？方其破荆州，下江陵，顺流而东也，舳舻千里，旌旗蔽空，酾酒临江，横槊赋诗，固一世之雄也，而今安在哉？

《前赤壁赋》（宋）苏轼

You see Xiakou in the west and Wuchang in the east. The hills and rivers are interlinked and enshrouded in a somber green. Is it not where Cao was ***besieged*** by Zhou Yu? At that time, Cao took Jingzhou, then sailed eastward down the Yangtze River, with ships in battle array, extending a thousand *li*, their flags and pennants eclipsing the sunlight. He filled his wine cup before the rolling waves, and holding his spear in both hands, composed and declaimed his poems. He was indeed the hero of his time. But where is he now?[12]

"Boating at the Red Cliff" (The Song Dynasty) Su Shi

山

由“**山**”组合的字，往往跟“山名”、“高大”等义有关。例字中除“**山**”外，余者均为形声字。其中，“**峦、嶅**”为下形上声，“**岩**”为上形下声，其他为左形右声。

岭

岭外音书断，
经冬复历春。
近乡情更怯，
不敢问来人。
《渡汉江》
（唐）宋之问

No news, no letters—all winter, all spring—
Beyond the ***mountains***.
With every homeward step more timid still
I dare not even inquire of passerby.[2]

"Crossing the Han River"
(The Tang Dynasty) Song Zhiwen

岫

诗思在灞陵桥上，微吟就，林**岫**便已浩然；野兴在镜湖曲边，独往时，山川自相映发。

《菜根谭》（明）洪应明

It is on ***Baling Bridge*** where the persons in parting would mostly fall into an exalted poetic mood. The lines murmured out on this bridge would permeate the forest and ***hills*** or thereabout with the artistic breath of poetry. It is beside Jinghu Lake and The Qu'e River where a person lingering about by himself would be mostly aroused to a feeling of wilderness. Though with no one in company, the brilliance enhanced between the mountains and the rivers would still make him intoxicated.[6]

"The Roots of Wisdom," (The Ming Dynasty) Hong Yingming

崎岖

人情反复，世路***崎岖***。行不去处，须知退一步之法；行得去处，务加让三分之功。

《菜根谭》（明）洪应明

Human relationships are inconstant. The road of life is ***rugged and rough***. When there is no enough room ahead on a path, you should have the sense to take a step back for others. Furthermore, even when you come to an open road, you should also take it as your merit to make way for them. [6]

"The Roots of Wisdom,"（The Ming Dynasty）Hong Yingming

峦（巒），屿

层***峦***耸翠，上出云霄，飞阁流丹，下临无地。鹤汀凫渚，穷岛***屿***之萦回；桂殿兰宫，即冈峦之体势。

《滕王阁序》（唐）王勃

The overlapping ***ridges***, bringing out their greenery, rise into the sky. The tower, poising in the air and overlooking a void, seems dripping with a vermilion sheen. The shoals inhabited by cranes and mallards present a whole zigzag of ***islets***. And the palaces built of laurel and orchid wood are arranged in keeping with the terrain of the mountains. [12]

"The Tower of Prince Teng"（The Tang Dynasty）Wang Bo

密

城上高楼接大荒， From the high city tower, a vast wilderness.
海天愁思正茫茫， Expanse of sky, and sea—and infinite this sorrow.
惊风乱飐芙蓉水， As whirlwinds riot over lotus waters,
密雨斜侵薜荔墙。 ***Sheets*** of rain pound vine-covered walls. [2]

《登柳州城寄漳汀封连四洲刺史》

"Mounting the City Tower of Liuzhou: Sent to the Magistrates of Zhangzhou, Tingzhou, Fengzhou and Lianzhou"

（唐）柳宗元 （The Tang Dynasty）Liu Zongyuan

"惊风乱飐芙蓉水，**密**雨斜侵薜荔墙"写夏日风雨急骤的景象：池中荷花本不畏风，但狂风偏要乱吹漫卷，使荷花倍受摧残；墙上薜荔，雨本难侵，暴雨偏要横扫斜侵，使薜荔遭受欺凌。这里"密"与"狂"相对，其雨之"暴"及"密"的程度非"滴"或"线"能够形容，故译文选用"**Sheets**"（very heavily)。英语中形容“大雨倾盆”往往使用到“Sheets”：The rain was coming down in sheets.

岩（巖）

渔翁夜傍西**岩**宿，	In the evening a fisherman shelters against West ***Cliff***.
晓汲清湘燃楚竹。	Early he draws clear water, and makes a fire of bamboo.
烟销日出不见人，	By sunrise, his smoke vanished, no one is seen.
欸乃一声山水绿。	As his song rings out, waters and mountains show green.[2]
《渔翁》	"A Fisherman"
(唐)柳宗元	(The Tang Dynasty) Liu Zongyuan

山：象形字。

1. 黄河远岸上白云间	The Yellow River reaches high beyond the clouds,
一片孤城万仞**山**。	Amid the massive ***mountains*** lies the solitary sliver of a town.
羌笛何须怨杨柳，	From a flute the Willow Song wails forth , but why?
春风不度玉门关。	Beyond Jade Gate Pass, spring winds will never climb.[2]
《凉州词》	"Liangzhou Lines"
(唐)王之涣	(The Tang Dynasty) Wang Zhihuan

2. 江流天地外，	It flows far beyond earth and heaven,
山色有无中。	The ***mountains*** on its banks are now visible and now hidden.[13]
《汉江临眺》	"Ascending a Height and Looking in the Distance at the Han River"
(唐)王维	(The Tang Dynasty) Wang Wei

【译法点滴】 综合与分析型思维在原文与译文中的体现

综合与分析型思维是人类思维的两种基本形式。[27] “综合”，即把事物的各个部分联为一个统一的整体。“分析”则把事物的整体分解为许多部分。由于传统文化的影响，“东方重综合，西方重分析”。两种思维方式在语言上的表现为：综合型思维注重语言的整体性，象征性和暗示性；分析型思维则重视语言的分析性，逻辑性和形式结构化。

在两种语言的结构上：综合型的思维方式使汉语条理层次呈隐性关系，词语、句子的意义要在全篇的整体网络中定位，因此不具有词形变化，语法形式的表达主要依靠词汇手段，组词造句依据语意逻辑和动作发生的时间次序；分析性思维方式使英语层次条理一目了然，具有明显的词形变化，语法形式多样，注重过渡连接词的关连作用，组词造句中语序的安排也较为灵活。

这里以“山”的翻译进行说明。

原文中，通过上下文即可理解到：此二“山”均非指一峰一峦，虽为多数，但看不到词形的变化。而译文中两个“**mountains**”皆为复数形式。**例 1**“一片孤城万仞***山***”中“山”的修饰词是“万仞”，故英语中用复数。**例 2**“***山***色有无中”的上句是“江流天地外”。这里的“江”指汉江，“天地外”即很远的地方，所以，“江”所流经的不止一峰、一峦，此“山”之译文用复数形式乃分型思维的体现。这里“山”的翻译不仅要通过上下文来理解其意义，还要考虑到综合与分析型思维方式的不同，使译文便于英语读者理解。

土

由“***土***”组合的字往往与“土”、“土地”及生长于其上的万物相关。例字中除“***城***、***埋***、***垒***、***尘***”外，余者为形声字。其中，“***壁***、***堂***、***垂***”为下形上声，其他为左形右声。

墙

宋有富人，大雨坏***墙***。
其子曰：“不筑，必将有盗。”
其邻人之父亦云。
暮而果大亡其财。
其家甚智其子，而疑邻人之父。

《韩非子》（战国）韩非

There was once a rich man in the state of Song. After a downpour of rain his ***wall*** began to crumble.

“If you don't mend that wall,” warned his son, “a thief will get in.”

An old neighbour gave the same advice.

That night, indeed, a great deal of money was stolen. Then the rich man commended his son's intelligence, but suspected his old neighbour of being the thief. [14]

“Han Fei Zi” (The Warring States Period) Han Fei

塘

沙河***塘***里灯初上，	By Sandy River ***Pond*** the new-lit lamps are bright.
水调谁家唱。	Who sings “the Water Melody” at night?
夜阑风静欲归时，	When I come back, the wind goes down, the bright moon paves

唯有一江明月碧琉璃。 With emerald glass the river waves. [1]

《虞美人、有美堂赠述古》

Tune: The Beautiful Yu, "Written for Chen Xiang at the Scenic Hall"

(宋)苏轼 (The Song Dynasty) Su Shi

堂

堂上谋臣帷幄,	Ministers in the ***court*** plan the campaign;
边头猛将干戈。	Generals spear in hand guard the frontier.
天时地利與人和,	When can we take back the lost Central Plain?
燕可伐與曰可。	Our men, united, should start now and here.
此日楼台鼎鼐,	Holding the premiership today,
他日剑履山河。	You'll win high honor tomorrow.
都人齐和大风歌,	The capital retaken, you may sing the lay
管领群臣来贺。	Of "Big Wind" and people will follow. [1]

《西江月》 Tune: The Moon over the West River

(宋)刘过 (The Song Dynasty) Liu Guo

城: 会意字, 由"土"、由"成"会意,"成"也表声。[9]

1. 渭**城**朝雨浥轻尘,	The tiny dust in Wei ***Town*** is wet with the morning rain,
客舍青青柳色新。	By the tavern the willows look all the more fresh and green.
劝君更尽一杯酒,	"Please drink up another cup of wine," I say,
西出阳关无故人。	"For west of the Sun Pass you'll see no friend on your way."[13]

《渭城送友人》 "Bidding Farewell to a Friend at Wei Town"

(唐) 王维 (The Tang Dynasty) Wang Wei

2. **城**上高楼接大荒,	From the high tower of ***Liuzhou*** I overlook a wilderness vast,
海天愁思正茫茫。	As boundless as the sea and the sky my gloomy thoughts last and last. [13]

《登柳州城寄漳汀封连四州刺史》

"A poem to Four Friends Demoted to Zhangzhou, Tingzhou, Fengzhou and Lianzhou after Ascending the Gate Tower pf Liuzhou"

(唐) 柳宗元 (The Tang Dynasty) Liu Zongyuan

3. 国破山河在，　The state broken up, the rivers still run and the mountains still tower,
城春草木深。　When spring comes, ***Chang' an*** is over green with weeds and thorns.
感时花溅泪，　Grieved at the turbulent times I am made to tear by a flower,
恨别鸟惊心。　Having the separation with family I am startled by the birds songs. [13]

《春望》　"Viewing Spring"
（唐）杜甫　(The Tang Dynasty) Du Fu

例 2 之诗题点明作者所登之城乃是柳州城。因其属专名，故使用音译的方法，**Liuzhou** 是按汉语拼音转写。**例 3** 用"**Chang' an**"对应"城"与诗的写作时代背景相关。唐玄宗天宝十五年（756），安史叛军攻陷长安，肃宗在灵武即位，改元至德。杜甫在投奔灵武途中，被叛军俘至长安，次年（至德二年）写此诗。所以，诗中之"城"即指"长安"。与例 2 相同，"长安"属专名，故音译，按汉语拼音转写。

【译法点滴】　汉语人名及地名的翻译：音译

汉语中的人名和地名属专名（英语的专有名词）的范畴，此类名词往往音译（音译是词语翻译中经常使用的手段之一），用汉语拼音转写。

埋：会意字，由"土"、由"里"会意。

凤凰台上凤凰游，　Phoenixes gathered on the Phoenix Terrace once,
凤去台空江自流。　Now the birds are gone, the Terrace is vacant, only the water of the Yangtze River by itself runs.
吴宫花草***埋***幽径，　The flowers and grasses in the Wu's palace ***keep*** the secluded paths ***from the eye***,
晋代衣冠成古丘。　The nobles of the Jin Dynasty all in graves lie. [13]
《登金陵凤凰台》　"Ascending the Phoenix Terrace in Jinling"
（唐）李白　(The Tang Dynasty) Li Bai

此例中的"埋"为意译。译诗需要考虑押韵的问题：选取"埋"之译文为"**keep…from the eye**"的一个考虑在于"eye"与后一句的句末"lie"押韵。

【译法点滴】　关于诗的翻译：押韵

在诗词歌赋中，某些句子的最后一个字用韵母相同或相近的字，使音调和谐优美，谓"押韵"。

译诗不仅要忠实于原作的内容、意境和情调，“押韵”也是翻译诗句时需要考虑的一个因素。对于原作押韵之处，也要大致与其保持一致。

垒、壁： 垒，会意字，由“厽”（象形字，像土块积累的样子）、由“土”会意。[9]

1. 大江东去，　The Great River eastward flows,
浪淘尽千古风流人物。　With its waves are gone all those
故**垒**西边，　Gallant heroes of bygone years.
人道是三国周郎赤**壁**。　West of the ancient ***fortress*** appears
The Red ***Cliff***. Here General Zhou won his early fame
When the Three Kingdoms were all in flame. [1]

《念奴娇 · 赤壁怀古》
Tune: Charm of a Maiden Singer, “Memories of the Past at Red Cliff”
（宋）苏轼　(The Song Dynasty) Su Shi

2. 夕阳依旧**垒**，　A beam of setting sun on the ruin ***terrace*** very slowly disappear,
寒磬满空林。　The old sound of the Buddhist percussion instrument echoes in the leafless woods far and near. [13]

《秋日登吴公台上寺远眺》
“Ascending the Temple on the Wugong Terrace on an Autumn Day and Looking Afar”
（唐）刘长卿　(The Tang Dynasty) Liu Changqing

3. 锦江春色来天地，　Spring spreads over the heaven and the earth and the River Brocade,
玉**垒**浮云变古今。　From the past and the present the flowing clouds have been changing over ***Mount*** Jade. [13]

《登楼》　“Ascending a Tower”
（唐）杜甫　(The Tang Dynasty) Du Fu

例 2“夕阳依旧**垒**”中之“垒”即诗题“秋日登吴公台上远眺”中的“吴公台”，意译为“**terrace**”，盖与“台”对应。**例 3** 之“玉**垒**”乃山名，在今四川都江堰市西。诗中虽为“垒”，实为“山”，译为“**Mount**”符合原文之意。

尘（塵）： 会意字，由“鹿”、由“土”会意。鹿行扬土。

汲井漱寒齿，　I draw the cool water from the well to rinse my teeth for a moment,

清心拂**尘**服。 Then to purify my heart I wipe the ***dust*** off my garment. [13]
《晨诣超师院读禅经》
"Coming to Monk Chao's Temple in the Morning to Read the Buddhist Scriptures"
（唐）柳宗元　(The Tang Dynasty) Liu Zongyuan

垂： 形声字，下形上声。"垂"意为遥远的边界。其下部为"土"，上部象形（音"chui"），表示草木和花叶下垂。

1. **垂**杨小院绣帘东，　The ***weeping*** willows stand east of the curtained bowers;
莺阁残枝蝶趁风。　Orioles and butterflies pass through the faded flowers.
大抵西冷寒食路，　But peach blossoms on Cold Food day are beautified
桃花得气美人中。　By beauties living or buried by the lakeside. [22]
《西湖》　"West Lake"
（明）柳如是　(The Ming Dynasty) Liu Rushi

2. 少小去乡邑，　While he was young, he left his native land;
扬声沙漠**垂**。　His name was known as far as ***border*** sand. [21]
《白马篇》　"Song of the White Horse"
（三国）曹植　(Three Kingdoms Period) Cao Zhi

3. 画阁朱楼尽相望，　Their carved and red towers in clusters are clearly seen,
红桃绿柳**垂**檐向。　Toward the eaves ***droop*** the peach trees red and the willow trees green. [13]
《洛阳女儿行》　"Song of a Young Lady in Luoyang"
（唐）王维　(The Tang Dynasty) Wang Wei

4. 头上何所有？　What do they have on their heads?
翠微盍叶**垂**鬓唇。***Down*** to their temples hang the flower-like headdresses. [13]
《丽人行》　"Song of the Beauties"
（唐）杜甫　(The Tang Dynasty) Du Fu

以上4例之"**垂**"均为直译。由于其所在上下文不同，所起作用不同，词性不同，故此译文各异。**例1**"**垂**杨"即垂柳，其树枝细长下垂。此"垂"为定语，修饰杨柳，译文选取形容词"**weeping**"［(of some trees) with branches that hang downwards］。**例2**"沙漠**垂**"之"垂"含"陲"（边地）意为名词，译文"**border**"与原文之意相符。**例3**"**垂**檐向"之"垂"在句中作谓语，表示树木下垂之状，其译文取动词"**droop**"(to bend, hang or move downwards)与其意对应。**例4**"**垂**鬓唇"之"垂"在原文中是动词，此处之"垂"需从原文的动词转换为译文的副词“**Down**”以符合译文语言规范及表达习惯。

女

由“***女***”构组的字一般与妇女有关。例字中除“***好***、***妙***、***如***、***婴***”外，余者为形声字：左形右声。

姥

海客谈瀛洲，	Speaking of the fairy isle Yingzhou,
烟涛微茫信难求。	The seafarers say it's really hard to find it because of the surging waves and the thick mist.
越人语天**姥**，	Speaking of the ***Tianmu*** Mountain,
云霓明灭或可睹。	The Yue people say it's sometimes visible because the rosy clouds flicker fleet. [13]

《梦游天姥吟留别》

"Song of the Trip in a Dream to the Tianmu Mountain in Farewell to My Friends"

（唐）李白　　(The Tang Dynasty) Li Bai

例中“天**姥**”即天姥山，属专有名词，故音译，用汉语拼音转写。

嫁

弟走从军阿姨死，	My brother went to war, my aunt died;
暮去朝来颜色故。	As dawn yields to dusk my beauty faded,
门前冷落鞍马稀，	And before my gate the carriages are few.
老大**嫁**作商人妇。	Two old, I ***married*** a merchant…. [2]

《琵琶行》　　"Song of the Pipa"

（唐）白居易　　(The Tang Dynasty) Bai Juyi

例中“**嫁**”的翻译体现出（1）英语词汇意义与汉语中有些词在意义上只有部分对应。它们在意义上概括的范围有广狭之分，如汉语有“嫁”、“娶”之分，而英语中的“**marry**”既可作“嫁”，又可用为“娶”。（2）综合与分析型思维的不同：原文“嫁”所发生的时间体现在语义逻辑上，其形式上没有任何变化；而译文过去时态的体现则是在语法及词形变化（marry 词尾+ed）上。

妍：“开”音“jian”。

雨余观山色，景象便觉新***妍***；夜静听钟声，音响尤为清越。

《菜根谭》（明）洪应明

Watch the hills after a shower of rain, and you will find that the view at your sight is exceptionally fresh and ***elegant***. Listen to the bell tone in the still of night, and you will find that the sound you pick up is especially clear and melodious. [6]

"The Roots of Wisdom" (The Ming Dynasty) Hong Yingming

原文中"妍"之意为"美丽"。译文"**elegant**"[(of clothes, places and things) attractive and designed well] 即含"妍"之意，体现出了雨后山色之清新悦目。

好：会意字，由"女"、由"子"会意。《段注》："本谓女子，引申为凡美之偁[9]。"

1. 丞相祠堂何处寻，　Where would I find the Prime Minister's shrine?
锦官城外柏森森。　Somewhere outside Jinguan, in a dense cypress glade
映阶碧草自春色，　Where the grass covered steps don the color of spring
隔叶黄鹂空***好***音。　And the orioles' ***fine*** songs go unheard. [2]
《蜀相》　"The Shu Prime Minister"
（唐）杜甫　(The Tang Dynasty) Du Fu

2. 向晚意不适，　Troubled in spirit, toward evening
驱车登古原。　I approach the ancient gardens.
夕阳无限***好***，　As the sun sets, unrivalled in its ***splendor***,
只是近黄昏。　My only thoughts are of impending night. [2]
《乐游园》　"At Le You Garden"
（唐）李商隐　(The Tang Dynasty) Li Shangyin

3. 明月如霜，　The bright moonlight is like frost white,
好风如水，　The ***gentle*** breeze like water clean:
清景无限。　Far and wide extends the scene serene. [1]
《永遇乐》　Tune: Joy of Eternal Union
（宋）苏轼　(The Song Dynasty) Su Shi

4. 沧江***好***烟月，　The misty moonlight on the blue river is ***good***,
门系钓鱼船。　And in front of the hotel gate is moored a boat with a fishing rod and a hook. [13]
《旅宿》　"Staying Overnight in a Hotel"
（唐）杜牧　(The Tang Dynasty) Du Mu

例1之“好”修饰黄鹂的声音。黄鹂的鸣声悦耳动听，以“**fine**”（of high quality）来修饰，意在凸显其音质之美。**例2**之“好”意译为“**splendor**”（grand and impressive beauty），在于对上下文的理解。这里夕阳“好”的含义是指其景色之“瑰丽”或“壮美”，译文“**splendor**”贴切原文之意。**例3**之“好”修饰的是“风”。就风而言，其好与坏的所指一般与其强度相关：“和风、微风、大风、狂风”，等等。根据上下文语境，上文：“明月如霜”即月色明亮，皎洁如霜；下文：“清景无限”表述出夜景之清幽并由此引发出无限之遐思，故此，“好风如水”，应是秋风和畅，清凉如水，译文“**gentle**”与此“好”对应。**例4**之“好”直译为“**good**”，既取其景色宜人之意。又考虑到押韵的问题。

妙：会意字，由“少”、由“女”会意。

素月分辉，　The skies with pure moonbeams o'er flow;
明河共影，　The water surface paved with moonshine;
表里俱澄澈。　Brightness above, brightness below.
悠然心会，　My heart with the moon becomes one,
妙处难与君说。　***Felicity*** to share with none.[1]

《念奴娇·过洞庭》　Tune: The Charm of A Maiden Singer, “Passing Lake Dongting”
（宋）张孝祥　(The Song Dynasty) Zhang Xiaoxiang

如：会意字，由“女”、由“口”会意。《段注》：“从必以口。从女者，女子，从人者也。”[9]

1. 燕草***如***碧丝，　The grasses on the Yan land look ***like*** green silk threads,
秦桑低绿枝。　The mulberry twigs on the Qin land, heavy with green leaves, bend their heads.[13]

《春思》　“Yearning in Spring”
（唐）李白　(The Tang Dynasty) Li Bai

2. 人生不相见，　Two persons can't meet for many years,
动***如***参与商。　***Just as*** the star Shen appears while the star Shang disappears.[13]

《赠卫八处士》　“To Hermit Wei the Eighth”
（唐）杜甫　(The Tang Dynasty) Du Fu

婴：会意字。“婴”本意为妇人颈上的装饰品。由“女”、由“贝贝”会意。“贝贝”表示用具相连。[9]

有过于江上者，见人方引**婴**儿，而欲投之江中，**婴**儿啼。
人问其故。
曰：“其父善游。”
其父虽善游，其子岂遽善游哉！

《吕氏春秋》（战国）吕不韦

A man walking along the river bank saw someone about to throw a ***small boy*** into the water. The ***child*** was screaming with terror.

“Why do you want to throw that child into the river?” asked the passer by.

“His father is a good swimmer,” was the answer.

But it does not follow that the son of a good swimmer can swim. [14]

“The Discourses of Lu Buwei”

(The Warring States Period) Lü Buwei

门

用“***门***”组合的字，字义往往与“门”的所含之义有所关联。例字中除“***门、闲***”外，余者为形声字。其中，“***问、闷***”为内形外声，其余为外形内声。

问

玄都观里桃千树，　In Royal Temple there are thousands of peach trees,
花落水空流。　Whence fallen blooms in vain with water flow.
凭君莫***问***：　Do not ***ask***, please,
清泾浊渭，　If water is not clear,
去马来牛。　Or cows will come or horses go. [5]

《人月圆 · 卜居外家东园》

Tune: Man and Moon, “Moving to My Mother's East Garden”

（元）元好问　(The Yuan Dynasty) Yuan Haowen

闷

风微浪息，　The waves are calmed when the wind light
扁舟一叶。　Blows on my leaflike boat at midnight.
1. 半夜心，　In my heart deep,

三生梦，　Of my past life I dream.
万里别，　I'll go far on the stream;
闷倚蓬窗睡些。　***Depressed*** in the lonely boat, I get a short sleep.[5]
《节节高 · 题洞庭鹿角庙壁》
Tune: Higher and Higher, "Written on the Temple Wall on Lake Dongting"
（元）卢挚　(The Yuan Dynasty) Lu Zhi

2. 败叶走庭除，　In the courtyard run riot withered leaves,
修竹扫苍楹。　The pale pillars caressed by bamboos tall.
唱到是人和***闷***可难争。　Can it be true that woman can fight the ***gloom***?[5]
《高平煞 · 宫词》　Ture: High Level Epilogue, "Palace Grief"
（元）曾瑞　(The Yuan Dynasty) Zeng Rui

例 1"***闷***倚蓬窗"之"闷"表示"倚"的状态，译文中使用过去分词"**Depressed**"作为状语。这里"闷"的翻译体现出了分析型思维之语法形式的多样。**例 2**"唱到是人和***闷***可难争"中之"闷"作为"争"的对象，故译文为名词"**gloom**"。

阔

剑河风急云片***阔***，　Over the Jian River blows a strong wind in which fly the clouds of ***huge*** flakes,
沙口石冻马蹄脱。　On the frozen stones at Shakou come off the horse-roofs.[13]
《轮台歌奉送封大夫出师西征》
"Song of Luntai for Seeing Off Official Feng on His Expedition to the West"
（唐）岑参　(The Tang Dynasty) Cen Shen

阁

绿叶阴浓，　Green leaves casting deep shade
遍池亭水***阁***，　Over pavilions and ***bowers*** by the pool
偏趁凉多。　Bring a delightful cool.[5]
《小圣乐 · 骤雨打新荷》
Tune: Minor Sacred Music, "Sudden Shower Beating on New Lotus Leaves"
（元）元好问　(The Yuan Dynasty) Yuan Haowen

阑

长江万里归帆，　On thousand-mile long River pass east-going sails.

西风几度阳关？　How many times at Sunny Pass has blown west breeze?
依旧红尘满眼。　Still I see a world of dust to my disgust.
夕阳新燕，　At sunset cry the new-come wild geese.
此情时拍***阑***干。　What can I do but beat now and then on the ***rails***. [5]

《天净沙·闲题》　Tune: Sunny Sand, "Written at Leisure"
（元）吴西逸　(The Yuan Dynasty) Wu Xiyi

此"***阑***"同栏杆之"栏"，译文取"**rails**"符合原文之意。

阃

其水之大，倍石渠三之一，亘石为底，达于两涯。若床若堂，若陈筵席，若限***阃***奥。

《永州八记》（唐）柳宗元

Water here was about one-third more voluminous than that in the rock flume. Its bed was formed with rocks from end to end, some of them resembling couches, parlor floors, banquet dishware, and some simply ***boudoirs***. [8]

"Eight Travel Journals on the State of Yong VII、The Rock Gorge" (The Tang Dynasty) Liu Zongyuan

阖

永有某氏者，畏日，拘忌甚异。以为已生岁值子；鼠，子神也，因爱鼠，不畜猫犬，禁童勿击鼠。……结果，某氏室无完器，椸无完衣，饮食大率鼠之余也。

数岁，某氏徙居他州。后人来居。……新来者假五六猫，***阖***门，撤瓦，灌穴，购僮罗捕之。杀鼠如丘。

《永某氏之鼠》（唐）柳宗元

In the state of Yong, there was such a householder so mindful of ominous days and meticulous of taboos that he thought mice were designated gods for Zi—the Year of the Mice. Because he was born in Zi, the householder pampered the mice, prohibiting his servants from killing them and never keeping cats of dogs at home. .... As a result, in his house, the mice gnawed away all his utensils, ripped open all his clothes in the closet and left no food undisturbed for him.

A few years later, as he was relocated to another state, a newcomer moved in, but the mice didn't change their behavior. ...The new dweller brought in a few borrowed cats, ***closed*** all the doors, removed the roof tiles, filled up all the holes with water, and hired servants to catch the mice. Those he had killed were piled up in a small mound. [8]

"The Rats of a Yong's Householder" (The Tang Dynasty) Liu Zongyuan

闲、门： 闲，会意字，由“门”中有“木”会意。[9]

1. 白云依静渚，　O’er the quiet islet the white clouds float about,
   芳草闭***闲***门。　By the green grass the ***unused door*** is blocked out and out.[13]
   《寻南溪常道士》　“Looking for Taoist Priest Chang at South Stream”
   （唐）刘长卿　（The Tang Dynasty） Liu Changqing

2. ***闲***依农圃邻，　***Leisurely*** I live near vegetable plots and the fields,
   偶似山林客。　Once in a while I move about like a hermit in the wooded hills.[13]
   《溪居》　“Living by a Stream”
   （唐）柳宗元　（The Tang Dynasty） Liu Zongyuan

例 1 中“芳草闭***闲门***”的“闲”修饰名词“门”，在句中作定语，故译文使用形容词“**unused**”。**例 2** 中“***闲***依农圃邻”的“闲”表示动词“倚”的状态，作为状语，故使用副词，译为“**Leisurely**”。

门： 象形字。

掩白沙翠竹柴***门***，　My wicket ***gate*** closed to bamboos green and sand white,
听彻秋来夜雨。　I listen to the rain throughout the autumn night.[5]
《黑漆弩 · 村居遣兴》
Tune: Varnished Black Bow, “Written at Random in the Village”
（元）刘敏中　（The Yuan Dynasty） Liu Minzhong

闲

隋朝有人敏慧，然而口吃。杨素每***闲***闷，即召与剧谈。尝岁暮无事对坐，因戏之云：“有大坑深一丈，方圆亦一丈，遣公入其中，何法得出？”此人低头良久，乃问云：“有梯出否？”素云：“只论无梯。若论有梯，何须更问。”其人又低头良久，问曰：“白白白白日？夜夜夜夜地？”素云：“何须云白日夜地，若为得出？”乃云：“若不是夜地，眼睛不瞎，为甚物入入里许？”素大笑。

《太平广记选》（宋）李昉等

Yang Su, a cabinet member during the Sui Dynasty, would often call in a stutterer for a witty chat when he was ***free from his office duty***.

One day near the end of the year, Yang and the stutterer sat facing each other.

“Suppose you were placed in a steep pit a dozen feet deep and a dozen across,” Yang teased, “how are you going to get out?”

Then the man dropped his head to think. After a long moment he asked, "Can I ... I have a ladder?"

"Say no, or why should I have asked?"

The man bent his head again. After another extended while, he asked, "Day...day ...daytime or ...ni...night?"

"Never mind if it's day or night. As long as you can get out, what does that matter?"

"If...if it were not p...pitch dark, and I...I were not b...blind, how ...how could I ... I've fallen into that it?"

Yang burst out laughing. [3]

"The Selections from Records of the Taiping Era"

(The Song Dynasty) Li Fang *et al.*

例中"***闲***"之译文"**free from his office duty**"为意译。

口

从"***口***"的字与嘴有关。例字中除"**鸣、吠、合、名、否、同、品**"外，其余为形声字：左形右声。

啼

1. 江雨霏霏江草齐，
六朝如梦鸟空**啼**。
无情最是台城柳，
依旧烟笼十里堤。

Raining, raining steadily along the River,
Luxuriant the grasses there.
Six Dynasties, as in a dream:
The empty ***call*** of birds.
Today, indifferently, in their green haze
Willows still embrace the ten-league banks of Taicheng. [2]

《台城》
（唐）韦庄

"Taicheng"
(The Tang Dynasty) Wei Zhuang

2. 问君何处天涯？
落日**啼**鹃，
流水桃花，
淡淡遥山，
萋萋芳草，
隐隐残霞。

Where are you going, spring's being? I ask,
While the sun is setting, birds ***chirping***,
Flowers falling and gone with the running stream.
And I am watching the distant hills
Over the sweet grass land at dusk. [10]

《蟾宫曲·送春》
（元）贯云石

Tune: Song of Moon Palace, "Farewell, Spring"
(The Yuan Dynasty) Guan Yunshi

3. 春山暖日和风，	The sun and gentle breeze warm hills in spring,
栏杆楼台帘栊。	The curtained bower girt with balustrade.
杨柳秋千院中。	Among the willows in the garden hangs the swing.
啼莺舞燕，	The swallows dance and crioles ***sing***
小桥流水飞红。	On running stream under the bridge fallen reds fade. [5]
《天净沙 · 春》	Tune: Sunny Sand, "Spring"
（元）白朴	(The Yuan Dynasty) Bai Pu

例 1 与例 2 中"**啼**"的译文为直译。**例 1** 中"鸟空**啼**"之"鸟"乃泛指，故其"啼"亦不必特指与其对应，译为"**call**"（to make the cry that is typical for it）其意与原文对应。其翻译同时涉及到了词类的转换：由原文中的动词转换为译文中的名词。**例 2** 中"**啼**鹃"乃"鹃"之"啼"，特指，译为"**chirping**"，专指小鸟所发出的吱喳、啁啾之声。译文"**chirping**"体现出分析型思维使英语具有明显的词形变化和多样的语法形式："chirp"通过词形变化（词尾+ing）构成现在分词"***chirping***"，"birds"为其逻辑主语；"birds chirping"构成分词的独立结构，作为状语，表示伴随情况。**例 3** 之"啼"为意译。其译文选取"**sing**"体现出了原文中所描述的春日里风和日丽、莺歌燕舞的景象。

【译法点滴】 翻译中的词类转换

在翻译实践中，如果机械地按原文词类"对号入座"，译文就可能变得生硬累赘。既要忠实于原文又要符合译文语言的规范，使译文通顺流畅，有时则需对原文的词类进行适当改变：把原文中属于某种词类的词在译文中转换成另一种词类，这就是翻译上通常所说的"词类转换"。汉语中，动词用得比较多，可以几个动词或动词结构连用，而英语句子中往往只用一个谓语动词，因此，要使译文符合英语的表达习惯，汉语动词在翻译中往往可以转换为名词、形容词、介词、副词以及各种非谓语动词等。根据译文的需要，其他词类也可进行转换，如：名词与副词、副词与形容词、形容词与动词之间的转换。

在上例"啼"的译文中，为符合译语的语言规范，对**例 1** 之"啼"的翻译即使用了词类转换这一手段。

咏

此地有崇山峻岭，茂林修竹，又有清流急湍，映带左右，引以为流觞曲水，列坐其次。虽无丝竹管弦之盛，一觞一**咏**，亦足以畅叙幽情。

《兰亭集序》（东晋）王羲之

The place was surrounded by sublime, high mountains clad in luxuriant forests and shapely bamboos, in addition to a limpid stream with swift rapids, which foiled each other in the whole scenic beauty. We used the sinuous brook for passing the floating cups and sat in order along its banks though we had no lutes or flutes for music, yet one cup of wine accompanied with the ***chanting*** of one poem was sufficient to make us air our deep feelings. [12]

"Preface to the Lanting Collection"
(The Eastern Jin Dynasty) Wang Xizhi

嚼、咽

客有曰："梨益齿而损脾，枣益脾而损齿。"

一呆子方思良久曰："我食梨**嚼**而不**咽**，不能伤我之脾；我食枣则吞而不嚼，不能伤我之齿。"

《湛渊静语》（元）白珽

A fool once heard someone say that pears were good for the teeth but harmful to the spleen, and that dates were good for the spleen but harmful to the teeth.

After pondering the matter a considerable while, he said:

"From now on, when I eat a pear, I will only ***chew*** and not ***swallow*** it. And when I eat a date, I will swallow it whole."[14]

"Zhan Yuan Jing Yu" (The Yuan Dynasty) Bai Ting

鸣：会意字，由"鸟"、由"口"会意。[9] 鸟叫为鸣。

1. 昨夜寒蛩不住**鸣**，
惊回千里梦，
已三更。
起来独自绕階行，
静悄悄，
帘外月胧明。
《小重山》
（宋）岳飞

The autumn crickets ***chirped*** incessantly last night,
Breaking my dream home-bound,
'T was already mid-night.
I got up and alone in the yard walk'd around,
On window screen the moon shone bright,
There was no human sound. [1]

Tune: Manifold Little Hill
(The Song Dynasty) Yue Fei

2. 微雨霭芳原，
春鸠**鸣**何处。
《东郊》
（唐）韦应物

On vast grassland the drizzle is falling,
Somewhere the spring turtledoves are ***singing***. [13]

" On the East Outskirts"
(The Tang Dynasty) Wei Yingwu

3. 浮云游子意，　You'll be like a piece of cloud floating on and on,
落日故人情。　My reluctance to part with you is like the sun slowly setting down.
挥手自兹去，　We wave our hands as you go on your way,
萧萧斑马**鸣**。　Our steeds ***neigh*** and neigh.[13]
《送友人》　" Seeing a Friend Off "
（唐）李白　（The Tang Dynasty）Li Bai

4. 风**鸣**两岸叶，　The leaves of trees on both banks ***rustle*** in the breeze light,
月照一孤舟。　The solitary boat of mine floats on the water under the moon bright.[13]
《宿桐庐江寄广陵旧游》
"To My Old Friend at Guangling While Staying Overnight on the Tonglu River"
（唐）孟浩然　（The Tang Dynasty）Meng Haoran

以上 4 首诗中"**鸣**"译文之不同主要基于其所处的上下文语境。**例 1**"昨夜寒蛩不住**鸣**"之"鸣"使作者从梦中惊醒，突出了蛩之较尖的叫声，译文"**chirp**"体现出小鸟之吱喳声［(of small birds and some insects) to make short high sounds.］。**例 2** 诗中"微、霭、芳、春"的使用体现出作者此时的心境尚好，使用"**singing**"即其心情之体现。此处" sing + ing"构成现在分词，表示进行时态，是分析型思维的具体体现。**例 3**"萧萧斑马**鸣**"之"鸣"出自"马"，其声为嘶鸣，译文使用"**neigh**"（When a horse neighs it makes a long high sound）即其鸣。**例 4**"风**鸣**两岸叶"之"鸣"是指在风中摇曳的树叶所发出的沙沙之声，故译为"**rustle**"（if sth dry and light rustles or you rustle it, it makes a sound like paper, leaves, etc. moving or rubbing together），与其意对应。

吠：会意字，由"犬"、由"口"会意。犬叫为"吠"。

日暮苍山远，　Bleak mountains at sunset stretching forever;
天寒白屋贫。　A white cottage even more pinched in the cold.
柴门闻犬**吠**，　In the night I hear a dog ***bark*** at the thatched gate:
风雪夜归人。　My host returns home in wind and snow.[2]
《逢雪宿芙蓉山主人》
" Spending the Night in a Mountain Village during a Snowstorm"
（唐）刘长卿　（The Tang Dynasty）Liu Changqing

合：会意字，由"两个人一张口"会意。

1. 人有悲欢离**合**，　Men have sorrow and joy, they part or ***meet*** again;

月有阴晴圆缺，　The moon may be bright or dim, she may wax or wane.
此事古难全。　There has been nothing perfect since the olden days.
但愿人长久，　So let us wish that man
千里共婵娟。　Will live long as he can!
Though miles apart, we'll share the beauty she displays. [1]

《水调歌头》　Tune: Prelude to the Melody of Water.
（宋）苏轼　(The Song Dynasty) Su Shi

2. 山无陵，　Till mountains crumble,
江水为竭，　Streams run dry,
冬雷震震，　Thunder rumbles in winter,
夏雨雪，　Snow falls in summer,
天地**合**，　And the earth ***mingles*** with the sky—
乃敢与君绝！　Not till then will I cease to love you! [4]
《上邪》　"A Pledge"
（汉）　(The Han Dynasty)

3. 每览昔人兴感之由，若**合**一契，未尝不临文嗟悼，不能喻之于怀。故知一死生为虚诞，齐彭殇为妄作。后之视今，亦犹今之视昔，悲夫！

《兰亭集序》（东晋）王羲之

Whenever I scrutinized the causes of the ancients' airing their sentiments, I found that they ***tallied*** exactly with each other, and did not fail to sigh with grief upon perusal of their writings, though I was not clear about the reason. I know for certain that to identify life with death is fallacious and to equate longevity to brief life is nonsensical. Men in the future will look upon us mortals in the same light as we look upon men in the past. How sad it must be! [12]

"Preface to the Lanting Collection"
(The Eastern Jin Dynasty) Wang Xizhi

4. 在我们一生中，生活有时会像河流一样，和另一条河流遇**合**了，又分开了，带来了某一种情绪的波流，永远萦绕着我们的心灵…… 淡淡的，却难忘！

《丁香花下》黄秋耘

Our life, like a river, sometimes ***joins*** another river only to separate again, thus leaving certain emotional ripples lingering in our mind... faint and unforgettable! [15]

"Under a Lilac Bush" Huang Qiuyun

5. 绿树村边**合**，青山郭外斜。 The village is ***surrounded*** by the trees green, Beyond the outer city wall slant the hills green.[13]

《过故人庄》 "Visiting an Old Friend's Village"

（唐）孟浩然 (The Tang Dynasty) Meng Haoran

以上例 1～例 4 中"**合**"的译文不同在于其上下文。**例 1**"悲欢离**合**"之"合"意在"相逢"，"**meet**"与原文之意相符。**例 2**"天地**合**"之"合"的译文取"**mingle**"（to bring or mix together or with something else usu. without fundamental loss of identity)，其含义是：此"合"之后的各自成分仍可分辨，不会完全融为一体，换言之，天与地合不到一起，即永远不会"与君绝"。**例 3**"若**合**一契"之"合"意在吻合，"**tally**"（match）即表此意。**例 4**"河流遇**合**"之"合"意在"汇合"，其意即"**join**"（come together to form are thing or group）。**例 5**"合"之意为"环绕"，"surround"（to be all around sth/sb）贴切原文之意。原文中"绿树村边合"为主动语态，其意思是"绿树合围了村庄"。由于本体与客体思维方式的不同，译文中则将被合围的"村庄"作为主语，谓语"合"的译文"**surrounded**"以过去分词的形式，表示出村庄被树所围。体现出本体与客体型思维方式的不同。

【译法点滴】 本体与客体型思维在原文与译文中的体现

中国文化以人本为主体[9]，以人生为本位。人本文化的长期积淀，形成了汉民族本体型的思维方式：以人为中心来观察、分析、推理和研究事物。西方文化以物本为主体[9]，以自然为本位，重视外向探索。这种较为偏重于对自然客体的观察和研究，逐渐形成了客体型的思维方式：把客观世界作为观察、分析、推理和研究的中心注重客观事物对人的作用和影响。

两种不同的思维方式反映在语言形态上，一个较为明显的表现就是在描述事物和阐述事理的过程中，习惯于本体思维方式的中国人，观察或叙述的视点往往落在动作的发出者，并以其作为句子的主语，因此汉语中主动语态句使用频繁。习惯于客体思维方式的西方人却常地把观察或叙述的视点放在行为、动作的结果或承受者上，并把他们作为句子的主语，所以英语中被动语态句的使用相当广泛。在例字的翻译上，原文中某些主动形式的例字，根据其所处语境，为符合译语的思维及语言习惯，在译文中有时则以被动的形式（过去分词）出现。

以上之**例 5** 即为此种情况。

名： 会意字，由"口"、由"夕"会意。夜晚因看不见彼此，所以要说出自己的名字。[9]

1. 钟鼓馔玉不足贵， Decious foods accompanied by bell-striking and drum-

	beat are not worthly to be prized,
但愿长醉不愿醒。	I only wish to get drunk forever and never soberized.
古来圣贤皆寂寞，	Already obscure are all the ancient sages,
惟有饮者留其**名**。	Only we drinkers will be ***well-known*** through ages.[13]
《将进酒》	" Please Drink Wine "
（唐）李白	(The Tang Dynasty) Li Bai

2. 千秋万岁**名**　His enjoyment of a high ***fame*** for ever and a day,
寂寞身后事。Will come only after his unknown life passes away.[13]
《梦李白二首》　"Dreaming of Li Bai (2)"
（唐）杜甫　(The Tang Dynasty) Du Fu

例 1 的题目"将进酒"原是汉乐府短箫铙歌的曲调，题意为劝酒歌。诗人在"古来圣贤皆寂寞，惟有饮者留其**名**"中，对比了圣贤与饮者身后之境遇：圣贤身后沉寂无闻，倒是饮者众所周知。此处"圣贤"与"饮者"均非特指，故对应寂寞（孤独冷情，含有被人冷落之意），"留名"之译文选取"**well-known**"贴切原文意思并考虑了译文的语法结构以及诗的押韵问题。**例 2** 的题目"梦李白"点出诗中所述乃李白其人，"千秋万岁**名**"之"名"所指乃李白之声名。译文选取"**fame**"着意于其声望显赫，同时也考虑到译文的语法结构。

否：会意字，由"口"、由"不"会意。[9]"口"中说"不"。

昨夜雨疏风骤，	Last night the wind was strong and rain was fine,
浓睡不消残酒。	Sound sleep did not dispel the taste of wine.
试问卷帘人，	I ask the maid who's rolling up the screen.
却道海棠依旧。	"The same crab-apple tree," she says, "is seen."
知**否**？	"***Don't*** you know,
知否？	Don't you know
应是绿肥红瘦。	The red should languish and the green must grow?"[1]
《如梦令》	Tune: Like a Dream
（宋）李清照	(The Song Dynasty) Li Qingzhao

同：会意字。意为"门内之人众口一词。"

1. 共看明月应垂泪，	We should shed tears when we look up at the moon bright,
一夜乡心五处**同**。	Though in five different places, we are all in the ***same*** sad mood homesick throughout the night.

"自河南经乱，关内阻饥，兄弟离散，各在一处。因望月有感，聊书所怀。……"

（唐）白居易

"Since the war chaos in Henan, the transportation in the Central Shanxi has been blocked, the people there have suffered from famine and my brothers and sisters have scattered here and there. Looking up the bright moon, I feel sad. So I write this poem to my brothers and sisters..."[13]

(The Tang Dynasty) Bai Juyi

2. ***同***是天涯沦落人，
相逢何必曾相识。

Both losers in this wide world,
By chance both here,
It mattered not that we had never met before.[2]

《琵琶行》
（唐）白居易

"Song of the Pipa"
(The Tang Dynasty) Bai Juyi

3. 睡去依依随雁断，
惊回故故恼蛩鸣。
醒时幽怨***同***谁诉，
衰草寒烟无限情。

In sleep the vision recedes with the flight of swans,
Around with a start we resent the chirp of crickets;
Awake, ***to*** whom can I describe my grief,
The infinite melancholy of cold mist and withered grass?[1]

《红楼梦》
（清）曹雪芹

" A Dream of Red Mansions"
(The Qing Dynasty) Cao Xueqin

4. 重来阊门万事非，
同来何事不同归？
梧桐半死清霜后，
头白鸳鸯失伴飞。
《鹧鸪天》（节选）
（宋）贺铸

All things hanve changed; once I pass the city gate.
We came ***together***; I go back without my mate.
Bitten by hoary frost, half of the plane tree dies.
Lifelong companion lost, one lonely lovebird flies.
Tune: Partridge in the Sky (Extract)
(The Song Dynasty) He Zhu

5. 大道之行，天下为公，选贤与能，讲信修睦。故人不独亲其亲，不独子其子，使老有所终，壮有所用，矜、寡、孤、独、废疾者皆有所养，男有分，女有归。货恶其弃于地也，不必藏于己；力恶其不出于身也，不必为己。是故谋闭而不兴，盗窃乱贼而不作，故外户而不闭，是谓大***同***。

《大道之行也》（春秋）孔子

The grand ideal, as realized in the remote antiquity, consists in creating a commonwealth for all, in which the sage and able are elected for office, faith is promoted and harmony between men fostered. One loves not only his own parents and his own children. The old are taken care of till the end of their lives, the able-bodied are put to good use, the children are duly brought up, and the widowed, orphaned and disabled are provided for. Every man has an occupation and every woman is married to form a family. Abandoning anything useful on the ground is disgusted. But the thing is not to be kept hidden by anyone for himself. Not exerting one's strength for a service is also detested. And the service need not be intended for oneself. Thus plots and intrigues are stifled. Robberies, thefts and riots are not committed. Doors need not be closed. And that is what is called a great ***commonwealth***. [12]

" The Grand Ideal" (The Spring and Autumn Period) Confucius

例 1"一夜乡心五处***同***"指分散中的兄弟均怀思乡之情，此"同"着意在"相同"，译文用"**same**"与原文之意相符。**例 2**"琵琶行"乃七言古诗。此长诗是白居易送客湓浦口，遇到琵琶女，故作此传世名篇。诗句"***同***是天涯沦落人"之"同"所指乃诗作者与琵琶女，"**both**"即其原文之意的表达。**例 3**之"同"为介词，根据对上下文的理解，其意与"跟"相同，引进动作对象，译文"**to**"与其对应。**例 4**之"同"为副词，其意"一同"；"一齐（从事）"，译文"**together**"（with each other）即含此"同"之意。**例 5**中所提之"大同"是我国古代一些思想家提出的一种天下为公，人人平等的社会政治理想。大同社会指的是理想社会，即国泰民安，人人安居乐业。此"同"的译文选用"**commonwealth**"(the general welfare)，较为贴切原文之意。

广

"***广***"部一般与房屋有关。例字均为形声字：外形内声。

庙（廟）

人生翕欻云亡，	Life will soon pass away like a flickering flame,
好烈烈轰轰做一场。	A man should work, come shine or rain,
使当时卖国，	With all his might and main.
甘心降虏，	If they had fallen to the foe,
受人唾骂，	They would have borne the blame
安得流芳？	And down in history ne'er their names could go.
古***庙***幽沉，	Their ***temple*** gloomy at the forest's side,
仪容俨雅，	Their statues awe-inspiring, dignified.
枯木寒鸦几夕阳。	How many times have they been worshipped with crows
邮亭下，	And ancient trees and setting sun which downwards goes!

有奸雄过此，　Should a traitor pass by
仔细思量。　This post-house, let him open wide his eye![1]
《沁园春·题潮阳张许公庙》　Tune: Spring in the Garden of Qin, "Written in the Temple of Their Excellencies Zhang Xun and Xu Yuan"
（宋）文天祥　(The Song Dynasty) Wen Tianxiang

廊

江皋楼观前朝寺，　By riverside stands ancient Temple of Sweet Dew,
秋色入秦淮。　Invaded by autumn hue.
败垣芳草，　Ruined walls overgrown with wild grass,
空***廊***落叶，　Empty ***gallery*** paved with fallen leaves, alas!
深砌苍苔。　Oldened steps covered with moss green.
远人南去，　No more tourists are seen.
夕阳西下，　Down in the west the sun goes,
江水东来。　The river to the east flows.
木兰花在，　Only the magnolia blows.
山僧试问，　I ask the monk for whom,
知为谁开？　The flowers are in bloom.[5]
《人月圆·甘露怀古》
Tune: Man and Moon, "The Ancient Temple of Sweet Dew"
（元）徐再思　(The Yuan Dynasty) Xu Zaisi

庖

良***庖***岁更刀，割也；族庖月更刀，折也。今臣之刀十九年矣，所解数千牛矣，而刀刃若新发硎。

《庖丁解牛》（战国）庄子

A good ***cook*** changes his knife every year, as it is blunted by cutting. An ordinary cook changes his knife every month, for it is injured by the bone-hacking. Now I have used my knife for nineteen years, carving thousands of oxen, but the blade of the knife is as incisive as if it were newly sharpened on a whetstone.[12]

"How a Cook Carved an Ox" (The Warring States Period) Zhuangzi

庐

1. 臣本布衣，躬耕于南阳，苟全性命于乱世，不求闻达于诸侯。先帝不以臣卑鄙，猥自枉屈，三顾臣于草***庐***之中，咨臣以当世之事，由是感激，遂许先帝以驱驰。

《前出师表》（汉）诸葛亮

I was originally a commoner, tilling my landing Nanyang, trying merely to survive in the troublous times, not seeking to be known to the nobility. The late Emperor, disregarding my humble birth and low position, condescended to pay me three visits in my thatched ***cottage***, consulting me on contemporary issues. I was therefore very grateful to him and promised him my whole-hearted service.[12]

"Memorial to the Emperor Before the Northern Expedition"

(The Han Dynasty) Zhuge Liang

2. ***庐***于翠微址最高，群山宫之，平畴崇田，参错其下，目之所周，大约数十里，故视勺庭为胜焉。于是高下其径，折而三之。松鸣于屋上，桃、李、梅、梨、梧桐、桂、辛夷之华，荫于径下，架曲直以为木栏，垩以蜃灰，光耀林木。

《吾庐记》（清）魏禧

The ***abode*** is situated at the highest point of Cuiwei Peak, surrounded by mountains, with interlocked level land and terraced fields below it, commanding a broad view of dozens of *li* in circumference. So it is even better than my own house. The path leading up and down from My Abode is divided into three sections, with pines soughing above the house, and the trees of peach, plum, pear, plane, osmanthus and magnolia shading the lower trails. And then twisted wood is used as railings, painted with clam ash which makes them glisten in the foliage.[12]

"My Abode" (The Qing Dynasty) Wei Xi

3. 清河张君梦得谪居齐安，即其***庐***之西南为亭，以览观江流之盛，而余兄子瞻名之曰"快哉"。

《黄州快哉亭记》（宋）苏辙

Zhang Mengde of Qinghe, having been relegated to a post in Qi'an, built an arbour to the southwest of his ***house*** to view the scenic splendour of the river, and my elder brother Su Zizhan exalted it with the name "ecstasy arbour".[12]

"The Huangzhou Ecstasy Arbour" (The Song Dynasty) Su Zhe

例 1 之"***庐***"为"草庐"，译文"**cottage**"（a small house, especially in the country）即其意。**例 2** 题目为"吾庐记"，其"***庐***"指"住所"或"家"，"**abode**"（the place where sb lives）即表此"家"之意。**例 3** 之"***庐***"着意于"建筑"，即"**house**"（a building for people to live in, usually for one family）。

庭

项脊轩，旧南阁子也。室仅方丈，可容一人居。…… 余稍微修葺，使不上漏。前辟四窗，垣墙门**庭**，以当南日，日影反照，室始洞然。又杂植兰桂竹木于庭，旧时栏楯，亦遂增胜。

《项脊轩志》（明）归有光

Xiangji Chamber was the south ***gezi*** of former days. It was a room one square *zhang* in area and could accommodate one person. …, I did a little repair to prevent the oozing of rain and opened four windows in the front, while surrounding the ***courtyard*** with walls, to screen the room from the sunlight from the south. With the reflection of the sunlight, the room brightened up. And then some orchids, sweet olives, bamboos and trees were planted in the courtyard, and the railings of former days were also carved and decorated. [12]

"Xiangji Chamber" (The Ming Dynasty) Gui Youguang

庥

自渴西南行不能百步，得石渠，民桥其上。有泉悠悠然，其鸣乍大乍细。……其流抵大石，伏出其下。……又北曲行纡余，睨若无穷，然卒入于渴。其侧皆诡石怪木，奇卉美箭，可列坐而***庥***焉。

《永州八记》（唐）柳宗元

Less than a hundred paces southwest of the tributary of the Yuans, I saw a rock flume, with a plank being thrown across it as a convenient bridge. Somewhere below, there was a spring bubbling, alternating abruptly in noise level. It gurgled along, … until it hit a boulder, and then crawled through from underneath it. …The spring continued to wind north as if it had no end, but it flowed abruptly into the tributary of the Yuans at last. All around the spring was a full range of unusually shaped rocks, rare trees, exotic flowers and graceful bamboos, with a clear space wide enough for a few visitors to sit in a row and ***relax***. [8]

"Eight Travel Journals on the State of Yong"
(The Tang Dynasty) Liu Zongyuan

马

用"***马***"组合的字，多与"马"、"马"的特性有关。除"***马***"外，其余皆为形声字。其中，"驚、驾"为下形上声，余者由左形右声构成。

驚

二十馀年如一梦，　O'er twenty years have passed like dreams,
此身虽在堪**驚**。　It is a ***wonder*** that I'm still alive.

闲登小阁看新晴。 Carefree, I mount the tower bathed in moonbeams.
古今多少事, So many things passed long
渔唱起三更。 Ago survive
Only in fishermen's midnight song. [1]

《临江仙 · 夜登小阁忆洛中旧游》
Tune: Immortal at the River, "Mounting a Tower at Night and Recalling the Old Friends Visiting Luoyang Together"
(宋) 陈与义 (The Song Dynasty) Chen Yuyi

原文之"**驚**"为动词。译文中转换为名词"**wonder**",考虑到了译语句子的结构、诗的押韵以及诗文的通顺流畅。

驻

淮左名都, In the famous town east of River Huai
竹西佳处, And scenic spot of Bamboo West,
解鞍少**驻**初程。 Breaking my journey, I alight for a short ***rest***.
过春风十里, In breeze the splendid three-mile road did I pass by,
尽荠麦青青。 'Tis now o'ergrown with wild green wheat and weeds.
自胡马去后, Since Southern shore was overrun by Jurchen steeds,
废池乔木, Even the tall trees beside the pond have been war-torn.
犹厌言兵。 As dusk is drawing near,
渐黄昏, Cold blows the horn,
清角吹寒, The empty town looks drear. [1]
都在空城。

《扬州慢》 Tune: Slow Tune of Yangzhou
(宋) 姜夔 (The Song Dynasty) Jiang Kui

押韵是诗词翻译中所要考虑的一个因素。上例"解鞍少**驻**初程"中"少"为副词,意"暂时","驻"为动词,意"停留"。译文中,根据句子结构,"少"从原文中的副词转换为形容词 short,其所修饰的"驻"也作出相应调整:从动词转换为名词,由此,使"rest"与其上面一句中的"west"押韵。此译文较为明显地体现出词类转换在翻译中的作用。

骢

花**骢**嘶断留侬住, Your dappled ***horse*** neighs when I ask you to stay.
满酌酒劝据鞍父。 I fill you cup with wine to detain you in vain.
柳青青万里初程, The green willows will see you go far, far away
点染阳关朝雨。 To see the Sunny Pass dotted with morning rain.

怨春风燕不回头， I complain why, without turning the head, the wild geese
一个个背人飞去。 Should fly away one by one with the vernal breeze.
望河桥敛衽悲啼， Gazing on the bridge, I wipe with my sleeves tear on tear.
早蓦到长亭短处。 Soon I find the Pavilion of Adieu is near. [5]

《鹦鹉曲·别意》 Tune: Song of Parrot, "Parting Grief"
（元）冯子振 (The Yuan Dynasty) Feng Zizhen

骑、驴

雪晴天地一冰壶， The sky and earth look like icy pot after snow.
竟往西湖探老逋， To seek after mume blossoms in West Lake I go.
骑驴踏雪溪桥路。 Treading on snow by the brook on an ***ass*** I ***ride***,
笑王维作画图， I' ve outdone the poet' s picture of the lakeside.
捡梅花多处提壶。 I bring a pot of wine where mume blossoms throng;
对酒看花笑， Wine cup in hand, I smile at the flowers for long.
无钱当剑沽， Wine drunk up, I may pawn my sword to buy;
醉倒在西湖。 Drunk down, by lakeside I would lie. [5]

《水仙子·西湖探梅》
Tune: Song of Daffodils, "Mume Blossoms at West Lake"
（元）杨朝英 (The Yuan Dynasty) Yang Chaoying

"**骑**"与"**驴**"在译文中次序的安排考虑到了译语的句子结构和曲的押韵。

驾

靖康耻， Our emperors captured,
犹未雪； It is a burning shame.
臣子恨， How could we generals
何时灭。 Quench our vengeful flame!
驾长车、 ***Driving*** our chariots of war, we' d go
踏破贺兰山缺。 To cut through our relentless foe.
壮士饥餐胡虏肉， Valiantly we' d cut off each head;
笑谈渴饮匈奴血。 Laughing, we' d drink the blood they shed.
待从头、收拾旧山河， When we' ve reconquered our lost land,
朝天阙。 In triumph would return our army grand. [1]

《满江红》 Tune: The River All Red
（宋）岳飞 (The Song Dynasty) Yue Fei

原文中"**驾**"为动词，其翻译体现出思维方式的不同：综合型思维方式使汉语"**驾**长车、**踏**破贺兰山缺"中"驾"与"踏"两个动作的次序依据语义逻辑和其发生的先后进行安排，词形上没有任何变化；“驾”之译文“**Driving**”则体现出分析型思维语法的多样：动词“驾”通过词形变化（词尾+ing）构成现在分词，在句中作状语，表示主语“we”的另一个动作。

驴（驢）

楚人有生而不知姜者，曰：“此从树上结成。”或曰：“从土里生成。”其人固执己见，曰：“请与予以十人为质，以所乘**驴**为赌。”已而遍口十人，皆曰：“土里出也。”其人哑然失色，月：“驴则付汝，姜还树生。”

《雪涛小说》（明）江盈科

In the state of Chu lived a man who did not know where ginger grew. He thought it grew on trees. Someone told him it grew in the ground.

He could not believe this was true, and said, “I will lay a bet with you with my ***donkey***. Let us ask ten people; if they all say it grows in the ground, the donkey is yours!”

They asked ten men who all said that it grew in the ground.

“Take the donkey!” said the man. “But, all the same, I know ginger grows on trees!”[14]

“Stories by Xue Tao” (The Ming Dynasty) Jiang Yingke

马：象形字。

但愿老死花酒间，	I would grow old and die among flowers and wine,
不愿鞠躬车**马**前；	Rather than bow before the ***steed*** and carriage fine.
车尘马足贵者趣，	The rich may love their dust-raising carriages and bowers;
酒盏花枝贫者缘。	The poor only enjoy their cup of wine and flowers.[22]
《桃花庵歌》	“Song of Peach Blossom Cottage”
（明）唐寅	(The Ming Dynasty) Tang Yin

弓

“**弓**”意为“从近射及远方的武器”[9]。例字中除“**引**”外，余者为形声字，“弯”为下形上声，其余为左形右声。

张

孔雀陶醉在自己的美丽中。…… 一个穿红衣服的孩子走过来了，她怕是与她媲美的，于是赶紧**张**屏，并左右摇摆，使出浑身解数。开屏后确乎引来大群观赏的人们，人们赞美，欢笑，她似乎全听懂了歌颂的语言，自己十分开心。只一句，她永远没听懂：你是一个可怜的女人。

《鸵鸟 · 孔雀 · 老鹰》吴冠中

The peacock is intoxicated with its own beauty. ...When a little kid in red happens to come near, the peacock, taking her for a potential strong rival, immediately ***erects and spreads out*** its tail feathers and sways now to the left and now to the right as best it can. That succeeds in attracting a large group of spectators. They marvel at its beauty and cheer. The big bird looks very happy with all the words of praise, which it seems to understand fully. Nevertheless, there is one sentence it can never understand, that is, "You're a miserable woman."[15]

"Ostrich · Peacock · Eagle" Wu Guanzhong

例中"**张**"之意译更进一步体现出孔雀开屏时的形态。

弦

吹牛也要认清对手方面的。不然的话必难打动他或她的心**弦**，那么就失掉吹牛的功效了。

《吹牛的妙用》庐隐

You've got to know enough about the person you are boasting to. Otherwise, you'll make a bungle of it and fail to touch a ***chord*** in his or her heart.[15]

"The Wonderful Use of Boasting" Lu Yin

弹

"明天我要回去了，告诉我，我们还能见面吗？"

不知怎的，这声音像一曲悲哀的调子，**弹**动了我的心弦，我突然感到凄凉起来。

"到前方见吧！我也希望你去从军。"

"……"

他没有回答，眼里闪着晶莹的泪光。

《初恋》谢冰莹

"I go back home tomorrow. Tell me if we can ever meet again."

His voice, like a melancholy tune, unexpectedly ***touched*** me to the heart. And a feeling of sadness suddenly came over me.

"Let's meet at the front! I hope you'll join up too."

"..."

He gave no reply, his eyes glittering with tears.[15]

"First Love" Xie Bingying

此例中，“**弹**动心弦”之“**弹**”的宾语是“心”而不是“琴”，故不能用弹拨乐器之“弹（play）”。译文中用“**touch**”来对应“弹”，准确地表达了原文的内容，使读者能够真正领会到作者的心情。

弯（彎）

1. 同样流行于20世纪30年代的一首外国歌曲是《伏尔加河船夫曲》。像我国四川号子一样，这里描绘的是伏尔加河上拉纤的俄罗斯河工的苦状。他们背着纤绳，**弯**着腰，哎哟嗬，哎哟嗬地吆喝着，呻吟着。一把又一把地捯着，吃力地向前踏步。

《从〈老黑奴〉说起》萧乾

Another foreign song popular in China during the thirties was ***The Song of the Volga Boatmen***. Like the Sichuan labor chant, it describes the misery of Russian boat-trackers along the Volga River. They ***bend*** their shoulders to the tow-line, chanting in a loud voice, "Yo heave oh! Yo heave oh!" They inch forward laboriously, pulling the line hand over hand. [15]

"Old Black Joe and Other Songs" Xiao Qian

2. 数十年风风雨雨中作了大批画，有心爱的、有带缺陷的、有很不满意但浸透苦劳的……任何一个探索都走过**弯**路和歧途，都会留下许多失败之作，蹩脚货，暴露真实吧，何必遮丑，然而，换了人间，金钱控制了人，进而摧毁了良知和人性。

《毁画》吴冠中

I produce a great many paintings during the scores of difficult years. Some of them were my favorites, some were defective, some, though unsatisfactory, were fruits of my painstaking labor. ... All art explorers are liable to take ***roundabout*** courses or lead themselves astray, thus ending up in fiascoes. Defective works should be exposed rather than covered up. But things on earth have changed and men are so much under the sway of money that they have become conscienceless and unfeeling. [15]

"Scrapping My Paintings" Wu Guanzhong

例1中“**弯**着腰”的“弯”为动词，其意是“使弯曲”。其译文“**bend**”即含此意：（especially of sb's body or head）to lean, or make sth lean, in a particular direction. **例2**中“**弯**路”的“弯”是形容词，其意为“弯曲；不直”，此处译为“**roundabout**”（not done or said using the shortest, simplest or most direct way possible），其意与此“弯”对应。

引：会意字。由弓和丨会意[9]（“丨”意为“上下通彻”）。其本意为“拉开弓”。现常用其引申意：“牵引，引导，引起，引用，惹”等。

1. 当时燕大教授多属学院派，不管教什么，都先***引***经据典，在定义上下功夫。而且，大都是先生讲，学生听。课堂上轻易听不见什么讨论。

《斯诺精神》萧乾

In those days, professors at Yenching University were mostly an academic type. Whatever they taught, they would, first of all, ***give*** copious references to the classics and spend very much time on definitions. More often than not, they did all the talking while the students did nothing but listen.[15]

"Spirit of Edgar Snow" Xiao Qian

2. 有些批评家说，中国的文人学士，尤其是诗人，都带着浓重的颓废色彩，所以中国诗文里，颂赞秋的文字特别的多。但外国的诗人，又何尝不然？我虽则外国诗文念得不多，也不想开出账来，做一篇秋的诗歌散文钞，但你若去一翻英德法意等诗人的集子，或各国的诗文的 anthology 来，总能够看到许多关于秋的歌颂与悲啼。各著名的大诗人的长篇田园诗或四季诗里，也总以关于秋的部分，写得最出色而最有味。足见有感觉的动物，有情趣的人类，对于秋，总是一样的能特别***引***起深沉，悠远，严厉，萧索的感触来。

《故都的秋》郁达夫

Some literary critics say that Chinese literati, especially poets, are mostly disposed to be decadent, which accounts for predominance of Chinese works singing the praises of autumn. Well, the same is true of foreign poets, isn't? I haven't read much of foreign poetry and prose, nor do I want o enumerate autumn-related poems and essays in foreign literature. But, if you browse through collected works of English, German, French or Italian poets, or various countries' anthologies of poetry or prose, you can always come across a great many literary pieces eulogizing or lamenting autumn. Long pastoral poems of songs about the four seasons by renowned poets are mostly distinguished by beautiful moving lines on autumn. All that goes to show that all live creatures and sensitive humans alike ***are prone to*** the feeling of depth, remoteness, severity and bleakness.[15]

"Autumn in Peiping" Yu Dafu

通过对上下文的理解，以上两例中“引”的译文均通过意译的方法给出。原文**例 1** 之“引”有“引用”之意。句子主语是“燕大教授”，“引经据典”属谓语部分。译者没有使用“quote”或“quotation”，而是通过“**give** copious references to the classics”表达出“引经据典”之意。译文在注意到了译语语言使用规范的同时，通过“copious”的使用，为后面“下功夫”（spend very much time）的翻译埋下了伏笔。**例 2**“引”所在句子的大致意思是：秋季易触发生灵的某种感触。此处之“引”含“容易感/受到”之意，译文选取“**are prone to**”（**be liable to**）贴切原文之意。

子

“***子***”之本意为“婴儿”。与“子”组合的字往往与“人、儿女、种子、卵、小而坚硬的块状物或粒状物”等有关。例字中，除“***孝***”外，余者为形声字：左形右声。

孺

抗战八年，中国死了二千多万，单是南京屠城就杀害了三十万，而且大都是老弱妇***孺***。

《忘了过去就是犯罪》冯亦代

During the eight-year War of Resistance Against Japan, Japanese troops killed a total of more than 20 million Chinese. In the Rape of Nanking alone, they slaughtered as many as 300,000, most of them old and weak and women and ***children***.[15]

"Forgetting the Past Is a Crime" Feng Yidai

孩

一九一一年秋，我们从山东烟台回到福州老家去。在还乡的路上，母亲和父亲一再地嘱咐我，“回到福州住在大家庭里，不能再像野***孩***子似的了，一切要小心。对长辈们不能没大没小的。祖父是一家之主，尤其要尊敬……”

《祖父和灯火管制》冰心

In the autumn of 1911, we returned from Yantai of Shandong Province to our native place Fuzhou. While on the way, my parents warned me again and again, "Since we'll beliving in a big family in Fuzhou, remember always to behave properly and never act like a naughty ***child***. Show respect for your elders, particularly your grandpa, who is head of the family..."[15]

"Grandpa and Nightly Blackout" Bing Xin

孤

1. 雨声渐渐的住了。窗帘后隐隐的透出清光来。推开窗户一看，呀！凉云散了，树叶上的残滴，映着月儿，好似荧光千点，闪闪烁烁的动着。—— 真没想到苦雨***孤***灯之后，会有这么一幅清美的图画。

《笑》冰心

As the rain gradually ceased to patter, a glimmer of light began to filter into the room through the window curtain. I opened the window and looked out. Ah, the rain clouds had vanished and the remaining raindrops on the tree leaves glistened tremulously under the moonlight like myriads of fireflies. To think that there should appear before my eyes such a beautiful sight after the miserable rain on a ***lonely*** evening![15]

"Smile" Bing Xin

2. 小时候，总感到年龄属于七老八十的长辈们，与自己无关。我的祖父六十岁早已蓄须，不免显得老态，那时我只有十岁。现在我年已八十，在浑浊的水中，犹如滚滚浪潮中的一叶***孤***舟。我闪避汽车开过的泥水飞溅，艰难地过马路，进弄堂，推入家门，厨房里满地积水，过道上也是积水，甚至地面较高的客堂后间也浸满大水。除了冰箱已提前移开，家具都被水淹，我只有望洋兴叹。

《困水记》何为

When I was a child, I used to think that age had nothing to do with me and associated it instead only with my elders in their sixties or eighties. When I was ten, my grandpa, at sixty, looked quite old for his age because of the beard he was wearing. Now, as an octogenarian, I was like a ***solitary*** small boat drifting at the mercy of a large flow of muddy water. I barely managed to cross the street, taking care to dodge the muddy water splashed over by cars. At last I entered the lane and, pushing open the door of my house, I found the kitchen, the passageway and even the place behind the drawing room all flooded. All furniture, except the fridge that had been previously moved elsewhere, was soaking wet. I felt simply helpless. [15]

"Stranded in a Flood" He Wei

以上两例中的"***孤***"均为直译。**例 1** 中"孤"的译文体现出语文联想对翻译的影响。《广雅 · 释诂三》对"孤"的解释中有一条是"孤，独也。""独"之意即"单一"，"只有一个"。译文并没有将"孤灯"译为"一盏灯"（a lamp/light）而是将从"孤灯"所联想到的，在凄风苦雨之夜孤身一人所感受的寂寞与凄凉之情译了出来。这里"**lonely**"（unhappy because you have no friends or people to talk to）的选用，贴切地再现了作者所要表达的内容及情感。**例 2** 中"孤"的译文"**solitary**"（alone, with no other people or things around）强调出了孤零零的状态。

【译法点滴】 文化差异对翻译的影响：语义联想及其译法——直译、意译

文化差异，顾名思义，即因文化的不同而产生的差异。

翻译不仅涉及到两种语言，同时也与两种文化密切相关。中、西方之间在文

学艺术、风俗习惯、生活方式、宗教信仰、行为规范、思维方式、价值观念等等方面都有存在着诸多的不同，而不同的文化观念之间局部的交叉、碰撞和冲突往往会给翻译带来不同程度的障碍和困难。根据本书的特点，这里主要介绍两种因文化差异而带来的翻译障碍：**语义联想**和**词汇空缺**，并针对具体例字介绍其所使用的翻译方法：直译、意译、音译、音译+注释。

语义联想是人在接收到语义信息时所产生的、超出该信息以外的、又有一定相关性的、连续的想象。换言之，语义联想即人们看到、听到一组或一段文字时，自然而然理解到的意思，这种理解是人脑不经过思考直接感受到的信息，这也是自然语言的一种基本属性。但由于文化差异和自然生态环境的影响，不同民族对于相同事物所产生的语义联想可能有所不同。如“早餐”一词，其意义虽然较为单一，但不同文化背景的读者对其所产生的联想也不尽相同：中国人想到的可能是豆浆、油条、包子；西方人所想的往往是牛奶、面包、果酱。

即景生情，托物寓意，这是日常生活及文学作品中常见的语言现象，也是各民族共同的思维方式。如上面**例 1** 中“**孤**”之原文及其译文即是语义联想在翻译中的体现：原文“真没想到苦雨**孤**灯之后，会有这么一幅清美的图画。”中的“孤灯”使人自然而然联想到的是“夜晚孤独一人”，而不会仅仅是“一盏灯”；基于对原文的理解，“孤灯”意译为“**on a lonely evening**”，贴切地表达出了作者所要表达的内容及情感，但就“孤”一字而言，可以说是直译，其译文选用“**lonely**”（unhappy because you have no friends or people to talk to），再现了单独一人的画面。

在文学翻译中，熟悉词语的文化背景知识很有必要。

孝：会意字。由老者、由子会意，表示子女承奉父老。[9]

近读大作，有“切望父灵能回到家园与先人同在”之语，不胜感慨系之。今老先生仍厝于慈湖，统一之后，即当迁安故土，或奉化，或南京、或庐山，以了吾弟**孝**心。吾弟近曾有言：“要把**孝**顺的心，扩大为民族感情，去敬爱民族，奉献于国家。”旨在斯言，盍不实践于统一大业！就国家民族而论，蒋氏两代对历史有所交代；就吾弟个人而言，可谓忠**孝**两全。否则，吾弟身后事何以自了。尚望三思。

《致蒋经国信》廖承志

Recently I was profoundly moved when I read one of your writings in which you expressed the “longing for my father’s soul to return to the homeland and be among the forefathers”. The remains of your father, now still temporarily placed at Cihu, shall, upon national reunification, be immediately moved to the final resting place in Fenghua, Nanking or Lushan in fulfillment of your ***filial*** wishes. You recently said, “***Filial*** devotion should be expanded into national devotion, which means love of the nation and dedication to the country." Well said! Why don't you apply it to the great cause of national reunification? As far as the country and the nation are concerned, you will have fulfilled the task imposed on you and your father by history; as far as you yourself are concerned, this will be an expression of both loyalty and ***filial*** piety. Otherwise how could you account for yourself after your passing away? I hope you will think more about it. [15]

"A Letter to Chiang Ching-Kuo" Liao Chengzhi

巾

"**巾**"本意为佩戴的巾帛。与"巾"一起构成的字往往与擦东西或包裹、覆盖东西的纺织品有关。例字中除"**巾**、**帘**"外，其余为形声字。其中，"常、幕、布、席"为下形上声，其他左形右声。

常

或一日得鱼稍大者某所，必数数往焉，卒未尝多得，且或无一得者。余疑钓之不善，问之**常**钓家，率如是。

《说钓》（清）吴敏树

It might occur that someday I did catch a bigger fish somewhere, and I would go to that place several times on end. But eventually I failed to get more, even none at all. I doubted whether my fishing skill was none too good and went to ask an ***experienced*** fisher. It turned out that it was a general case. [12]

"On Fishing" (The Qing Dynasty) Wu Minshu

"**常**"此处为意译。根据上下文"问之**常**钓家，率如是"，说明因经常垂钓，故有经验，才能够说出"率如是"。译文选取"**experienced**"体现出原文之意。

幕

严闭的心**幕**，慢慢的拉开了，涌出五年前的一个印象。—— 一条很长的古道。驴脚下的泥，兀自滑滑的。田沟里的水，潺潺的流着。近村的绿树，都笼在湿烟里。弓儿似的新月，挂在树梢。一边走着，似乎道旁有一个孩子，抱着一堆灿白的东西。驴儿过去了，无意中回头一看。—— 他抱着花儿，赤着脚，向着我微微的笑。

《笑》冰心

A ***scene*** of five years ago slowly unveiled before my mind's eye. It was a long ancient country road. The ground under my donkey's feet was slippery with mud. The water in the field ditches was murmuring. The green trees in the neighbouring village were shrouded in a mist. The crescent new moon looked as if hanging on the tips of the trees. As I passed along, I somewhat sensed the presence of a child by the roadside carrying something snow white in his arms. After the donkey had gone by, I happened to look back and saw the child, who was barefoot, looking at me smilingly with a bunch of flowers in his arms. [15]

"Smile" Bing Xin

"严闭的心**幕**，慢慢的拉开了"：作者用比喻的手法生动形象地写出封闭的记忆逐渐开启。此处"心幕"之"幕"非舞台所用之"幕（布）"，乃作者之心扉；"**scene**"亦非具体之场景，而是作者心中所浮现出的景象。译文通过使用具体的"**unveiled** "（拉开帷幕）将抽象之"幕"的含意体现在译文之中，而非与某个单词或词组对应。

布

1. 母亲亲手纺出线，请人织成***布***，染了颜色，我们叫"家织布"，有铜钱那样厚，一套衣服老大穿过了，老二老三接下来穿还穿不烂。

《母亲的回忆》朱德

Mother would spin cotton into yarn and then asked somebody to have it woven into ***fabric*** and dyed. We called it "home-spun fabric" . It was as thick as a copper coin and was so durable that after the eldest brother had grown out of the home-spun garment, it could still be used by the second and third brothers in turn without being worn out. [15]

"Loving Memories of Mother" Zhu De

2. 外边看不到什么颜色了，我只好在屋子里"创造"些颜色。我在堂屋里挂上绿色的窗帘，铺上绿色的桌***布***，窗台上摆上些朋友送的一品红、仙客来，和孩子们自己种的吊兰。

《春的消息》冰心

Disappointed at the drab surroundings, I had to turn to "creating" colour under my roof. I decorated my room with green-coloured window curtains, spread a green ***cloth*** on the table, placed on windowsills some poinsettias and, cyclamens given by a friend and some diaolan planted by my children. [15]

"Tidings of Spring" Bing Xin

例 2 之"***布***"是"桌布"，译文"**cloth**"（ a piece of cloth, often used for a special purpose, especially cleaning thing or covering a table)，即此"布"之意。

席

1. 诗情放，剑气豪，	With a poetic mood, and
英雄不把穷通较。	A spirit of swordsmanship—
江中斩蛟，	A hero never cares about the ups and downs in life.
云间射雁，	You kill the dragon in the river,
席上挥毫。	Or shoot the eagle in the air,
他得志笑闲人，	Or write big characters at the ***party***.
他失脚闲人笑。	And you laugh at others as you like,
	Or be laughed by them, woe![10]

《庆东原 · 次韵马致远先辈韵》

Tune: Blessed East Plain, "Rhyming with Mr. Ma Zhiyuan"

（元）张可久　　(The Yuan Dynasty) Zhang Kejiu

2. 绿树当门酒肆，	By a wine shop amid green trees,
红妆映水鬟儿。	A ring-haired girl in red shows up,
眼底殷勤***席***间诗。	Who once served us at the ***feasts***
尘埃三五字，	While we were reciting new poems.
杨柳万千丝，	Now, our words turned into dust,
记年时曾到此。	And willows faded into memories.
	Oh, here is the place we once were![10]

《红绣鞋 · 春日湖上》

Tune: Embroidered Red Shoes, "Spring: Once More by the Lakeside"

（元）张可久　　(The Yuan Dynasty) Zhang Kejiu

"***席***"之意为 1. 用苇篾、竹篾、草等编成的片状物，用来铺炕、床、地或搭棚子等；2. 成桌的饭菜、酒席。此两例之"席"皆属第二意"酒席"。根据上下文语境，**例 1**"***席***上挥毫"之"席"着意于"聚会"，译文选取"**party**"（a social occasion, often in a person's home, at which people eat, drink, talk, dance and enjoy themselves）符合原文之意。**例 2**"酒肆"中之"席"着意在"宴会"，译为"**feasts**"（a large special meal, especially for a lot of people and to celebrate sth）即此"宴"之意。

帐

我用力把眼睛睁大，我撩开蚊***帐***，我在漆黑的空间中找寻你的影子。

但是从两扇开着的小窗，慢慢地透进来灰色的亮光，使我的眼睛看见了这个空阔的房间。

没有你，没有你的微笑。有的是寂寞、单调。雨一直滴——滴地下着。

《梦》巴金

Forcing my eyes to open wider and drawing aside the mosquito ***net***, I began to search for you in the pitch darkness.

A greyish light, nevertheless, edged in through two small windows to enable me to see the spacious room.

You and your smile were no more. Only loneliness and monotony remained. The rain kept pitter-pattering. [15]

"Dreams" Ba Jin

帷

我白天是写不出文章的。"楼上书房"的光线太大，多呆了会头疼，用了太厚的窗***帷***又会闷气。"楼下书房"事实上又是会客间，我的客人又多，文章写到一半，来了几个朋友，反而大家不舒服。……"三楼书房"现已放了一个床，我的表弟睡在里面，所以我寻了书便不常去了。

事实上，我已不应当对我的书斋发什么牢骚，虽然不大，可是究竟容得下我。况且它们也不算对不起我，自从去年秋天搬到此地，真名假名的文章，将近十五万字了。

《我的书斋生活》邵洵美

I can't work efficiently in the daytime. The "Upstairs Study" is too lit up by the sun, so that I get a headache after staying there a bit too long. And a thick window ***curtain*** would only make the room stuffy. The "Down Study" is in fact a drawing room-cum-study. I have frequent visitors. When they call, I have to break off writing to the discomfort of both parties. ... As to the "Third-floor Study", a bed has now been placed there for my younger male cousin. So I seldon go there unless when I need a book.

In fact, I shouldn't have complaints about my studies. Small as they are, they are tolerable. Since I moved to the resent lodgings in the autumn of last year, I've produced writings, under my real name or a pseudonym, totaling about 150,000 words. [15]

"My Private Library" Shao Xunmei

帽

我走出这户人家，回头望一眼门牌号码，靠着蓝布大褂和呢***帽***的掩护，谁也看不出我是个被打伤的"逃犯"，拐了个弯，到了骑河楼清华同学会，坐上直开清华园的校车，我就这样安然无恙地脱险了。

《丁香花下》黄秋耘

On stepping out of the house, I turned my head to take a look at the house number. Now, under cover of the blue long gown and the felt ***hat***, nobody could recognize me as the injured "criminal" at large. After turning a corner, I arrived at Tsinghua University Alumni Association on Qihelou Street where a school bus took me straight back to the university campus. So I was at last safe and sound. [15]

"Under a Lilac Bush" Huang Qiuyun

帻

西湖七月半，一无可看，只可看看七月半之人。看七月半之人，以五类看之。…… 其一不舟不车，不衫不**帻**，酒醉饭饱，呼群三五，跻入人丛，昭庆、断桥，嚣呼嘈杂，装假醉，唱无腔曲，月亦看，看月者亦看，不看月者亦看，而实无一看者，看之。

《西湖七月半》（明）张岱

The fourth category is of those who have neither boats nor chariots and are neither clad in gowns nor crowned with ***headgears***. Drunk and surfeited, they call their associates to squeeze into the crowds of merrymakers, bawling and roistering at Zhaoqing Temple and Duanqiao Bridge. They sham intoxication and sing tuneless ditties, looking at the moon and the people admiring the moon as well as those who are not admiring the moon, yet seeing actually nothing at all. [12]

"The West Lake in the Middle of the Seventh Month"
(The Ming Dynasty) Zhang Dai

幡

金鱼玉带罗兰扣，
皂盖朱**幡**列五侯。
山河判断在俺笔尖头。
得意秋，
分破帝王忧。

《喜春来》
（元）伯颜

Adorned with gold fish and belt of jade,
I button my robe of brocade,
Under black canopy and ***banners*** red,
Of the five highest lords I'm at the head.
The land is ruled at the tip of my pen.
What pride over all men!
I bear my share of the imperial care. [5]

Tune: Welcome to Spring
(The Yuan Dynasty) Bo Yan

巾：象形字。

别了，我爱的中国，我全心爱着的中国，当我倚在高高的船栏上，见着船渐渐的离岸了，船与岸间的水面渐渐的阔了，见着许多亲友挥着白**巾**，挥着帽子，挥着手，说着 Adieu，adieu！听着鞭炮噼噼啪啪的响着，水兵们高呼着向岸上的同伴告别时，我的眼眶是润湿了，我自知我的泪点已经滴在眼镜面了，镜面是模糊了，我有一种说不出的感动！

《离别》郑振铎

Farewell, China, my beloved homeland! Learning over the high railing, I watched the ship rearing itself away slowly from the shore, leaving a widening expanse of water in between. Many relatives and friends of mine were waving their hats and white ***handkerchiefs*** amidst shouts of "Adieu, adieu!" Firecrackers were cracking and spluttering, and sailors shouting goodbye to their buddies on the shore. I was seized with violent emotion, tears welling up in my eyes and blurring my eyeglasses.[15]

"Parting Sorrows" Zheng Zhenduo

帘：会意字。由穴、由巾会意。"穴"本意为"土室"。

傍午的时候，雾变成了牛毛雨，像**帘**子似的老是挂在窗前。两三丈以外，便只见一片烟云——依然遮抹一切，只不是雾样的罢了。没有风。门前池中的残荷梗时时忽然急剧地动摇起来，接着便有红鲤鱼的活泼泼的跳跃划破了死一样平静的水面。

《雾》矛盾

About noon the fog turned into a fine misty rain like a ***curtain*** hanging still at the window. Some 30 feet away, a cloud of misty vapour prevailed, blotting out everything. The air was windless. Every now and then, the withered lotus stems in the pond in front of my door gave a sudden violent jerk as a red carp was seen splashing briskly out of the water to break the death-like silence.[15]

"Fog" Mao Dun

三、四画

欠

其甲骨文的字形像一个人跪坐着，张着嘴巴正在打呵欠。后来引申为"亏欠""欠缺"义[26]。由"**欠**"构成的字有些与张口吐气的动作相关。例字中除"**吹**"外，其余为形声字：右形左声。

歇

愁因薄暮起，	I feel sad when dusk is coming near,
兴是清秋发。	Yet my interest is aroused by the autumn clear.
时见归村人，	From time to time I see villagers home-returning,
沙行渡头**歇**。	They are walking on the sands, and then ***taking a rest*** at the ferry-crossing. [13]

《秋登万山寄张五》

"To Zhang the Fifth After Ascending Mount Wan in Autumn"

（唐）孟浩然　　（The Tang Dynasty）Meng Haoran

欲

1. 臣闻求木之长者，必固其根本；**欲**流之远者，必浚其泉源；思国之安者，必积其德义。

《谏太宗十思疏》（唐）魏征

I, your humble subject, have learned that to expect a tree to grow, one must strengthen its roots, to ***hope*** that a river runs far, one must dredge its source, to wish a state stability, one must make himself abound in virtues. [12]

"Ten Points of Deliberation Recommended to Emperor Taizong"

（The Tang Dynasty）Wei Zheng

2. 鱼，我所**欲**也；熊掌，亦我所欲也。二者不可兼得，舍鱼而取熊掌者也。

《鱼我所欲也》（战国）孟子

Fish is what I ***desire***, and so are bear ' s paws. If I cannot have both, I would choose the latter and forsake the former. [12]

"Fish Is What I Desire"（The Warring States Period）Meng Zi

3. 夫钓，适事也，隐者之所游也，其趣或类于求得。终焉少系于人之心者，不足可**欲**故也。

《说钓》（清）吴敏树

As for fishing, it is just a matter of pastime, a delight for those who live in retirement. Its fun might be likened to that of seeking gains. But after all, it is by no means a thing that one attaches so much to heart and considers as deserving of a strong ***desire***. [12]

"On Fishing"（The Qing Dynasty）Wu Minshu

4. 人有枯梧树者，其邻父言："枯梧之树不祥。"其邻人遽而伐之。邻人父因请以为薪。其人乃不悦，曰："邻人之父，徒**欲**为薪，而教吾伐之也，与我邻若此其险，岂可哉！”

《列子》（战国）列子

A man had a withered plane tree. “It’s unlucky to keep a withered tree,” said his neighbor. But when the first man had felled the tree, his neighbor asked him for some of the wood as fuel. “The old man simply ***wanted*** some fuel,” thought the owner of the tree indignantly. “That’s why he told me to fell my tree. We are neighbors, and yet he tricks me in this way—this is really going too far!”[14]

“Lie Zi” (The Warring States Period) Lie Zi

以上4例“**欲**”之译文均为直译，但基于所处之上下文，译文不尽相同。**例1**“**欲**流之远者”之“欲”着意于“希望”或“期待”；**例2**“鱼，我所**欲**也”和**例3**“不足可**欲**”之“欲”表示“渴望”和“愿望”；**例4**“徒**欲**为薪”之“欲”意在表达渴求所需之物。译文“hope, desire 和 wanted”分别表达出其各自原文之“欲”的含意。例4之“**wanted**”通过动词 want+ed 所构成的过去时态是分析型思维的体现。

歔欷

唯佳人之独怀兮，	With fragrant Herbs I ease my Heart,
折芳椒以自处。	And long for the Elect.
曾***歔欷***之嗟嗟兮，	Alone I ***sigh***, and Tears fall down,
独隐伏而思虑。	As deeply I reflect.[7]
《悲回风》	“The Ill Wind”
（战国）屈原	(The Warring States Period) Qu Yuan

欣欣

兰叶春葳蕤，	In spring the orchid grows lush and green,
桂华秋皎洁，	In autumn the osmanthus flowers look bright and clean.
欣欣此生意，	They are so ***thriving and flourishing***,
自尔为佳节。	That they naturally make beautiful the seasons they are in.[13]
《感遇》	“Some Thoughts on the Orchid and the Osmanthus Flowers”
（唐）张九龄	(The Tang Dynasty) Zhang Jiuling

歌

笙***歌***正浓处，便自拂衣长往，羡达人撒手悬崖；更漏已残时，犹然夜行不休，笑俗士沉身苦海。

《菜根谭》（明）洪应明

The person, who can leave the theatre without the least hesitation just when the show of dancing and ***singing*** is at its height, is an enlightened man who knows how to rein in at the brink of the precipice. Such a man deserves to be admired. The person, who is still busy rushing about for his worldly purpose even late at midnight, is a mean fellow who is deeply submerged by the sea of bitterness. Such a fellow is destined to be held up to ridicule. [6]

"Rein in at the brink of the precipice so as to avoid falling into the sea of bitterness."

"The Roots of Wisdom"

(The Ming Dynasty) Hong Yingming

吹：会意字，由“口”、由“欠”会意[9]。气从口中吐出。

朔风寒**吹**下银沙，	The northern wind ***blows*** snow down like silver sand,
蠹气穿帘，	It erodes the steps where I stand,
拂柳惊鸦。	Passes through the screen, caresses willow trees,
轻若鹅毛，	And startles crows. It's light as feather of geese,
姣如柳絮，	As willow down it's tender,
瘦似梨花。	And as pear flower it's slender. [5]
《折桂令·微雪》	Tune: Plunking Laurel Branch, "Slight Snow"
（元）无名氏	(The Yuan Dynasty) Anonymous

“**吹**”在原文中没有任何词形上的变化；而译文却需通过语法来表达出主语的数以及时态：“**blows**”即其体现。

车

用“**车**”组合的字，与车、车的零件以及具有与车之性质相近的物品有关。

例字中除“**军、辇、车**”外，余者为形声字：左形右声。

转

转轴拨弦两三声，	She ***turned*** the tuning-pegs and plucked twice or thrice each string,
未成曲调先有情。	Though a tune was not played, we could feel her deep feeling. [13]
《琵琶行》	"Song of a Female Pipa-Player"
（唐）白居易	(The Tang Dynasty) Bai Juyi

输

汉女**输**橦布，To pay taxes the Han women there kapok cloth would ***contribute***,
巴人讼芋田。And to get potato fields the Ba people would start a lawsuit. [13]
《送梓州李使君》 "Seeing Off Provincial Governor Li of Zizhou"
(唐) 王维 (The Tang Dynasty) Wang Wei

“**输**”的含义除“运输”之外，书面语中，还有“捐献（财物）”之意，根据诗意，译文“**contribute**”表达出此“输”之意。

辘轳

月皎惊乌栖不定， The crow feels restless, startled by moonlight,
更漏将阑， The water-clock drips out as later grows the night,
辘轳牵金井。 ***The windlass*** lifts water from the well painted gold.
唤起两眸清炯炯， She wakes me with her beaming eyes so bright,
泪花落枕红棉冷。 I find the pillow wet with tears and cold. [1]
《蝶恋花 · 早行》
Tune: Butterflies Lingering over Flowers, "Parting in the Early Morning"
(宋) 周邦彦 (The Song Dynasty) Zhou Bangyan

军：会意字，由“冖”、由“车”会意。小篆体的“冖”是一个“∩”，“军”的意思是“包围”。

上将拥旄西出征， General Feng carries a commander's tally to lead the troops on the westward expedition,
平明吹笛大**军**行。 At dawn the ***troops*** set out as soon as the fifes are blown.
四边伐鼓雪海涌， The drums are beaten in all directions and Xuehai seems to ripple,
三军大呼阴山动。 The whole troops shout and the Yinshan Mountain seems to tremble. [13]
《轮台歌奉送封大夫出师西征》
"Song of Luntai for Seeing Off Senior Official Feng on His Expedition to the West"
(唐) 岑参 (The Tang Dynasty) Cen Shen

原文诗中虽为“大军”（大队人马），但“军”之词形不变；译文“**troops**”则需通过名词后+s 来表达其复数的形式：综合与分析型思维方式使然。

辇：会意字，由表示两人的“夫夫”在“车”前牵引会意。[9]

那堪独坐青灯。 How can I bear to sit alone by dim lamplight,

想故国、	Thinking of Northern land now lost to sight
高台月明。	With palaces steeped in moonlight;
辇下风光,	Of Southern ***capital*** in days gone by;
山中岁月,	Of my secluded life in mountain high;
海上心情。	Of grief of those who seawards fly![1]
《柳梢青》	Tune: Green Tip of Willow Branch
(宋) 刘辰翁	(The Song Dynasty) Liu Chenweng

此处通过层层语义联想意译出“**辇**”的内涵:通过“辇”使人联想到乘“辇”之人,即古代的皇帝;通过皇帝所在之地,联想到“都城”。因此使用“**capital**”来对应“辇”,贴切原文所要表达之意。当时南宋的都城为临安,现今的杭州,“capital”前使用“southern”,凸显出作者的故国之思。

车:象形字。

徒令上将挥神笔,	Zhuge Liang was asked by Shu to write with a deity brush but in vain,
终见降王走传**车**。	Because Liu Chan finally surrendered to Wei and was sent to Luoyang in a post-house ***wagon***.
管乐有才真不忝,	By all means Zhuge Liang was as good as Guan Zhong and Yue Yi in talent,
关张无命欲何如?	Yet what could he do when Guan Yu and Zhang Fei died a death violent?[13]
《筹笔驿》	"At the Choubi Posthouse"
(唐) 李商隐	(The Tang Dynasty) Li Shangyin

日

“***日***”组合的字与“太阳、炎热、白天、时间、光亮”等有关。例字中除“***明、旦、日***”外,其余为形声字。其中,“**景**”为上形下声,其他:左形右声。

晓

岱宗夫如何?	Oh, what on earth is Mount Tai like?
齐鲁青未了。	On the states of Qi and Lu its green ranges out of sight.
造化钟神秀,	The nature gathers on it all its miracle and beauty,
阴阳割昏**晓**。	Its southside is ***bright*** while its northside is shady.[13]
《望岳》	"Gazing in the Distance at Mount Tai"
(唐) 杜甫	(The Tang Dynasty) Du Fu

诗题“望岳”之“**岳**”本意为高大的山，这里指泰山。山之南为阳，其北面为阴，阳面光线充足，译文“**bright**”表达了诗中“晓”的含意。

【译法点滴】 文化差异对翻译的影响：词汇空缺及其译法——意译

翻译中的词汇空缺指原语的某些表达在目的语中没有现成的表达与之对应。如中国传统文化中的阴阳、节气、生肖等词在英语中没有现成的对等之词；英语中的 karaoke，hippie 等在汉语中也没有词语与之对应。在此情况之下，译者要使其读者获得与原文读者相同的反应，需在熟悉文化知识、正确理解原文的基础上，考虑到读者的接受能力，选择适当的翻译方法。如上例诗中的“造化”“阴”“阳”在英语中无完全对等之词。译者在充分理解原文的基础上，根据汉文化的传统表达习惯，将“造化”意译为“nature”，“阴”“阳”则通过“northside”和“southside ”与之对应。中国位于北半球，以我们的视点来观察太阳，它是从东方升起经由南方最后落到西方，山的南面是向阳坡，山的北面是背光坡，南面的日照一定比北面充足，所以山南为阳，山北为阴。再如诗句“少小虽非投笔吏”，其中所提及的“投笔吏”源于东汉班超投笔从戎的典故。班超为西域的回归、促进民族融合，做出了巨大贡献，官至西域都护，封定远侯。这一文化信息在译语中没有与其相对应的词语，从整句诗的译文“Though，when young，I didn't give up pen for sword as Ban Chao did（*Translated by Wang Fulin*）”来看，译者即运用意译的方法，通过“as Ban Chao did”在一定程度上表达出“投笔吏”的文化内涵。

晴

晴川历历汉阳树，	Across the ***sunlit*** river，clearly seen are Hanyang's trees，
芳草萋萋鹦鹉洲。	And Parrot Island's teeming，fragrant grasses.[2]
《黄鹤楼》	“Yellow Crane Tower”
（唐）崔颢	（The Tang Dynasty）Cui Hao

晚

一竿为活计，	With fishing rod I earn a living without rest，
往来西又东。	Coming and going east and west.
笑着荷衣不叹穷。	Wearing a straw cloak，I don't sigh
翁，	For I am poor. Old and drunk，I
醉眠杨柳风。	Lie down in the breeze under willow trees.
波微动，	On rippling waves afloat，
晚来舟自横。	At ***dusk*** athwart the stream lies my boat.[5]

《阅金经》 Tune：Reading Golden Classics
（元）无名氏 （The Yuan Dynasty）Anonymous

此处“**晚**”的译文为“**dusk**”乃意译。古代把晚上戌时作为一更，亥时、子时、丑时、寅时分别为二、三、四、五更。晚上前半夜7时至9时为戌时，故晚上基本上从19时算起。根据《庄子· 让王》：“日出而作，日入而息”的生活方式，当时归舟时间估计在日落之前，故此处的“晚”意译为“dusk”，贴切词意。

暝

平林漠漠烟如织， O'er far-flung wooded plain wreaths of smoke weave a screen,
寒山一带伤心碧。 Cold mountains stretch into a belt of sorrowful green.
暝色入高楼， The ***dusk*** invades the tower high
有人楼上愁。 Where someone sighs a longing sigh. [1]
《菩萨蛮》 Tune：Buddhist Dancers
（唐）李白 （The Tang Dynasty）Li Bai

景

此去经年， I'll be gone for a year.
应是良辰好**景**虚设。 In vain would good times and fine ***scenes*** appear!
便纵有千种风情， However gallant I am on my part,
更与何人说。 To whom can I lay bare my heart?[1]
《雨霖铃》 Tune：Bells Ringing in the Rain
（宋）柳永 （The Song Dynasty）Liu Yong

暖

1. 几处早莺争**暖**树， Here and there first orioles contend in ***sunny*** trees;
谁家新燕啄春泥。 To which households do new swallows wing, bearing their spring mud?[2]
《钱塘江春行》 "A Spring Outing by Qiantang Lake"
（唐）白居易 （The Tang Dynasty）Bai Juyi

“暖树”之“**暖**”的翻译在于其所修饰的“树”：“树”无冷暖之分，此处之“暖”意指“光照”，“暖树”即沐浴在阳光之下的树木，译文“**sunny**”，体现出此处之“暖”意。

2. 歌台**暖**响，春光融融；舞殿冷袖，风雨凄凄。
《阿房宫赋》（唐）杜牧

The platform for singing was full of ***heart-warming*** sounds and the light of spring, while the hall for dancing was chilled as if by wind and rain, with the cold air stirred up by the moving sleeves. [12]

"Efang Palace" (The Tang Dynasty) Du Mu

此处"***暖***响"之"暖"的译文"**heart-warming**"为意译。之所以称"暖响"，盖因其声使人内心感到温暖之故。译文用词贴切。

晖

予观夫巴陵胜状，在洞庭一湖。衔远山，吞长江。浩浩汤汤，横无际涯；朝***晖***夕阴，气象万千。此岳阳楼之大观也。

《岳阳楼记》(宋) 范仲淹

In my view, the grandeur of Baling lies solely in Lake Dongting, which looks as if it were holding in its mouth the distant mountains and gulping down the Yangtze River. Boundless and marvelous, it presents in the morning ***sunshine*** and the evening twilight a most gorgeous spectacle. This is the general view from the tower. [12]

"Yueyang Tower" (The Song Dynasty) Fan Zhongyan

明：会意字，由"日""月"会意。

1. 不才***明***主弃，　I have no talent , so the ***wise*** emperor has abandoned me,
   多病故人疏。　I'm all sickness, so my old friends have kept away from me. [13]
   《岁暮归南山》　"Returning to the South Mountain at the End of the Year"
   (唐) 孟浩然　(The Tang Dynasty) Meng Haoran

2. 春江潮水连海平，　In spring the river swells level with the sea,
   海上***明***月共潮生。　The ***bright*** moon rises mounting the tide.
   滟滟随波千万里，　Waters flash with infinite light,
   何处清江无月***明***。　Where on the spring river is there so ***bright*** moon? [2]
   《春江花月夜》　"Spring, the River, the Moon": Night
   (唐) 张若虚　(The Tang Dynasty) Zhang Ruoxu

以上两例"***明***"之译文均为直译。因其所修饰之词的不同，其译文自然有异。"***明***主"之"明"修饰的是人，指人之"明智、英明"，译文选取"**wise**"[(of people) able to make sensible decisions and give good advice because of experience and knowledge that you have] 与原文意思相符。"***明***月"之"明"修饰月，指的是月之光，月光皎洁，译文"**bright**"(full of light shining strongly) 即显此月之"明"。

旦：会意字，由“日”出现在“一”之上会意。“一”表示“地”。

住近湓江地低湿，	I live near the bank of the Pen River, a low and damp ground,
黄芦苦竹绕宅生。	My house is surrounded by the yellow reeds and the bamboos all around.
其间**旦**暮闻何物？	Here what do I hear from ***morns*** to evens?
杜鹃啼血猿哀鸣。	Only the bitter cry of the cuckoos and the wailing of the gibbons.
春江花朝秋月夜，	On the flowery spring morns or the autumn nights lit by the moon,
往往取酒还独倾。	Oft I get some wine and drink it alone. [13]
《琵琶行》	"Song of a Female Pipa-Player"
（唐）白居易	(The Tang Dynasty) Bai Juyi

日：象形字。

泉声咽危石，	Hindered by the big stones the stream produces low and deep sound,
日色冷青松。	Shedding through the green pines the ***sunlight*** seems to be cool on the ground. [13]
《过香积寺》	"Visiting the Xiangji Temple"
（唐）王维	(The Tang Dynasty) Wang Wei

木

用“**木**”组合的字，跟木本植物或用木头制作的物品有关。例字中除“**杳、林**”外，其余皆为形声字。其中，“**檠**”为下形上声，其他为左形右声。

檠

挑短**檠**，	Turning up ***candlelight***,
倚云屏，	Standing by cloudy screen,
伤心伴人清瘦影。	Heart-broken, I'm accompanied by shadow lean.
薄酒初醒，	Awakened from thin wine,
好梦难成，	For vain sweet dreams I pine.
斜月为谁明？	Why should the slanting moon be bright? [5]
《塞儿令》	Tune: Song of Frontier
（元）周文质	(The Yuan Dynasty) Zhou Wenzhi

“挑短**檠**”之“檠”在此译作“烛光”，而不是与其意相应的“烛台”或“蜡台”，在于其前面的“挑”和“短”。“挑”针对烛芯而言，“短”指正在点燃并逐渐变短的蜡烛，所以“檠”在这里译作“**candlelight**”才可体现出词之原本之意。

松

疏***松***影落空坛静，　The shadows of the sparse ***pine*** trees lie on the empty altar still,
细草香生小洞幽。　The tender grasses smell sweet and the small caves are tranquil. [13]

《同题仙游观》　“Writing Poems Together with Others at the Xian You Temple”
（唐）韩翃　（The Tang Dynasty） Han Hong

枫

青***枫***江上秋帆远，
白帝城边古木疏。

In autumn on Green ***Maple*** River, the sails in the distance will be seen,
Near White Emperor Town, the sparse old trees will be seen. [13]

《送李少府贬峡中王少府贬长沙》
“Farewell to Vice-Prefect Li Demoted to Xiazhong and Vice-Prefect Wang Demoted to Changsha”
（唐）高适　（The Tang Dynasty） Gao Shi

梅

兰烬落，　Candle-wick burned,
屏上暗红蕉。　Red cannas painted on the screen dark turned.
闲梦江南***梅***熟日，　I dreamed of ***mume-fruit*** ripping on the Southern shore,
夜船吹笛雨潇潇，　Of flute-songs played adrift one rainy night of yore,
人语驿边桥。　Of whispers lost
In running stream below the bridge beside the post. [1]

《忆江南》　Tune：The South Recalled
（唐）皇甫松　（The Tang Dynasty） Huangfu Song

枝

1. 明月别***枝***惊鹊，　Startled by magpies leaving the ***branch*** in moonlight;

清风半夜鸣蝉，　I hear cicadas shrill in the breeze at midnight.
稻花香里说丰年，The ricefields' sweet smell promises a harvest great,
听取蛙声一片。　I listen to the frogs' croak when the night grows late. [1]

《西江月 · 夜行黄沙道中》　Tune: The Moon over the West River, "A Summer Night on My Way Home from the Yellow Sand Ridge"
（宋）辛弃疾　(The Song Dynasty) Xin Qiji

2. 机中锦字论长恨，　Her circular poem to her husband expresses her sorrow hour after hour,
楼上花**枝**笑独眠。　Her sleep alone is oft sniggered at by the ***twigs*** with flowers reaching the tower. [13]

《春思》　"Yearning in Spring"
（唐）皇甫冉　(The Tang Dynasty) Huangfu Ran

以上两例中虽然所含同一“枝”字，其译文根据所处语境而有所不同。**例 1**“明月别**枝**惊鹊”中，鹊所落之枝往往是树木不断分杈而向四处伸展的分枝或从分枝上长出的杈枝，译文“**branch**”（a part of a tree that grows out from the main stem and on which leaves, flowers and fruit grow）即属此枝。**例 2**“楼上花**枝**笑独眠”中所言之“枝”，通常较为柔嫩：伸入楼中的花枝一般不会是粗大的树枝。“**twigs**”（a small very thin branch that grows out of a larger branch on a bush or tree）之意即小枝、嫩枝。

栏

1. 独自莫凭**栏**，　Don't lean alone on the ***railings*** and
无限江山。　Yearn for the boundless land!
别时容易见时难。　To bid farewell is easier than to meet again.
落花流水春去也，　With flowers fallen on the waves spring's gone amain,
天上人间！　So is the paradise of men. [1]

《浪淘沙》　Tune: Ripples Sifting Sand
（南唐）李煜　(The Nontang Dynasty) Li Yu

2. 绕水恣行游，　Along the river I go where I will,
上尽层城更上楼。　Up city-walls and watch-towers I gaze my fill.
往事悠悠君莫问，　Do not ask what has passed without leaving a trail!
回头，　To what avail?
栏外长江空自流。　The endless river rolls in vain beyond the ***rail***. [1]

《南乡子》 Tune: Song of a Southern Country
(宋) 王安石 (The Song Dynasty) Wang Anshi

杖

莫听穿林打叶声。 Listen not to the rain beating against the trees.
何妨吟啸且徐行。 Why don't you slowly walk and chant at ease?
竹**杖**芒鞋轻胜马, Better than a saddle I like sandals and ***cane***.
谁怕! I'd fain,
一蓑烟雨任平生。 In a straw cloak, spend my life in mist and rain. [1]
《定风波》 Tune: Calming the Waves
(宋) 苏轼 (The Song Dynasty) Su Shi

杪

山中一夜雨, If it rains in the mountains the whole night,
树**杪**百重泉。 From the tree ***tops*** hang hundreds of springs white. [13]
《送梓州李使君》 "Seeing Off Provincial Governor Li of Zizhou"
(唐) 王维 (The Tang Dynasty) Wang Wei

楼

1. 云溪初起日沉阁, Mist rises from the river; the sun sets behind the Pavilion.
   山雨欲来风满**楼**。 Wind fills the ***tower***, heralding mountain rain. [2]
   《咸阳城西楼晚眺》 "Evening Prospect from the West Gate Tower of Xianyang"
   (唐) 许浑 (The Tang Dynasty) Xu Hun

2. 金陵城上西**楼**, I lean on western ***railings*** on the city wall
   倚清秋。 Of Jinling in the fall.
   万里夕阳垂地, Shedding its rays o'er miles and miles, the sun hangs low
   大江流。 To see the great River flow. [1]
   《相见欢》 Tune: Joy of Meeting
   (宋) 朱敦儒 (The Song Dynasty) Zhu Dunru

例 2“金陵城上西**楼**”中“**楼**”的翻译主要在于“倚”字。“倚清秋”意为在清秋之季，作者登楼，倚在楼栏杆上俯视夕阳和江流。此处“楼”意译为“**railings**”，具体地表达出了作者词中的“倚清秋”之意。

枯

1. 草**枯**鹰眼疾， Keen are the falcon's eyes above the ***withered*** grasses,

雪尽马蹄轻。	And light the horses' hoofbeats in the melted snow. [2]
《观猎》	"Watching the Hunt"
（唐）王维	(The Tang Dynasty) Wang Wei

2. 离离原上草，	Green green the grass upon the plain,
一岁一**枯**荣。	That each ***dies*** to flourish anew,
野火烧不尽，	That's scorched by flames yet unsubdued,
春风吹又生。	Surging back when spring winds blow. [2]
《赋得古原草送别》	"The Grass upon the Ancient Plain: A Song of Parting"
（唐）白居易	(The Tang Dynasty) Bai Juyi

3. **枯**藤老树昏鸦，	***Dry*** vines, old trees, and crows at dusk;
小桥流水人家，	A bridge over a rivulet, and a cottage.
古道西风瘦马。	An ancient road, a skinny horse in the west wind.
夕阳西下，	The sun is setting—heart-broken,
断肠人在天涯。	The traveler is dragging his way Towards the end of the world. [10]
《天净沙·秋思》	Tune: Sunny Sand, "Autumn Thoughts"
（元）马致远	(The Yuan Dynasty) Ma Zhiyuan

4. 蜀道之难难于上青天，	Oh, the road to Shu is harder than that to climb up the sky!
使人听此凋朱颜。	Hearing this the tourists' faces would lose the ruddy dye.
连峰去天不盈尺，	The distance is less than a foot from the continuous peaks to the sky,
枯松倒挂倚绝壁。	The ***dried up*** pines hang head-down on the cliffs high. [13]
《蜀道难》	" Hard Is the Road to Shu"
（唐）李白	(The Tang Dynasty) Li Bai

例 1 之"枯"指的是"草"。根据上下文，时值冬季，草已枯萎，直译为"**withered**"[(of plants) dried up and dead]，凸显出其枯竭之状貌。**例 2** 的译文选择"**dies**"，在于"春风吹又生"之"生"："生"与"死"相对。**例 3** 之"枯"所修饰的是"藤"，直译为"**Dry**"(not wet, damp or sticky; without water or moisture)，表达出藤之"干、缺乏水分"。**例 4**"枯"之译文"**dried up**"(having lost all moisture) 体现出干枯的程度。

桔，枳

桔生淮南则为橘，生于淮北则为***枳***，叶徒相似，其实味不同。

《晏子春秋 · 内篇杂下》

Oranges grown south of the Huai River are true oranges; once transplanted to the north of the river, they become ***trifoliate oranges***. Although they resemble in the shape of leaves, yet they differ widely in taste. [12]

"Yanzi Chunqiu"

杳：会意字，由"日"在"木"下会意[9]："阳光"被树木遮挡，光线幽暗。

采芳人***杳***，　Maidens gathering flowers now are ***few***,
顿觉游情少。I find no joy within the natural view. [1]
《清平乐》　Tune: Pure Serene Music
（宋）张炎　(The Song Dynasty) Zhang Yan

"***杳***"之本意为"远得看不见踪影"。"采芳人***杳***"即看不到采芳人的影子，暗含"人少"之意。译文使用"**few**"不仅体现出"人少"，而且与"view."押韵。

林：会意字，双木为"林"。

1. 清晨入古寺，　When I walked into the old temple in the early morning,
   初日照高***林***。　On the tall ***trees*** the early sun is shining. [13]
   《破山寺后禅院》
   "A Visit to the Buddhist Abode in the Back of the Poshan Temple"
   （唐）常建　(The Tang Dynasty) Chang Jian

2. ***林***表明霁色，　On the ***tree*** tops the daylight just after the snowing glitters on and on,
   城中增暮寒。　At dusk the snow has added cold to Chang'an. [13]
   《终南望馀雪》
   "Gazing in the Distance at the Piled-Up Snow on Mount Zhongnan"
   （唐）祖咏　(The Tang Dynasty) Zu Yong

3. 晚年惟好静，　Old age must cherish only quietude,
   万事不关心。　A heart untouched by worldly cares.
   自顾无长策，　For myself I have no long-term strategy,
   空知返旧***林***。　Except returning to my native ***woods***. [2]

《酬张少府》 “ For Vice-Magistrate Zhang”
（唐）王维 （The Tang Dynasty）Wang Wei

4. 空山不见人， Remote the mountains, where no one is seen,
但闻人语声。 Though human voices resound.
返景入深**林**， At dusk, reflected sunlight enters the ***forest*** deep,
复照青苔上。 Once again setting the green moss aglow. [2]
《鹿砦》 “The Deer Enclosure”
（唐）王维 （The Tang Dynasty）Wang Wei

例 1 中，“初日照高**林**”之“林”即高耸的树林，故译文中选择复数形式的“**trees**”与“林”对应。从**例 2** 题目即可看出诗中所咏乃雪后之景。“霁色”说明雪后天已放晴。“**林**表明霁色”生动地描绘出初晴的阳光照在树梢上的景色。此“林”为“表”的定语。按照译语语言的使用规范，作定语的名词一般用单数，故此“林”之译文取“**tree**”，“林表”则译为“tree tops”。**例 3** 与**例 4** 之“林”的区别在于“林”之大、小不同。“forest”之意为森林，大片林区；“**woods**”指树林、林地。Woods 小于 forest。“空知返旧林”意指作者的归隐山林之意。作为可供归隐的居住之地，“**woods**”（an area of trees, smaller than a forest）与原文之意较为贴切。**例 4** 之“空山不见人”和“深**林**”说明了此“林”的面积之大，“**forest**”与其意相配。

心

用“**心**”组合的字一般与心、由“心”（作为思想器官）所生之思想和情感相关。例字中除“**忘**”外，其余为形声字：下形上声。

愁

1. 移舟泊烟渚， Mooring the boat among the mist—
日暮客**愁**新。 Day wanes
野旷天低树， A wanderer' s ***ache*** persists.
江清月近人。 In the vast wilds the sky descends to touch the trees
As brightening waters bear the moon to me[2].
《宿建德江》 “Spending the Night on the Jiande River”
（唐）孟浩然 （The Tang Dynasty）Meng Haoran

2. 杨花落尽子规啼， The popular catkins have all fallen; the cuckoo' s begun to cry.

闻道龙标过五溪。	I've heard it said that Wang Changling must pass beyond the River Five.
我寄**愁**心与明月，	To the bright moon I entrust an ***anxious*** heart:
随君直到夜郎西。	May it see you as far west as the country of Yelang. [2]

《闻王昌龄左迁龙标，遥有此寄》

"Sent to Wang Changling After Hearing of His Demotion to Longbiao"

（唐）李白　　(The Tang Dynasty) Li Bai

3\. 日暮乡关何处是，　Dusk has fallen, where is my hometown?
烟波江上使人**愁**。　Looking at the mist-covered waves on the river, I ***worry*** on and on. [13]

《黄鹤楼》　　"The Yellow Crane Tower"

（唐）崔颢　　(The Tang Dynasty) Cui Hao

4\. 雕栏玉砌应犹在，　Carved balustrades and marble steps must still be there,
只是朱颜改。　But rosy faces cannot be as fair.
问君能有几多**愁**？　If you would ask me how my ***sorrow*** has increased,
恰似一江春水向东流。Just see the over-brimming river flowing east! [1]

《虞美人》　　Tune: The Beautiful Lady Yu

（南唐）李煜　　(The Nontang Dynasty) Li Yu

5\. 月落乌啼霜满天　The setting moon, a cawing crow, the frost filled sky;
江枫渔火对**愁**眠。　River maples, fishermen's flares, and ***troubled*** sleep.
姑苏城外寒山寺，　From the Cold Mountain Temple, outside Suzhou,
夜半钟声到客船。　The tolling of the midnight bell reaches the wanderer's boat. [2]

《枫桥夜泊》　　"Mooring at Night by Maple Bridge"

（唐）张继　　(The Tang Dynasty) Zhang Ji

6\. 一杯**愁**绪，　In my heart ***sad*** thoughts throng:
几年离索。　We've severed for years long. [1]

《钗头凤》　　Tune: Phoenix Hairpin

（宋）陆游　　(The Song Dynasty) Lu You

7\. 而今识尽**愁**滋味，　I know what ***grief*** is now that I am old,
欲说还休，　I would not have it told.
欲说还休，　I would not have it told

却道天凉好个秋！　But only say I'm glad that autumn's cold. [1]

《采桑子》　Tune: Song of Picking Mulberry

（宋）辛弃疾　(The Song Dynasty) Xin Qiji

以上译文共7个“**愁**”字。**例1**是“客**愁**”。“愁”因“客”起，“愁”随“客”同在，只要身为他乡“客”，其“愁”则会日日相伴。此处译文使用“**ache**”（a continuous dull pain）不仅说明作者内心的痛苦，同时也着意于此“愁”的持续性。**例2**是“**愁**心”。因朋友远赴夜郎，为朋友旅途安危担心，译文使用“**anxious**”（feeling nervous），表示出内心的担忧和紧张。**例3**是“乡**愁**”。在沉沉暮色、茫茫雾气之中，作者被思乡之情所搅扰，内心难以安宁。这里译文使用“**worry**”（to think about unpleasant things that make sb feel anxious），着意于作者的焦虑不安。**例4**之“**愁**”是指作者不绝的忧愤和苦闷。“**sorrow**”（a feeling of great sadness because sth very bad has happened）的使用体现出了作者之悲伤。**例5**之“**愁**”乃是因作者的难以入眠而起。“月落、乌啼、江枫、渔火”再加上“霜满天”，衬托出作者孤寂的心情。此情此景使作者夜不能寐，使用“**troubled**”（worried and anxious）表明了作者内心的烦（苦）恼。**例6**之“**愁**”来自于分离之苦，译文使用“**sad**”（unhappy），表明其忧伤之情。**例7**中之“而今”说明作者亦非年少，“识尽”表明作者对“人生不如意事十之八九”已有所体验。译文选用“**grief**”（a feeling of great sadness, especially when sb dies; problems and worry）来对应词中之“愁”，使读者对此“愁”之“滋味”有了一个较深层次的体会和了解。

悲

1. 白发**悲**花落，　I, a white-haired man, feel ***sad*** to see the fallen flowers on the ground lie,

青云羡鸟飞。　I envy other's promotion in the way birds fly up into sky. [13]

《寄左省杜拾遗》　"To Remonstrator Du of the Left Court"

（唐）岑参　(The Tang Dynasty) Cen Shen

2. 关山难越，谁**悲**失路之人？萍水相逢，尽是他乡之客。

《滕王阁序》（唐）王勃

Mountains are insurmountable. Who ***deplores*** a man who has lost his way? An incidental meeting only brings one into a company of strangers. [12]

"The Tower of Prince Teng" (The Tang Dynasty) Wang Bo

原文中**例1**之“**悲**”为动词，译文中转换为形容词“**sad**”。

忍

不***忍***登高临远，　I cannot ***bear***
望故乡渺邈，　To climb high and look far, for to gaze where
归思难收。　My native land is lost in mists so thick
Would make my lonely heart homesick. [1]

《八声甘州》　Tune: Eight Beats of a Ganzhou Song
（宋）柳永　(The Song Dynasty) Liu Yong

慰

1. 何当重相见，　When we meet again some day,
樽酒***慰***离颜。　Let us drink to ***drive*** our parting ***sorrow away***. [13]
《送人东游》　"Seeing Off a Friend Going on a Tour of the East"
（唐）温庭筠　(The Tang Dynasty) Wen Tingyun

2. 欲持一瓢酒，　I'd like to carry a gourd of wine to your place,
远***慰***风雨夕。　On this raining and windy night to ***give*** you some ***solace***. [13]
《寄全椒山众道士》　"To the Taoist Priest in Mount Shen in Quanjiao"
（唐）韦应物　(The Tang Dynasty) Wei Yingwu

此两例之译文凸显出了诗韵之美：away→day, place→solace。

愚

南亩耕，　Having tilled the southern field, I
东山卧，　At the foot of eastern hill lie.
世态人情经历多。　I've known the world and its ways,
闲将往事思量过。　And ponder at leisure the past days.
贤的是他，　O wise is he
愚的是我，　And ***foolish*** me!
争什么？　What should I contend to be? [5]

《四块玉·闲适》　Tune: Four Pieces of Jade, "Life of Easy Leisure"
（元）关汉卿　(The Yuan Dynasty) Guan Hanqing

志

穷且益坚，不坠青云之***志***。酌贪泉而觉爽，处涸辙以犹欢。北海虽赊，扶摇可接；东隅已逝，桑榆非晚。

《滕王阁序》（唐）王勃

Though poor, one should have a firmer integrity, never forsaking his soaring ***aspiration***! ***Having drunk from the Fountain of Avidity, one may still keep clean and be free of corruption***. Placed in a dried rut, one may still feel gay. Though the North Sea is far away, one may reach it with the help of a whirlwind. Though the youth is gone, it is not too late to retrieve what is lost in the old age. [12]

"The Tower of Prince Teng" (The Tang Dynasty) Wang Bo

愿

富贵非吾**愿**，帝乡不可期。怀良辰以孤往，或植杖而耘耔。登东皋以舒啸，临清流而赋诗。

《归去来兮辞》(东晋) 陶渊明

Wealth and honor are not my ***wish***, and paradise is beyond my hope. Cherish my time and take lonely saunters in the splendid morn. Or planting my stick in the ground, do some weeding in the fields. Ascend the eastern hills and shout to my heart's content or, standing before a limpid stream, compose and declaim my poetic prose. [12]

"Sentiments on My Homecoming" (The Eastern Jin Dynasty) Tao Yuanming

惑

古之学者必有师，师者，所以传道、授业、解**惑**也。人非生而知之，孰能无惑？惑而不从师，其为惑也，终不解矣。

《师说》(唐) 韩愈

Ancient scholars certainly had teachers. A teacher is one who passes on the truth, imparts knowledge and solves ***puzzles***. Man is not born with knowledge. Who can be free of puzzles? These would remain unsolved, should one refuse to be instructed by teachers. [12]

"On Teachers" (The Tang Dynasty) Han Yu

忘：会意字，由"心"、由"亡"会意。"亡"也表声[9]。

耕者**忘**其犁，	The ploughman ***leaves*** ploughing,
锄者忘其锄。	The hoer his hoeing,
来归相怨怒，	And back in their houses
但坐观罗敷。	Find fault with their wives. [4]
《陌上桑》	"By the Roadside Mulberry"
(汉)	(The Han Dynasty)

火

用"**火**"组合的字，往往含有火、光或性质如火之意。例字皆为形声字：左形右声。

炬

相见时难别亦难，	Difficult it was for us to meet, and difficult to part.
春风无力百花残。	Now the east wind has failed, and all the flowers wither.
春蚕到死丝方尽，	The silkworm labors until death its fine thread severs;
蜡**炬**成灰泪始干。	The ***candle***'s tears are dried when it itself consumes. [2]
《无题》	"Untitled"
（唐）李商隐	(The Tang Dynasty) Li Shangyin

灯

去年元夜时，	Last year on this moonlit spring night,
花市**灯**如画。	***Lanterns*** in Flower Fair were bright.
月上柳梢头，	The moon rose above the willow tree,
人约黄昏后。	At dark he had a tryst with me. [1]
《生查子》	Tune: Mountain Hawthorne
（宋）欧阳修	(The Song Dynasty) Ouyang Xiu

烟

1. 夫天地者，万物之逆旅；光阴者，百代之过客。而浮生若梦，为欢几何？古人秉烛夜游，良有以也。况阳春召我以**烟**景，大块假我以文章。

《春夜宴桃李园序》（唐）李白

The universe is but an inn for milliards of creatures of nature, and time is but a passenger hastening through hundreds of generations. The ephemeral life is like a dream. How long can one have joy? The ancients made nocturnal promenades by candle light—it was too sensible! And then the warm spring appeals to us with its ***hazy*** scenery. The good earth presents to us its embroidery-like patterns of landscape. [12]

"A Spring Night Feast in the Peach-Plum Garden"

(The Tang Dynasty) Li Bai

2. 六朝旧事随流水，	The running water saw Six Dynasties pass;
但寒**烟**、	But I see only chilly ***mist*** and withered grass.
衰草凝绿。	E'en now the songstresses still sing

至今商女，　　The songs composed by captive king.[1]
时时犹唱，
后庭遗曲。
《桂枝香 · 金陵怀古》
Tune: Fragrance of Laurel Branch, "Memories of the Past at Jinling"
（宋）王安石　　(The Song Dynasty) Wang Anshi

例1之“***烟***”为意译。译文以“**hazy**”与此处之“烟”对应，体现出了被云霭和烟雾所缭绕的景色。**例2**中“衰草”表明天气转凉，已是秋季。由于地面温度较低，时常会有雾气产生。词中“寒***烟***”之“烟”即指雾气之朦胧，如烟一般，这里的“烟”意译为“**mist**”（薄雾），尽显此意。

烛（燭），烧，炽

一阃帅，寒天夜宴，***炽***炭***烧***烛，引满浮白，酒后耳热，叹曰：“今年天气不正，当寒而暖。”

兵卒在旁跪禀曰：“较似小人们立处，天气觉正。”

《雪涛小书》（明）江盈科

A general was drinking in the camp in a cold winter's night. ***Candles*** were ***lighted*** and coal was ***burning*** well in the stove. After a few bowlfuls of wine, beads of sweat appeared on his forehead. "Extraordinary weather we're having this year!" said the general. "When it should be cold, it's warm."

His words were heard by his orderly, who was standing outside in the cold. Entering the tent, he knelt respectfully before the general and said, "The weather seems normal enough where your servant was standing, sir."[14]

"Notes of Xue Tao" (The Ming Dynasty) Jiang Yingke

本例中“烧”和“炽”的翻译涉及到三种译法的运用。（1）通过上下文理解字义。此处“烧”的英译取决于语篇中的“烛”。汉语中常用“红烛高烧”来形容点着的红色蜡烛。“烧”即“点着（zhao）”之意，译文以“**light**”（to make sth start to burn）与其对应，与原文之意相符。（2）本、客体的思维方式在此例中均有所体现：汉语习惯于用表示人或生物的词作主语（或潜在的主语），原文中，“烧”的潜在主语是“人”（军营中的兵卒），“烧烛”为主动形式，“烛”为宾语；译文中，“烛”转换为主语，动词“烧”通过“were+lighted”构成被动语态，由此体现出了不同的思维方式在语言形态上的表现：当涉及到行为主体时，英语常用非生物名词作主语，故其被动语态出现的频率多于汉语。（3）综合与分析型思维的体现：“***炽***炭”之“炽”在原文中无词形变化，燃烧状态的体现在于词汇手段，即从“炽”（烹煮，热烈旺盛）本身之义表达出来。而译文中“炽炭”的含义则是通过词形的变化“burn+ing”以及语法形式的多样（现在进行时）来体现。

户

用“**户**”组合的字与“门”及与门相关的结构有关。例字中除“**扁**、**启**、**扇**、**户**”外，其他为形声字：外形内声。

房

曲径通幽处，　A winding path leads to a secluded and quiet place, where,
禅**房**花木深。　A Buddhist ***abode*** is sheltered by the flowers and trees there.[13]
《破山寺后禅院》
“A Visit to the Buddhist Abode in the Back of the Poshan Temple”
（唐）常建　(The Tang Dynasty) Chang Jian

扉

行当浮桂棹，　You'll take a delicate boat to go back to your hometown,
未几拂荆**扉**。　And you'll knock at the wicker ***door*** of your house before long.[13]
《送綦毋潜落地还乡》　“Seeing Off Qiwu Qian Who's Going Home After Failing the Palace Graduate Examination”
（唐）王维　(The Tang Dynasty) Wang Wei

扃

金阙西厢叩玉**扃**，　Knocking at the jade ***door*** of the west wing of the gold palace, he bade,
转教小玉报双成。　The maid Xiaoyu who then informed Shuangcheng, Yang Guifei's maid.[13]
《长恨歌》　“Song of Everlasting Remorse”
（唐）白居易　(The Tang Dynasty) Bai Juyi

扁：会意字，由“户”、由“册”会意，表示题署门户的文字[9]。

雨晴云散，　After the rain clouds clear away;
满江明月。　Over the lake the moon sheds its ray.
风微浪息，　The waves are calmed when the wind light

扁舟一叶。 Blows on my ***leaf-like*** boat at midnight. [5]

《节节高 · 题洞庭鹿角庙壁》

Tune: Higher and Higher, "Written on the Temple Wall on Lake Dongting"

（元）卢挚 (The Yuan Dynasty) Lu Zhi

这里"**扁**"的译文在于"叶"。物体平而薄为"扁"，似舟之形，当其行驶于江中，如叶漂浮于水面。这里"扁"与"叶"同为"舟"之修饰语，二者俱指其外形，"扁"中含有"叶"之形，"叶"则体现"扁"之状，译文"**leaf-like**"体现了原文之意。

启：会意字，由"户"、由"口"会意[9]。

节义之人济以和衷，才不**启**纷争之路；功名之士承以谦德，方不开嫉妒之门。

《菜根谭》（明）洪应明

A man of rectitude and moral integrity should temper himself with amiability, and thus he will not ***evoke*** a dispute with others. A man of scholarly honor and rank should cultivate himself with the virtue of modesty, and thus he will not arouse jealousy from others. [6]

"The Roots of Wisdom" (The Ming Dynasty) Hong Yingming

扇：会意字，由"户"、由"羽"会意。意为"门扇"及摇动生风的器具。

1. 奉帚平明金殿开， At daybreak when the golden palace door opens, she begins to sweep with a broom,
   暂将团**扇**共徘徊。 Then with a moon-shaped ***fan*** in her hand, she paces up and down in deep gloom.
   玉颜不及寒鸦色， Alas, her beautiful face is even inferior to the color of a crow,
   犹带昭阳日影来。 Because flying from the Zhaoyang Palace in the east, it carries the emperor's favor in a glow. [13]

   《长信怨》 "Ban Jieyu's Resentment"
   （唐）王昌龄 (The Tang Dynasty) Wang Changling

2. 长江万里白如练， For miles and miles the endless river flows silk-white;
   淮山数点青如淀。 Dots on dots of southern hills stand indigo-blue.
   江帆几片疾如箭， Sails on sails go past as fast arrows do;
   山泉千尺飞如电。 The waterfall dashes down like lightning from the height.

晚云都变露，	All evening clouds turn into dew;
新月初学**扇**。	The crescent moon imitates a ***bow***;
塞鸿一字来如线。	The wild geese from the frontier fly in a row. [5]

《塞鸿秋·浔阳即景》

Tune: Autumn Swan on Frontier, "By the River of Xunyang"

（元）周德清　(The Yuan Dynasty) Zhou Deqing

"新月初学**扇**"之意为初月冉冉升起，就像一把半圆形的团扇。扇之半圆形弧线又具"弓"形，此处之"扇"取"弓"之英译"bow"，不仅具体体现出原文描述之生动，同时还具有押韵的作用：bow→row。

户：象形字。

西风穿***户***冷，	The west wind blowing through the ***door*** brings me chill.
檐马隔帘鸣。	Iron bells ring across the curtain still. [5]

《塞儿令》　Tune: Song of Frontier

（元）周文质　(The Yuan Dynasty) Zhou Wenzhi

王（玉）

用"**玉**"组合的字，一般与玉石、玉器的名称及制玉手工业有关。例字中除"**玉**"外，其余皆为形声字：左形右声。

瑾瑜

任重载盛兮，	I feel my Task too hard for me;
陷滞而不济。	Despairing of Success,
怀***瑜***握***瑾***兮，	I do not know to whom to show
穷不知所示。	The ***Jewels*** I possess. [7]

《楚辞选》　"Selected Elegies of the State Chu"

（战国）屈原　(The Warring States Period) Qu Yuan

珊瑚

鸾翔凤翥众仙下，	The hand writing looks like the phoenix flying, followed by the fairs descending,
珊瑚碧树交枝柯。	Or like the twigs of a ***coral*** or a green tree intertwining. [13]

《石鼓歌》　"Song of the Stone Drums"

（唐）韩愈　(The Tang Dynasty) Han Yu

珠玑

落日外萧山翠微， Beyond the setting sun the hills appear green still,
小桥边古寺残碑。 Besides the bridge the temple ruins loom.
文藻**珠玑**， Your words flow like ***pearls*** in a stream;
醉墨淋漓。 Drunk, you spilt your ink at will.
何似班超， Is it not better to be a man of men,
投却毛锥？ Who for the sword gave up the pen?[5]

《蟾宫曲·江淹寺》 Tune: Song of Moon Palace, "Temple of Literary Genius"
（元）徐再思 (The Yuan Dynasty) Xu Zaisi

玲珑

玉：像形字。甲骨文"玉"字像用一根绳子穿着几块玉石。金文和小篆作三横一竖，与"王"字相似；它们的区别是"玉"字三横等距，而"王"字不是而已。隶书以后"玉"字才加点。[11]

里湖， In inner lake
外湖， And outer lake,
无处是无春处。 There's nowhere but spring is awake.
真山真水真画图， True hills and water make the picture true,
一片**玲珑玉**。 No ***carved jade*** can outdo.
宜酒宜诗， It's good for verse and for wine,
宜晴宜雨。 Rain or shine.[5]

《朝天子·西湖》 Tune: Skyward Song, "West Lake"
（元）徐再思 (The Yuan Dynasty) Xu Zaisi

在作者眼中，西湖景色如同美玉，且是"**玲珑玉**"。"玲珑"本意是指物品之精巧细致，而"玉"经过雕琢之后才会更进一步显现出它的晶莹、明澈、无暇。译文用"**carved**"与"玲珑"对应，较完美地体现出诗人眼中的西湖之美非寻常玉可比，只有雕琢后的宝玉才可与之匹配。

琼

开**琼**筵以坐花，飞羽觞而醉月。

《春夜宴桃李园序》（唐）李白

We sit against flowers to enjoy a ***sumptuous*** feast and, passing around the goblets, we fall drunk under the moon.[12]

"A Spring Night Feast in the Peach-Plum Garden"
(The Tang Dynasty) Li Bai

"琼"之本意为美玉，泛指精美的东西。"筵"此处之意为"筵席"：宴饮时陈设的座位，借指酒席。此处"琼"修饰"筵"，表明酒席之丰盛，译文选取"**sumptuous**"即表此意。

珍

标节义者，必以节义受谤；榜道学者，常因道学招尤。故君子不近恶事，亦不立善名，只浑然和气，才是居身之***珍***。

《菜根谭》（明）洪应明

The one who flaunts his moral rectitude will surely be slandered by others in the name of the same. The one who flaunts his virtue and learning will normally be censured by others for the sake of the same. Therefore, the accomplished man should keep clear of wrongdoings and avoid prettifying himself, merely maintaining an easy-going manner all round. This is ***the golden rule*** of conducting oneself in the world. [6]

"The Roots of Wisdom" (The Ming Dynasty) Hong Yingming

这里"***珍***"是指"居身"，而非"物品"，译文"**the golden rule**"（an important principle that should be followed when doing sth in order to be successful）与此"***珍***"对应。

贝

古时以贝壳为财富，以龟甲为珍宝。一些由"***贝***"组合的字往往含有财宝之意。例字中，除"***贫***"外，其他皆为形声字。"贝"在下的由下形上声构成；"贝"在左侧的由左形右声构成。

资

吾***资***之昏，不逮人也，吾才之庸，不逮人也，旦旦而学之，久而不怠焉，迄乎成，而不知其昏与庸也。

《为学一首示子侄》（清）彭端淑

Being obtuse, I am surpassed by others in ***intelligence***. Being mediocre, I am outstripped by others in ability. But if I work hard on my learning with perseverance till I achieve success, then no one would make much of my obtuseness and mediocrity. [12]

"On Learning—to My Nephew" (The Qing Dynasty) Peng Duanshu

根据上下文语境，此处之"***资***"意指人的"资质"而言，故译文为"**intelligence**"。

赏

落红满地湿胭脂，	Petals fallen on the ground,
游**赏**正宜时。	Leaves of rouged faces.
呆木料不顾蔷薇刺，	A nice time to go ***sightseeing***.
贪折海棠枝。	A girl ventures to pluck the rose
蚩，	Despite of its sharp thorns.
抓破绣裙儿。	Hiss—
	Dear me!
	Her silk skirt is torn![10]

《游四门 · 落红满地》 Tune: Around the Gates, "Petal Fallen"

（元）无名氏 (The Yuan Dynasty) Anonymous

原文中"**赏**"为动词，其译文"**sightseeing**"则为名词，其所在句型结构使然："A nice time to go sightseeing."是一个省略句，其主语和谓语（It's）被省略。不定式短语"to go sightseeing"做"time"的定语，常用来表达去游览、观光之意。这里转变"赏"的词性以符合译语语言规范和表达习惯。

贱、贵

贱日岂殊众，She's no different from the ordinary people when she's ***lowly and in poverty***,

贵来方悟稀。She feels for her beauty is rare when she rises ***high in society***.[13]

《西施咏》 "Song of Xi Shi"

（唐）王维 (The Tang Dynasty) Wang Wei

诗题为"西施咏"，作者所述自然是"西施"其人。所以，此处"贵"与"贱"并非针对物品，而是指"人"。诗中通过"贱"与"贵"来表明"西施"身份的变化，译文使用"**lowly and in poverty**"和"**high in society**"表达出诗中所含之意。

贱

原来姹紫嫣红开遍，	So many colors splendid and splashing,
似这般都付予断井颓垣。	You are given to the deserted well and broken wall.
良辰美景奈何天，	So nice a natural scene, but for the other day!
赏心乐事谁家院！	So gay an hour, but to whom is it merry?
朝飞暮卷，云霞翠轩；	From morning to evening, twilights flying

丝雨风片，烟波画船一锦屏	Over the pavilion by the rippled pond,
人忒看的这韶光**贱**！	A drizzle carried by a breeze puzzles the boat
	In a distance—a misty view.
	Youthful hour is felt so ***cheap***
	By one who is locked in the room![10]

《皂罗袍·原来姹紫嫣红开遍》　Tune: Black Silk Gown, "So Many Colors Splendid"

（元）汤显祖　(The Yuan Dynasty) Tang Xianzu

赊

世情别，	Shunning society,
故交绝，	Without old company,
床头金尽谁行借？	From whom can I borrow when I've spent my gold?
今日又逢冬至节。	Again it's winter solstice today.
酒，何处**赊**？	Where's wine ***on credit*** sold?
梅，何处折？	Where's mume against the cold?[5]

《山羊坡·冬日写怀》　Tune: Sheep on the Slope, "Thoughts in Winter"

（元）乔吉　(The Yuan Dynasty) Qiao Ji

赋

杜郎俊赏，	The place Du Mu the poet prized,
算而今、	If he could come again today,
重到须惊。	Would make him feel surprised.
纵豆蔻词工，	His verse on the cardamom spray
青楼梦好，	And on sweet dreams in Mansions Green
难**赋**深情。	Could not ***express***
二十四桥仍在，	My deep distress.
波心荡、	The Twenty-four Bridges can still be seen,
冷月无声。	But the cold moon floating among
念桥边红薬，	The waves would no more sing a song.
年年知为谁生。	For whom should the peonies near
	The Bridges grow red from year to year?[1]

《扬州慢》　Tune: Slow Tune of Yangzhou

（宋）姜夔　(The Song Dynasty) Jiang Kui

赒

齐人有东郭敞者，犹多愿，愿有万金。其徒请***赒***焉，不与，曰："吾将以求封也。"其徒怒而去之宋。曰："此爱于无也，故不如以先与之有也。"

《商子》（战国）商鞅

In the state of Qi there was one Mr. Dongguo Chang who was a man of many ambitions. Among other things, he wanted to possess ten thousand taels of gold.

A student of his, knowing of his ambition, asked ***to be favored*** with a small sum, for he was very poor.

Mr. Dongguo Chang refused to grant his request. "I need all my money to buy myself a post in the government," he said.

His student became angry and left for the state of Song. Before he went he said to the teacher, "Since I shall have no share in the fortunes that you are covering, I'd better seek them elsewhere. Maybe I can come by them earlier than you do."[14]

"Shang Zi" (The Warring States Period) Shang Yang

原文中"***赒***"虽为主动形式，但语篇中之"请"字体现出其被动的含义，此即汉语语法所依靠的词汇手段；译文中则是通过语法形式"**to be favored**"来表达被动。

赠

一贫士遇故人于途，故人已得仙术矣。相劳苦中，因指道旁一砖成赤金***赠***之。士嫌其少，更指一大石狮为***赠***，士嫌未已。

仙曰："汝欲如何？"

士曰："愿乞公此指。"

《笑府》（明）冯梦龙

A poor man one day met an old friend who had become an immortal. After hearing his friend complain of his poverty, the immortal pointed his finger at a brick by the roadside, which immediately turned into a gold ingot. He ***presented*** it to his friend. When the man was not satisfied with this, he ***gave*** him a big gold lion. But the man was still not appeased.

"What more do you want?" asked his immortal friend.

"I want your finger!" was the reply.[14]

"Xiao Fu" (The Ming Dynasty) Feng Menglong

此例中两个"***赠***"之译文的不同在于对语篇的理解。"相劳苦中，因指道旁一砖成赤金赠之"之"赠"的译文为"**presented**"（to give sth to sb, especially formally at a ceremony）表达出相逢之初的较为客气或正式。“士嫌其少，更指一大石狮为**赠**”之“士嫌其少”表现出二人之间已不再客气，此“赠”的译文取“**gave**”（to hand sth to sb as a present），与原文之意相符。

赡、财

汉世有人，年老无子，家富，性敛啬，恶衣蔬食。……或人从之求丐者，不得已而入内，取十钱。自堂而出，随步辄减；比至于外，才余半在。闭目以授乞者，寻复嘱云：“我倾家**赡**君，慎勿他说，复相效而来。”

老人俄死，田宅没官，货**财**充于内帑也。

《太平广记选》（宋）李昉等

In the Han Dynasty there was an heirless old man. He was rich but stingy. What he wore was rags; what he ate was coarse rice and vegetables.... If a beggar could not be driven off, sometimes he might go inside and count out 10 coins. Caressing them in his palm, he would put away a coin every few steps on his slow return. By the time he reached the counter, only half of the coins would remain in his hand. Always shutting his eyes to the painful sight as he placed them in the beggar's hand, he would repeatedly say, "I'm ruining my business to ***assist*** you. Don't let others know, lest they follow you here."

Before long, the old man died. His house and land were confiscated by the government; his store and ***money*** went into the imperial coffer. [3]

"The Selections from Records of the Taiping Era"

(The Song Dynasty) Li Fang *et al.*

“**赡**”本意是“赡养”（供给生活所需）。从上下文可以看出，此处之“赡”并非出其本意：“取十钱……才余半在”，因此只能算作“赒济”。译文取“**assist**”（help sb to do sth），即含此意。

贫： 会意字，由“分”、由“贝”会意[9]。

日暮苍山远，　Bleak mountains at sunset stretching forever;
天寒白屋**贫**。　A White cottage even more ***pinched*** in the cold.
柴门闻犬吠，　In the night I hear a dog bark at the thatched gate;
风雪夜归人。　My host returns home in wind and snow. [2]

《逢雪宿芙蓉山主人》

" Spending the Night in a Mountain Village During a Snowstorm"

（唐）刘长卿　(The Tang Dynasty) Liu Changqing

从上下文可看出其时正值雪天。译文此处使用“**pinched**”，表达出了原文中“贫”之含意：在白雪覆盖之下、寒风瑟瑟之中、本就简陋的茅屋显得更加矮小破旧。此处“pinch”之意为：to cause to appear shrunken or thin; to cause to shrivel or wither.

月（肉）

“***月***（***肉***）”之本意为“大块肉”。用“月”组合的字往往与肉食及身体的某个部位相关。例字均为形声字，其中，“***背***”为下形上声，其余左形右声。

胸

“呀！好眼熟的地方！”我不禁失声地喊了起来。于是潜藏在心底的印象，陡然一幕幕地重映出来，唉！我的心有些抖颤了，我是被一种感怀以往的情绪所激动，我的双眼怔住，***胸***膈间充塞着悲凉，心弦凄紧地搏动着。

《异国秋思》庐隐

“Ah, this place looks so familiar to me,” I blurted out. Scene after scene of the bygone days, long tucked away in the depth of my memory, now reemerged all of a sudden. The nostalgic recollections made my heart thump with emotion, my eyes glaze over and my ***chest*** fill with sadness. [15]

“Autumn in a Foreign Land” Lu Yin

胀、肚

口渴时就张开嘴来，站在自来水的龙头下，一扭开来，就让水灌进嘴里，喝得***肚***子***胀***得饱饱的，又冷又痛，那滋味真有说不出的难受。

《饥饿》谢冰莹

When I was thirsty, I would stand under a tap and let its running water pour down my throat through my wide-open mouth. I felt ***bloated***. There was a pain and chill in my ***stomach***. I cannot tell you enough how miserable I was. [15]

“Hunger” Xie Bingying

脸

我仰起头，天空低垂如灰色的雾幕，落下一些寒冷的碎屑到我***脸***上。一只远来的鹰隼仿佛带着愤怒，对这沉重的天色的怒愤，平张的双翅不动地从天空斜插下，几乎触到河沟对岸的土阜，而又鼓扑着双翅，作出猛烈的声响腾上了。那样巨大的翅膀使我吃惊。

《雨前》何其芳

When I look up at a gray misty pall of a low-hanging sky, some dust particles feel chilly on my ***face***. A hawk, seemingly irked by the gloomy sky, swoops down sideways out of nowhere, with wings wide-spread and immovable, until it almost hits the hillock on the other side of the brook. But it soars skywards again with a loud flap. I am amazed by the tremendous size of its wings. And I also catch sight of the grizzled feathers on its underside. [15]

"Praying for Rainfall" He Qifang

腥、腹

这天晚上海丽琪罕熬了一大锅牛杂碎汤，我只觉得**腥**，勉强吃了半碗就不肯再吃，使房东二老颇觉疑惑。第二天一早，我**腹**痛如绞，腹泻如注。从这一件事情上，我已经看准了自己的无用。

《宰牛》王蒙

That evening, Hailiqi prepared a potful of chopped beef tripe stew. It was too ***smelly*** for me, so I managed to eat only half a bowl.

That very much perplexed my landlord and his wife. Early the next morning, I suffered from a severe ***stomach***-ache and diarrhea. I blamed myself for being so fragile. [15]

"Ox-Slaughtering" Wang Meng

膀、背

我北来后，他写了一信给我，信中说道，"我身体平安，惟**膀**子疼痛厉害，举箸提笔，诸多不便，大约大去之期不远矣。"我读到此处，在晶莹的泪光中，又看见那肥胖的，青布棉袍，黑布马褂的**背**影。唉！我不知何时再能与他相见！

《背影》朱自清

After I arrived in Beijing, he wrote me a letter, in which he says, "I'm all right except for a severe pain in my ***arm***. I even have trouble using chopsticks or writing brushes. Perhaps it won't be long now before I depart this life." Through the glistening tears which these words had brought to my eyes I again saw the ***back*** of father's corpulent form in the dark blue cotton-padded cloth long gown and the black cloth mandarin jacket. Oh, how I long to see him again! [15]

"The Sight of Father's Back" Zhu Ziqing

斤

"**斤**"之本意为"砍削木头的横刀小斧"。用"斤"组合的字往往与砍伐相关。例字中，除"**匠**"外，其他为形声字，"**新**"为右形左声，"**斧**"为下形上声。

新

那时正是大革命之后，时代的激荡当然会在文学的领域里反映出来。那两年，《小说月报》上出现了许多有***新***意的作品，也出现了许多新的名字，最惹人注意的是茅盾、巴金和丁玲。当时大家不知道茅盾就是沈雁冰兄。他过去不写小说，只介绍国外的作品和理论。巴金和丁玲两位都不相识，是以后才见面的。

《我和商务印书馆》叶圣陶

It was the post-Great Revolution days when the stirring times found expression in literature. For two consecutive years, there appeared in *Fiction Monthly* a great many works full of ***new*** ideas and also a great many new manes, of which the most conspicuous were Mao Dun, Ba Jin and Ding Ling. People at that time did not know that Mao Dun was the pseudonym for Shen Yanbing. He had up to then written no fiction, but articles introducing foreign literary works and theories. I was not acquainted with Ba Jin and Ding Ling. I met them later.[15]

"The Commercial Press and I" Ye Shengtao

斧

一块粗糙的木头经过了***斧***子劈，锯子锯，刨子刨，就变成了一方或者一条光滑整齐的木板，再经过钻子、凿子等工具以后，又变成了各种各样的东西；像美丽的窗格，镂花的壁板等细致的物件，都是这样制成的。

《木匠老陈》巴金

A piece of coarse wood, after being processed with the ***hatchet***, saw and plane, would become pieces of smooth and tidy wood, square or rectangular in shape. After further treatment with the chisel, drill, etc., they would end up as various kinds of exquisite articles, such as beautiful window lattices, ornamental engravings on wooden partitions.[15]

"Carpenter Lao Chen" Ba Jin

（木）匠：会意字，由匚、由斤会意[9]。"匚"意为盛物的器具。

"老陈，你还在省城！人家说你吃粮去了！"我快活地大声叫起来。

"我只会做***木匠***，我就只会做木匠！一个人应该安分守己，"他摇摇头微微笑道，他的笑容里带了一点悲哀。他没有什么大改变，只是人瘦了些，脸黑了些，衣服脏了些。

《木匠老陈》巴金

"Lao Chen," I yelled out in joy, "You're still here in the provincial capital! People say you've joined up!"

"I'm good at nothing else but ***carpentry***, I'm good at nothing else but carpentry! One should be content with one's lot." He shook his head, wearing a faint smile with a touch of sorrow. There was not much change in him except that he was thinner, his face darker and his clothes dirtier. [15]

"Carpenter Lao Chen" Ba Jin

四、五画

田

用"***田***"组合的字，与农田、田猎、农事耕作有关。除"***畋***、***里***、***奋***、***田***"外，其他为形声字，其中"***畔***"为左形右声，余者下形上声。

畔

1. 沉舟侧***畔***千帆过， One ship sinks, a thousand sails go ***by***.
病树前头万木春。 One tree is sicken, spring brings ten thousand more to bloom. [2]

《酬乐天扬州初逢，席上见赠》

"In response to a Poem by Bai Juyi, Composed upon Our First Meeting at a Banquet in Yangzhou"

（唐）刘禹锡 (The Tang Dynasty) Liu Yuxi

2. 凤凰台上青山旧， From Phoenix Tower I find the changeless hill blue;
秋千墙里垂杨瘦， Beside the swing within the wall
琵琶亭***畔***野花秋。 The weeping willow slender grows;
长江自流。 ***Before*** the pavilion late autumn flowers fall,
But heedless, the endless river still flows. [5]

《醉太平·怀古》 Tune: Drunk in Time of peace, "Thinking of the past"

（元）张可久 (The Yuan Dynasty) Zhang Kejiu

例 1 之"***畔***"意为：旁边、附近。译文取"**by**"的"经过"（past）之意，与"go"进行搭配，表达出诗中沉舟之侧千帆驶过之意。"by"此处为副词。**例 2** 中，作者登临凤凰台，身处琵琶亭，"野花"与"长江"是其眼前之景，译文"**before**"体现出"附近"之意。

當

对潇潇暮雨灑江天， Shower by shower

一番洗清秋。	Besprinkles evening rain the sky
渐霜风凄紧，	Over the river,
关河冷落，	Washing cool the autumn air both far and nigh.
残阳**當**楼。	Gradually frost falls and blows the wind so chill
是处红衰翠减，	That few people pass by hill or rill,
苒苒物华休。	In fading sunlight ***drowned*** is my bower.
唯有长江水，	Everywhere the red and the green wither away,
无语东流。	There's no more splendor of a sunny day.
	Only the waves of River Long Silently eastward flow along. [1]

《八声甘州》 Tune: Eight Beats of a Ganzhou Song
（宋）柳永 （The Song Dynasty） Liu Yong

此处之“**當**”意为“面对着，向着”，译文“**drown**”虽为意译，但其所含“盖没、淹没”之意则含蓄地体现出诗中之“當”：漫射的阳光将作者所居之楼笼罩其中。阳光漫射，洒在作者所居之楼，意即“當楼”。这里“當”的翻译还体现出主、客体之不同的思维方式：原文“残阳當楼”：主动语态；译文“In fading sunlight ***drowned*** is my bower”为被动形式。

思：囟（xin）声[9]。

1. 黯乡魂，	A homesick heart
追旅**思**。	Lost in ***thoughts*** deep,
夜夜除非，	Only sweet dreams each night can retain me in sleep.
好梦留人睡。	Don't lean alone on rails when the bright moon appears!
明月楼高休独倚。	Wine in sad bowels would turn into nostalgic tears. [1]
酒入愁肠，	
化作相思泪。	

《苏幕遮》 Tune: Screened by Southern Curtain
（宋）范仲淹 （The Song Dynasty） Fan Zhongyan

2. 雕栏外，红日低；	The red sun is sinking by the rail,
画栋畔，彩云飞。	And the twilights, splashing in the air.
十二栏杆在天外倚，	I am looking into China proper,
我这里望中原，**思**故里，	From far away, from another world.
不由我感叹酸嘶，	I'm ***thinking*** of my homeland
越搅得我这一片乡心碎！	With a nostalgic mood, and
	My heart is broken for my homesickness! [10]

《望中原》 Tune: Looking into China Proper
（元）马致远 （The Yuan Dynasty） Ma Zhiyuan

例 2“***思***”之译文体现出与原文不同的思维方式。原文中诗人所表达的“正在思念”依靠的是词汇手段和语意逻辑：“我这里望中原，思故里”之“这里”既含“此处”，又蕴有“当时正在”之意；“望”先于“思”，但“望”与“思”皆是作者在此处（当时）之所为，而“思”的词形并没有任何的改变。如此的词汇手段及动作顺序的安排即综合型思维方式使然。对于同一诗意的表达，分析性思维方式则需通过词形的变化（think+ing）以及语法中的进行时态加以体现。

留（畱:“田”的上部取“丣”音）

鹤飞去兮，西山之缺。高翔而下览兮，择所适。翻然敛翼，宛将集兮，忽何所见，矫然而复击。独终日于涧谷之间兮，啄苍苔而履白石。鹤归来兮，东山之阴。其下有人兮，黄冠草屦，葛衣而鼓琴。躬耕而食兮，其馀以汝饱。归来归来兮，西山不可以久***留***。

《放鹤亭记》（宋）苏轼

Oh, to the west mount crack, the cranes are let to fly;
For where to frolic and lark, they look from the sky.
With a swing, they close their wings to descend;
For a new lure, they lift to re-ascend.
They ramble in dales and rills, sunrise to sunset,
Aloof, pecking at lichen and treading on grit.

Oh, to the east mount shady slope, the cranes fly back;
Under their roost, a hermit resides in a shack.
Straw sandals, a coarse robe, and a Taoist hat,
Are his garb, when he plucks a ***zheng*** instrument.
He grows his own crops, but they are also the cranes' food;
Oh, come home; west mount isn't a crane's ***homestead***.[8]

"The Crane Pavilion" (The Song Dynasty) Su Shi

“***留***”之本意为“不离去”。一般而言，久留之地即是“家”，此处“**homestead**”(a house with the land and buildings around it, especially a farm) 与“留”之意相符。

畋：会意字，由“攵（攴）”、由“田”会意[9]。其意为平治田地。“攴”意为“小击”，凡举有做事之意，皆从之。现为打猎之意。

临江之人，***畋***得麋鹿，畜之。入门，群犬垂涎，扬尾皆来，其人怒怛之。自是日抱就犬，习示之，使勿动；稍使与之戏。……犬畏主人，与之俯仰甚善，然时啖其舌。

三年，麋出门，见外犬在道甚众，走欲与为之戏。外犬见而喜且怒，共杀食之，狼藉道上，麋至死不悟。

《柳河东集》（唐）柳宗元

A man in Linjiang ***captured*** a fawn. When it was brought home, the dogs came licking their chops and wagging their tails. The man angrily drove them off. Afterwards, he took the fawn among the dogs, warning them to keep their peace, and making them frolic with it. ...The dogs, fearing their master, had to suppress their natural desires and fraternize with it.

One day after three years, the deer went outside the gate. There were many strange dogs in the street, so it went up and tried to play with them. The dogs were surprised, but being glad to see a meal come their way, fell upon it and killed it. As it was breathing its last, the deer was at a loss to understand why it had come to such an untimely end.

"Collected Works of Liu Zongyuan" (The Tang Dynasty) Liu Zongyuan

里：会意字，由“田”、由“土”会意[9]。

吾尝终日而思矣，不如须臾之所学也；吾尝跂而望矣，不如登高之博见也。登高而招，臂非加长也，而见者远；顺风而呼，声非加疾也，而闻者彰。假舆马者，非利足也，而致千**里**；假舟楫者，非能水也，而绝江河。君子生非异也，善假于物也。

《劝学篇》（战国）荀子

I used to take to thinking all the day, yet I found that it was not as fruitful as a moment's learning. I tried to stand on tiptoe to look far. But it was unlike my ascending to a high place that gave me a broad view. I waved someone on an elevation and it could be seen by him at a greater distance. It was not because my arm was lengthened. I cried in the direction of a wind, though my voice was not any louder, yet it could be heard more clearly. Those who ride a horse or take a chariot can cover a thousand ***li*** a day. It is not because they have prodigious feet. Those who travel by boats can make little of rivers. It is not because they can swim. A man is not born with extraordinary abilities. The point is that they are capable of making use of various things.[12]

"On Learning" (The Warring States Period) Xun Zi

原文“假舆马者，非利足也，而致千**里**”之“**里**”是中国传统的长度单位，虽可译成“miles”，毕竟与原文意思有所差距：一里相当于500米，一英里相当于1609米，此处之“里”音译为“**li**”，尽量保留了中国独特的文化意象。

【译法点滴】 文化差异对翻译的影响：词汇空缺及其译法——音译

音译是词语翻译中经常使用的手段之一。中国传统文化中的有些词语，如天干地支、阴阳八卦等在西方文化中没有与其相对等的词语，翻译时一般采用音译，用汉语拼音转写。此外，还有些词，如上例中的“**里**”，虽可译成“miles”，毕竟与原文的意思有所差距，所以，为了尽量保留中国独特的文化意象，有时也使用音译的方法。

奋（奮）：会意字，由“隹（短尾鸟的总名）”在“田”上会意[9]。

公明仪为牛弹清角之操，伏食为故。非牛不闻，不合其耳矣。转为蚊虻之声，孤犊之鸣，即掉尾、***奋***耳，蹀躞而听。

牟子

One day Gong Mingyi, the celebrated musician, was playing an elegant tune on his harp to amuse a browsing ox.

The ox, however, continued to munch, paying no heed to him at all.

Then he struck up some different notes, which sounded like mosquitoes droning and calves bleating. Whereupon the ox flicked its tail, ***pricked up*** its ears, and began frisking round and round, evidently absorbed in the music. [14]

Mou Zi

译文“**pricked up**”［（of an animal, especially a horse or dog） to raise the ears］形象地表达出了“奋耳”（竖起耳朵）之“奋”。

田：象形字。

1. 玉鉴琼***田***三万顷，　Like thirty thousand ***acres*** of jade bright
   着我扁舟一叶。　Dotted with the leaf-like boat of mine. [1]

   《念奴娇 · 过洞庭》

   Tune: The Charm of a Maiden Singer, “Passing Lake Dongting”

   （宋）张孝祥　（The Song Dynasty） Zhang Xiaoxiang

2. 求***田***问舍，　I’d be ashamed to see the patriot,
   怕应羞见、　Should I retire to seek for ***land*** and cot. [1]
   刘郎才气。

   《水龙吟 · 登建康赏心亭》

   Tune: Water Dragon Chant, “On Riverside Tower at Jiankang”

   （宋）辛弃疾　（The Song Dynasty） Xin Qiji

例1之原文“**田**”，虽“三万顷”，但没有词形变化；译文则采用了其复数形式“**acres**”，便于不同思维形式的译语读者理解。

鸟

用“**鸟**”组合的字，与鸟的类别、名称及鸟的活动有关。例字中除“**枭**”外，余皆为形声字，其中，“**鹭**”和“**莺**”为下形上声，其余右形左声。

鹂

独怜幽草涧边生，	Most lovely are there grasses that grow hidden by the banks
上有黄***鹂***深树鸣。	Where ***orioles*** sing from deep within the overhanging boughs.
春潮带雨晚来急，	Quickened by the evening rain, the spring flood swells the rustic crossing;
野渡无人舟自横。	No one aboard, the ferryboat rights itself upon the tide. [2]
《滁州西涧》	“Chuzhou's West Valley Stream”
（唐）韦应物	(The Tang Dynasty) Wei Yingwu

鹏

九万里风***鹏***正举。	The ***roc*** soars up to ninety thousand miles and nine.
风休住，	O wind mine!
蓬舟吹取三山去。	Don't stop but carry my boat to three isles divine! [1]
《渔家傲·记梦》	Tune: Pride of Fishermen, “A Dream”
（宋）李清照	(The Song Dynasty) Li Qingzhao

鸡（鷄）

1\. 半壁见海日，　Halfway, already sunlight crowns the sea;
空中闻天***鸡***。　Above, the Heavenly ***Rooster*** crows. [2]
《梦游天姥吟留别》
“Dream Journey to the Heavenly Mother Mountain: A Song of Parting”
（唐）李白　(The Tang Dynasty) Li Bai

2\. 谁道人生无再少，　Who says an old man can't return once more unto his spring?
门前流水尚能西。　Before Clear Fountain's temple the water still flows west.
休将白发唱黄***鸡***。　Why can't the ***cock*** still crow at dawn though with a snow-white crest? [1]
《浣溪沙》　Tune: Sand of Silk-washing Stream
（宋）苏轼　(The Song Dynasty) Su Shi

鸥

1. 飘飘何所似，　What do I resemble, after all?
天地一沙**鸥**。　A lone ***gull***, poised between earth and sky.[2]
《旅夜书怀》　"Night Thoughts on a Journey"
（唐）杜甫　(The Tang Dynasty) Du Fu

2. 寒光亭下水如天，　Water looks like the sky below Bower Cold-Light,
惊起沙**鸥**一片。　It's ruffled only by the ***water-birds*** in flight.[1]
《西江月》　Tune: The Moon Over the West River
（宋）张孝祥　(The Song Dynasty) Zhang Xiaoxiang

例 2 中之"**鸥**"的译文取"**water-birds**"在于"沙**鸥**一片"。"一片"盖泛指，故这里"鸥"之译文取"water-birds"（水禽中自然包括沙鸥），与一片之意对应。

鹭

闲**鹭**栖长早，　The leisurely ***egrets*** oft go back to their nests earlier,
秋花落更迟。　The autumn flowers here wither and fall much later.[13]
《谷口书斋寄杨补阙》　"To Official Yang from My Study at Gukou"
（唐）钱起　(The Tang Dynasty) Qian Qi

鹤、莺

松影一庭唯见**鹤**，　Only a ***stork*** can be seen in the pine-shadowed court,
梨花满地不闻**莺**。　No ***oriole*** sings in the snow which has drifted like pear-blossom.[17]
《冬夜即事》　"Winter Night"
（清）曹雪芹　(The Qing Dynasty) Cao Xueqin

鸦

声声啼乳**鸦**，　Nursing ***crows*** caw out cry on cry,
生叫破韶华。　Breaking the early day of spring.
夜深微雨润堤沙，　Last night the drizzle moistened the sand far and nigh,
香风万家。　Thousands of homes sweetened by the breeze on the wing.[5]
《醉太平·寒食》　Tune: Drunk in Time of Peace, "Cold Food Day"
（元）王元鼎　(The Yuan Dynasty) Wang Yuanding

鸿

孤村落日残霞，	At sunset over lonely village rainbow clouds glow;
轻烟老树寒鸦，	Over mist-veiled old trees flies a cold crow.
一点飞**鸿**影下。	The shadow of a dot of ***swan*** in flight
青山绿水，	Over green hills and bluish rills
白草红叶黄花。	Sees leaves red, flowers yellow and dewy grass white. [5]
《天净沙 · 秋》	Tune: Sunny Sand, "Autumn"
（元）白朴	(The Yuan Dynasty) Bai Pu

此例的原文与译文突出体现了具象与抽象思维的不同：原文的五行诗句中使用了十二个名词，列出了十二种具象，使秋日之景跃然纸上，而且强调了色彩的对比。严密的抽象逻辑思维以及英语遣词造句的语法要求在译文中的表现为：通过增添动词、连词、介词和冠词，使原文中的具象组合改换成了三个完整的逻辑语句。此译文句式工整，语言通顺流畅，词义贴切对应，韵律和谐自然，并最大限度地保留了原始具象。

【译法点滴】　具象思维与抽象思维在原文与译文中的体现

中、西传统文化的一个重要特征分别是“尚象”与“尚思”。“尚象”形成了偏重具象的思维方式，“尚思”则形成了偏重抽象的思维方式。具象思维活动以物象为媒介，要求取象与取义相结合，特定的思想要寄寓于具体的物象之中。其特点在于它的直感性，即它与被思维对象直接联系，其叙事说理、表情达意往往离不开具体形象的借助。而抽象思维则是人们在认识活动中运用概念、判断、推理等思维方式，对客观现实进行间接的、概括的反映过程。通过对物象的统摄，以词作为中介来反映现实，以严密的逻辑语句叙事说理、表达概念、情感和意向。从上例对白朴“***秋***”之原文与译文的分析即可看出两种思维方式的不同。通过对下例“***春***”及其译文的对比亦可看到两种思维方式对各自文学作品在艺术结构和表达形式上的影响。

《春》原文：　春山暖日和风，
栏杆楼台帘栊。
杨柳秋千院中。
啼莺舞燕，
小桥流水飞红。

《天净沙 · 春》
（元）白朴

原文的五行诗句中使用了十三个名词，列出了十三种具象，使春日之绚丽和清新凸显而出。

译文：　The sun and gentle breeze warm hills in spring,
The curtained bower girt with balustrade.
Among the willows in the garden hangs the swing.
The swallows dance and orioles sing
On running stream under the bridge fallen reds fade. [5]

Tune：Sunny Sand，"Spring"
（The Yuan Dynasty）Bai Pu

与"**秋**"相同，出于英语遣词造句的语法要求及其严密的抽象逻辑思维表达形式的需要，根据其句法结构，译文中增添了动词、连词、介词和冠词，使原文中的具象组合改换成了三个完整的逻辑语句。

鹊、枭、鸠： 枭，会意字，由鸟头在木（"母"的谐音）上会意。枭为不孝鸟。

鹊巢于木，巢之远人者；燕巢于梁，巢之袭人者。凤之巢，人瑞之；***枭***之巢，人覆之。雀不能巢，或夺燕巢，巢之暴者也；***鸠***不能巢，伺鹊育雏而去，则居其巢，巢之拙者也。

《书巢记》（宋）陆游

A ***pie*** builds its nest in a tree. It is meant to be farther from the crowds. A swallow builds its nest on a beam. It is intended to closer to men. The nest of a phoenix is considered to be propitious, while that of an ***owl*** is to be destroyed. A sparrow is incapable of building a nest, and it may seize that of a swallow, which is therefore much exposed. Likewise, a ***turtle-dove*** would occupy the nest of a pie after it has bred its young and left. So the nest must be a shabby one. [12]

"The Nest Built of Books"（The Song Dynasty）Lu You

穴

"**穴**"的本意是土室。用"穴"组成的字与岩洞、地上某些建筑物上的坑或孔、动物的窝以及墓穴有关。例字中除"**帘**、**穿**"外，余者为形声字：上形下声。

空

1. 吾在天地之间，犹小石小木之在大山也。方存乎见少，又奚以自多？计四海之在天地间也，不似礨空之在大泽乎？

《秋水》（战国）庄子

I am but a pebble or a tiny piece of wood on a large mountain. I can only be ashamed of my smallness. How can I feel proud and complacent? Just imagine, are not seas in the universe comparable to small ***cavities*** in a vast lake?[12]

"Autumnal Floods" (The Warring States Period) Zhuang Zi

2. 每至晴初霜旦，林寒涧肃，常有高猿长啸，属引凄异，**空**谷传响，哀转久绝。故渔者歌曰，"巴东三峡巫峡长，猿鸣三声泪沾裳！"

《三峡》（北魏）郦道元

On the first sunny days and frosty mornings when the woods look chilly and the dells seem somber and grave, apes are heard to be whining on high, causing a prolonged feeling of disconsolation, and the sound, vibrating in the ***hollow*** ravines, only vanishes after a long melancholy echoing. That accounts for the fishermen's song: "The Wu Gorge is the longest of the three in the Ba region's eastern part, three cries of the monkeys bring forth your tears, wetting your sleeves and distressing your heart."[12]

"The Three Gorges" (The Northern Wei Dynasty) Li Daoyuan

3. 闲云潭影日悠悠， 物换星移几度秋。 阁中帝子今何在？ 栏外长江**空**自流。	Along with the idle clouds and the shadows in the ponds, pass the days in a leisurely way. Things have changed, stars have shifted—how many years have gone away? Where are now the princes who once in the tower stayed? Only the Yangtze is seen to be flowing ***vainly*** outside the palisade![12]
《滕王阁序》 （唐）王勃	"The Tower of Prince Teng" (The Tang Dynasty) Wang Bo

例1中的"**空**"为名词；**例2**为形容词（修饰"谷"）；**例3**为副词（修饰"流"），译文中对此均有体现，其意与原文相符。

窝："呙"音 guo。

懒云**窝**， 醒时诗酒醉时歌。	In my ***nest*** for Idle Clouds, Sober, I drink and write; while drunk, I croon aloud.[5]
《殿前吹 · 懒云窝》 （元）阿利西瑛	Tune: Joy before Palace, "My Nest for Idle Clouds" (The Yuan Dynasty) Ali Xiying

窍

徐而察之，则山下皆石穴罅，不知其深浅，微波入焉，涵澹澎湃而为此也。舟回至两山间，将入港口，有大石当中流，可坐百人，空中多**窍**，与风水相吞吐，有窾坎镗鞳之声，与向之噌吰者相应，如乐作焉。

《石钟山记》（宋）苏轼

I took the time to observe and saw that hollowed into the foot of the cliff were rock caves and clefts. I didn't know how deep they were, but when water ruffled in, the surging and lashing waves produced bell-like chimes. We skirted back into a spot between two hills. Situated right in the middle of the mouth of the stream, where we were about to head, was a gigantic boulder, which was spacious enough for a hundred people to sit on. It was hollow inside, with many ***clefts*** in it to usher the water and wind in and out. This created lapping and chiming sounds that were in harmony with the booming sound springing out of the water, like an ongoing band concert.[8]

"Mount Rock Bell" (The Song Dynasty) Su Shi

窥

听静夜之钟声，唤醒梦中之梦；观澄潭之月影，**窥**见身外之身。

《菜根谭》（明）洪应明

Listen to the sound of a temple bell afar on a still midnight, and so you will awaken yourself from the dream of life. Gaze upon the moon reflection on the surface of a limpid pool, and so you will ***perceive*** the true characters of your nature.[6]

"The Roots of Wisdom" (The Ming Dynasty) Hong Yingming

踰

昔曾子处费，费人有与曾子同名族者，而杀人。
人告曾子母曰："曾参杀人!"
曾子之母曰："吾子不杀人!"织自若。
有顷焉，人又曰："曾参杀人!"
其母尚织自若也。
顷之，一人又告之曰："曾参杀人!"
其母惧，投杼，**踰**墙走。

《战国策》（汉）刘向

Once, when Zeng Shen went to the district of Fei, a man with the same name there committed a murder. Someone went to tell Zeng Shen's mother: "Zeng Shen has killed a man!"

"Impossible," she replied. "My son would never do such a thing."

She went calmly on with her weaving.

After a while, someone else came to report: "Zeng Shen has killed a man."

Still the old lady went on weaving.

Then a third man came to tell her: "Zeng Shen has killed a man!"

This time his mother was frightened. She threw down her shuttle and escaped ***over*** the wall.

For although Zeng Shen was a good man and his mother trusted him, when three men accused him of murder, much as she loved him she could not but begin to doubt him.[14]

"Warring States Anecdotes" (The Han Dynasty) Liu Xiang

例中之“**窬**”为动词，其意“从墙上爬过去”。如果只翻译“窬”之意，不足以表现出曾子之母因害怕越墙而逃的情景。通过对上下文的理解，译文中使用了动词“逃”（escaped），更贴切地表达出原文所含之意，故“窬”的词性也随之在译文中发生变化：转换为介词“**over**”，介词短语“over the wall”用作状语，表示出逃的方式。

帘：会意字，由“穴”、由“巾”会意。

苔痕上阶绿，草色入**帘**青。

《陋室铭》（唐）刘禹锡

The green moss creeps up my doorsteps. The verdant grass reflects its light upon my window ***curtains***.[12]

"Eulogy to My Humble Chamber" (The Tang Dynasty) Liu Yuxi

穿：会意字，由“牙”在“穴”中会意[9]。

绳锯木断，水滴石**穿**，学道者须加力索；水到渠成，瓜熟蒂落，得道者一任天机。

《菜根谭》（明）洪应明

A wood can be cut off by sawing with a rope; a stone can be ***worn away*** by dripping water. Enlightened by this, those who intend to learn the Way must constantly exhort themselves to explorations. When water flows, a channel is formed; when a melon is ripe, it falls off its stem. So those who have comprehended the Way should allow things to follow their natural bent. [6]

"The Roots of Wisdom" (The Ming Dynasty) Hong Yingming

禾

用"**禾**"组合的字，与谷类植物和农作物有关。例字中除"**利**、**禾**"外，余者为形声字，左形右声。

稼

社坛烟淡散林鸦。	The incense on the altar fades
把酒观多**稼**。	And crows disperse into the glades.
霹雳弦声斗高下，	Wine cup in hand and bumper ***harvest*** in view,
笑喧哗，	I hear strings rumbling low and high,
壤歌亭外山如画。	Mingle with cheerful cry.
朝来致有	Beyond Labor Pavilion hills look like pictures fair.
西山爽气，	At dawn the western hills exhale fresh air.
不羡日夕佳。	Why should I envy Southern Mountain hue? [5]

《平湖乐·尧庙秋社》

Tune: Joy of Calm Lake, "Autumn Festival at Emperor Yao's Temple"

（元）王恽　(The Yuan Dynasty) Wang Yun

稀

翠荷残，	Lotus blooms fade,
苍梧坠。	Green plane leaves fall.
千山应瘦，	Hills on hills appear lean;
万木皆**稀**。	Woods on woods cast ***less*** shade. [5]

《普天乐》　Tune: Universal Joy

（元）滕宾　(The Yuan Dynasty) Teng Bin

种

问荆溪溪上人家，	I ask people by the riverside why
为甚人家	Mume trees are not
不**种**梅花?	***Planted*** near by. [5]

《折桂令·荆溪即事》

Tune: Plucking Laurel Branch, "The Riverside Land"

（元）乔吉　(The Yuan Dynasty) Qiao Ji

此例之原文的“***种***”与译文之“**Planted**”体现出本体与客体型思维方式的不同。

秣

昔者瓠巴，鼓瑟而沈鱼出听，伯牙鼓琴而六马仰***秣***。故声无小而不闻，行无隐而不形。玉在山而草木润，渊生珠而崖不枯。

《劝学篇》（战国）荀子

In the past Huba played the Chinese zither, the swimming fish came out of the water to listen to it. And when Boya played the lute, six horses raised their heads from the ***manger*** for the same joy. Therefore, no sounds so faint but are heard. No actions so hidden but are discovered. A jade buried in a mountain makes the grass look lustrous. A pearl grown in an abyss makes the cliff abound in water. [12]

"On Learning" (The Warring States Period) Xun Zi

“***秣***”意为“牲口的饲料”。例中典故“伯牙鼓琴六马仰秣”之意：因伯牙琴声之美妙，连正在槽中吃饲料的马也仰起头来（不再继续吃其饲料），将此处之“秣”与“manger（饲料槽）”对应之与原文之意更为贴切。

利：会意字，由“禾”、由“刂”会意。

大凡君子与君子以同道为朋，小人与小人以同***利***为朋，此自然之理也。……

小人所好者，利禄也；所贪者，财货也。当其同***利***之时，暂相党引以为朋者，伪也；及其见***利***争先，或***利***终而交疏，则反相贼害，虽其兄弟亲戚，不能相保。……君子则不然：所守者道义，所行者忠信，所惜者名节。以之修身，则同道而相益；以之事国，则同心而共济；始终如一，此君子之朋也。

《朋党论》（宋）欧阳修

Generally speaking, noble men group together as friends for common avocations while ignoble men bundle up as friends, so to speak, for personal ***interests***. That is inevitable. ...What ignoble men are interested in is gaining and taking, and what they desire is money and goods. When they share the same ***interest***, they can, for the time being, band together as friends. But that is a fake friendship, for where there is a ***gain***, there they each vie to lay his hands on it. When the ***profit*** runs out, they estrange themselves from one another and even harm each other, despite being brothers or relatives. ...

Noble men prove the contrary. What they abide by is morality and justice; what they adhere to, faith and honesty; what they value, reputation and integrity. With these as principles for self-cultivation, when they group together, they can better themselves by learning from each other; with these as guidelines in serving the country, they can share the same goals, make concerted efforts, and persist in pursuing them. These are the noble men's coterie![8]

"On Coterie" (The Song Dynasty) Ouyang Xiu

此例中，四个"***利***"，其含义有三：第一，"小人与小人以同利为朋"；第二，"当其同利之时"，此二"利"有"兴趣与利益"双重含义。第三，"见利争先"之"利"偏重于收益。第四，"利终而交疏"之"利"的含义中既有"好处"，又有实际的收益。第一个与第二个"利"的译文为"**interest**(s)"；第三个为"**gain**"(an advantage)；第四个为"**profit**"(the advantage that you get…，及 money that you make…)。此 4 个"利"的译文均体现出其原文的所含之意。

禾：象形字。

1. 锄***禾***日当午， When ***crops*** are worked at noon,
汗滴禾下土。 It is sweat that moistens the soil.
谁知盘中餐， Who stops to think, before a bowl of food,
粒粒皆辛苦。 That every grain comes only through long toil?[2]
《悯农二首》 "Sympathy for the Peasants"
（唐）李绅 (The Tang Dynasty) Li Shen

2. 亭以雨名。志喜也。古者有喜，则以名物，示不忘也。周公得***禾***，以名其书；汉武得鼎，以名其年；叔孙胜敌，以名其子。其喜之大小不齐，其示不忘一也。

《喜雨亭记》（宋）苏轼

Using rain to name the arbor—it is to denote my joy of it. The ancients had their joy denoted by a certain things to show that it would never be forgotten. Thus Lord Zhou, having come by an ear of ***wheat***, entitled his book The *Book of Wheat*. Emperor Wu of the Han Dynasty, having been presented a bronze cauldron, used it to name that year of his reign. Shu Sun, having defeated his enemy, had his son called Qiao Ru, the latter's name. Joy may be greater or lesser, but to do like that is to manifest its unforgettableness.[12]

"The Arbor of Joyful Rain" (The Song Dynasty) Su Shi

例 1 中"锄***禾***日当午"之"***禾***"，译文用"**crops**"（庄稼），盖泛指。**例 2** 中"周公得***禾***"之"***禾***"源于历史典故：周成王的同母弟唐叔得到一种奇异的禾，两株禾生在不同的田埂上，却合生一穗，便献给成王。成王转送周公。周公因而作《嘉禾》。此"禾"的译文取"**wheat**"（小麦），强调了"穗"。**例 1** 中"禾"与其译文 crops（复数形式）体现出综合与分析型思维的不同，同时还反映出本体与客体型思维的区别：由于汉语习惯于用表示人或生物的词作主语（或潜在的主语），原文中“锄禾”的潜在主语是“人”，即农民，“禾”是宾语，而英语则常用非生物名词作主语，故译文中“禾”为主语。

目

用“***目***”组合的字一般与眼睛、视力等有关。例字中除“***睡***、***眇***、***眉***”外，余者为形声字，其中，“**盲**、***瞽***”为下形上声，其他为左形右声。

盲

寇难至，躄者告**盲**者，盲者负而走，两人皆活。得其所能也。

《淮南子》（汉）刘安

A certain country was invaded by its enemy. When a lame man there told a ***blind*** man of this, the blind man carried the lame one on his back and they escaped together. They did this by making use of each other's strong points. [14]

"Huai Nan Zi" (The Han Dynasty) Liu An

瞽

瞽者与人同坐。人有所见而笑，瞽者亦笑。或问汝何所见而笑？瞽答曰：“诸君所笑，定然不差，难道是骗我的。”

《笑赞》（明）赵南星

A ***blind*** man was in the company of others. When his companions saw something funny, they laughed. The blind man laughed, too.

When they asked him why he was laughing, the blind man replied, "Since there must be something worth laughing at. Can you be cheating me there?" [14]

"Xiao Zan" (The Ming Dynasty) Zhao Nanxing

眠

一江秋水淡寒烟，	On autumn stream pale smoke and cold mist rise,
水影明如练。	With water crystal-clear and silk-white.
眼底离愁数行雁。	A few rows of wild geese bring parting grief to the eyes.
雪晴天，	After snow the sunny sky's bright,
绿苹红蓼参差见。	Green duckweed and red knotweed high and low appear.
吴歌荡桨，	The rower sings a Southern song on the stream,
一声哀怨，	So plaintive and so drear,

惊起白鸥***眠***。　　A white gull's startled from its ***dream***.[5]

《小桃红》　　Tune: Red Peach Blossoms

（元）倪瓒　　(The Yuan Dynasty) Ni Zan

此例中"惊起白鸥***眠***"之"***眠***"的译文取"**dream**"（梦）为意译。"梦"即睡眠时局部大脑皮层还没有停止活动而引起的脑中之表象活动。"dream"含有"眠"之意。此译文与原文意思相符；而且"dream"的选取起到了押韵的作用：stream→dream。

瞒

叹世间多少痴人，　　How many in the world are people unwise?
多是忙人，　　Most of them early rise;
少是闲人。　　Few are idle guys.
酒色迷人，　　Some bewitched by women and wine lose their health;
财气昏人，　　Others are greedy for wealth.
缠定活人。　　The living to death are bound;
钹儿鼓儿终日送人，　　The dead are sent to burial mound.
车儿马儿常时迎人。　　Carriages and horses welcome the new,
精细的***瞒***人，　　The crafty will ***deceive*** you,
本分的饶人。　　The un-crafty will forgive.
不识时人，　　If you do not know how to live,
枉只为人。　　You are a swain living in vain.[5]

《折桂令》　　Tune: Plucking Laurel Branch

（元）无名氏　　(The Yuan Dynasty) Anonymous

此处"***瞒***"的译文选取"**deceive**"，不仅在于其含义"to cause to accept as true or valid what is false or invalid"，且起到押韵的作用：new→you。

瞻

然将适西山，行於松柏之间，羊肠九曲，而获小平。游者至此必息，倚怪石，荫茂木，俯视大江，仰***瞻***陵阜，旁瞩溪谷，风云变化，林麓向背，皆效于左右。

《武昌九曲亭记》（宋）苏辙

To get to the West Hill, however, one has to thread across pine and cedar woods and wind along narrow, meandering paths to finally reach a relatively flat spot, when everyone will pause for a rest, either leaning against an anomalous rock, or sitting in thick tree shade, or surveying the great river, or ***looking*** up to loft peeks, or gazing at the streams of dales by its side. This is a spot from where one can behold the vacillations of winds and clouds and both the front and back views of the mountain forests.[8]

"The Pavilion on the Winding Mountain Ranges in Wuchang"

(The Song Dynasty) Su Zhe

例中之"***瞻***"为动词。其译文"**looking**"即 look+ing 所构成的现在分词，与译文中 leaning、sitting、surveying、gazing 一起在句中充当状语，表示伴随情况。此例字的翻译体现出英语语法形式的多样—分析型思维方式使然。

睇眄："丏"音 mian。

穷***睇眄***于中天，极娱游于暇日。天高地迥，觉宇宙之无穷；兴尽悲来，识盈虚之有数。

《滕王阁序》（唐）王勃

One can, stretching his ***sight*** far into the sky, enjoy himself to the utmost in the leisurely days. Contemplating the high sky and the boundless earth, one conceives the infinity of the universe. And, as joy is oft followed by sorrow, one comes to know the cycles of good and ill fortunes as destined by Heaven.[12]

"The Tower of Prince Teng" (The Tang Dynasty) Wang Bo

睡：会意字，由"目"、由"垂"会意[9]。

低茅舍，	Among the thatched cottages low
卖酒家，	There is a shop selling wine.
客来旋把朱帘挂。	When comes a drinker, they will soon up roll
长天落霞，	The curtain red.
方池***睡***鸭，	In endless sky the rainbow clouds overspread,
老树昏鸦。	Ducks ***sleep*** here and there around a pond square,
几句杜陵诗，	Over old trees hovers crow on crow.
一幅王维画。	It's like a poetic line
	Or a painters' scroll.[5]
《庆东原·江头即事》	Tune: Blessed Eastern Plain, "The Rivershore"
（元）曹德	(The Yuan Dynasty) Cao De

眇：会意字，由"目"、由"少"会意。"少"也表声[9]。

生而***眇***者不识日，问之有目者。
或者之曰："日之状如铜盘。"扣盘而得其声，他日闻钟，以为日也。
或者之曰："日之光为烛。"扪烛而得其形，他日揣籥，以为日也。
日之与钟、籥亦远矣，而眇着不知其异，以其未尝见而求人也。

《苏轼文集》（宋）苏轼

A man who was born ***blind*** wanted to know what the sun looked like, so he asked others to describe it.

"It looks like this, like a bronze disc," said one, tapping a gong as he spoke. Some time later, when the blind man heard a gong, he said, "Isn't that the sun?"

Another told him, "The sun has light like this candle," and let him feel the candle. Some time later, the blind man picked up a flute and exclaimed, "Ah! This is surely the sun."

A sun is a far cry from a gong or a flute, but the blind cannot make out the difference because they cannot see and have to ask others. [14]

"Collected Essays of Su Shi" (The Song Dynasty) Su Shi

眼

浪中一叶扁舟，　My leaflike boat braves the perilous waves.
睡煞江南烟雨，　I've slept through Southern rain and smoke.
觉来是满**眼**青山，　My ***eyes*** are filled with green mountains when awake;
抖擞绿蓑归去。　I come back, shaking water off my green straw cloak. [5]
《鹦鹉曲》　Tune: Song of Parrot
（元）白贲　(The Yuan Dynasty) Bai Ben

译文体现出"满眼青山"中所潜在的被动含义。

眉：象形字。

花自飘零水自流。　As water flows and flowers fall without leaving traces,
一种相思，　One and the same longing
两地闲愁。　O'erflows two lonely places.
此情无计可消除，　I cannot get rid of this sorrow: kept apart
才下***眉***头，　From my ***eyebrows***,
却上心头。　It gnaws my heart. [1]
《一剪梅》　Tune: A Twig of Mume Blossoms
（宋）李清照　(The Song Dynasty) Li Qingzhao

石

用"***石***"组合的字，词义大都与石头、坚硬、石制品及石的性质有关。例字中除"***碧***、***磬***、***石***"外，其余为形声字：左形右声。

碑

水落鱼梁浅，	The water subsides and the Yuliang Islet comes out,
天寒梦泽深。	The weather is cold and the depth of the Dream Swamp Land shows a lot.
羊公**碑**尚在，	The stone ***tablet*** to Yang Hu still stands erect and old,
读罢泪沾襟，	After reading the inscriptions on it my tears wet the front part of my coat. [13]

《与诸子登岘山》 "Ascending Mount Xian Together with Several Friends"

（唐）孟浩然 (The Tang Dynasty) Meng Haoran

砖

风流贫最好，	Poor though, be honest, and
村沙富难交。	Be a gentleman in the country.
拾灰泥补砌了旧**砖**窑，	Prepare an old ***brick*** kiln, and
开一个教乞儿市学。	Make it small school campus.
裹一顶半新不旧乌纱帽，	Put on your thinking cap of shabby style,
穿一领半长不短黄麻罩，	Wearing an overcoat of jute fiber,
系一条半联不断皂环绦。	With a black belt around the waist.
做一个穷风月训导。	Aha, I am a good school teacher. [10]

《醉太平》 Tune: Intoxicated in Time of Peace

（元）钟嗣成 (The Yuan Dynasty) Zhong Sicheng

砧

关城树色催寒近，	At Tong Pass the color of the trees seems to hasten the cold season to come near,
御苑**砧**声向晚多。	At dusk in Chang'an a lot of sound of the ***anvil*** you'll hear. [13]

《送魏万之京》 "Seeing Wei Wan Off to Chang'an"

（唐）李颀 (The Tang Dynasty) Li Qi

碾

无意苦争春，	Let other flowers their envy pour.
一任群芳妒。	To Spring she lays no claim.
零落成泥**碾**作尘，	Fallen in mud and ***ground*** to dust, she seems no more,

只有香如故。　But her fragrance is still the same.[1]

《卜算子 · 咏梅》　Tune: Song of Divination, "Ode to the Mume Blossom"

（宋）陆游　(The Song Dynasty) Lu You

例中“**碾**”之原文无词形变化，其译文“**ground**”为过去分词形式，体现出原文中潜在的“被碾”含义。

碧：会意字，由“玉（王）”、由“石”会意[9]。

暮从**碧**山下，　At dusk from the ***green*** Zhongnan Mountain I come down,
山月随人归。　The moon o'er the mountain follows me all along.
却顾所来径，　Looking back at the pathway I just passed, where,
苍苍横翠微。　I see in the boundless dusk the green mountain slants in the air.[13]

《下终南山过斛斯山人宿置酒》

"Descending from the Zhongnan Mountain, Visiting the Hermit Husi, Staying Overnight and Being Entertained with Wine"

（唐）李白　(The Tang Dynasty) Li Bai

磬：会意字，由“石”、由“声殳”会意。“殳”表示用器具敲击石磬[9]。

独敲初夜**磬**，　He alone beats the Buddhist ***percussion*** instrument at the first watch at night,
闲倚一枝藤。　At his leisure he leans against a rattan light.
世界微尘里，　The whole world is merely a particle of dust,
吾宁爱与憎？　So for me to love or hate, is it a must?[13]

《北青萝》　"Visiting a Solitary Monk"

（唐）李商隐　(The Tang Dynasty) Li Shangyin

石：象形字。

凡河中失***石***，当求之于上流。盖石性坚重，沙性松浮，水不能冲石，其反激之力，必于石下迎水处啮沙为坎穴，渐激渐深，至石之半，石必倒掷坎穴中。如是再啮，石又再转。转转不已，遂反溯流逆上也。

《河中石兽》（清）纪昀

All ***stones*** fallen into the river must be looked for upstream. Because stone is solid and heavy while sand is loose and soft. Water cannot wash a stone away, but the force of its dashing against it can erode the sand and scoop a pit beneath it where it is exposed to the water, whose constant dashing and pounding keep it sinking deeper and deeper. When half of the stone is thus affected it overturns into the sand pit. The water's continuous scooping of the sand gives the stone one turn after another. Given the incessant overturning process, it moves against the currents and travels up the river. [12]

"Stone Animals in the River" (The Qing Dynasty) Ji Yun

皿

"**皿**"本意为盛饭食的用器。用"皿"组合的字往往与盛物之器具相关。例字中，除"**盈**、**益**"外，余者为形声字：下形上声。

盎

我久久徘徊于霍墓雕刻间，远看，浑然一体；近看，耐人寻味，在粗犷的斧凿中行走着蜿蜒的线。斯是顽石，却生意**盎**然，全世界的艺术家到此不能不肃然起敬！

《哭》吴冠中

I loitered for quite a long while among the sculptures, which were an integrated mass when viewed from afar and very intriguing when scrutinized close by. Traceable among the rough marks of hatchet and chisel were delicate lines zigzagging. Insensate as they were, the carved stone were ***brimming*** with life and vigor. Artists from all over the world cannot help feeling awed when they visit this place. [15]

"On the Verge of Tears" Wu Guanzhong

盒

日本富人区，小巧、幽静、精致，每座房子都像一个首饰**盒**，也挺美。

《富人区》冯骥才

Japanese houses were small, quiet and exquisite, and each was like a beautiful jewellery ***box***. [15]

"The Wealthy Quarter" Feng Jicai

盆（1）

五十年代的上海寒冬腊月，气候比现在冷得多。寒夜，窗上玻璃结满冰凌，呵气如雾。我拉上窗帘，以炭**盆**烤火取暖，让身边的小水壶在炭火上嘶嘶作响，伴随我逐渐投入创作境界。

《书房》何为

In the fifties, Shanghhai was much colder in winter than now. The window panes would ice up and one's breath would freeze in the cold air. I would, with the window curtains drawn together, warm myself by a charcoal ***brazier*** over which a small kettle was sizzling away, and gradually move into the best state of readiness for creative writing.[15]

"My Study" He Wei

盛、盆（2）

我带着这只有疤痕的茶缸进了抗日根据地。它的用途倒意外地多起来了——喝水、**盛**饭、热菜，给生病的同志煮粥，必要时还可以代行“面**盆**”、“浴缸”的职责。

《搪瓷茶缸》万全

I went to the anti-Japanese base area carrying with me the enamel mug with a chip in it. Unexpectedly, over there it turned out to be a multipurpose utensil. It was used for ***carrying*** drinking water or cooled rice, for heating up food, cooking congee for sick comrades, and when necessary, as a substitute for a ***basin*** or bathtub.[15]

"The Enamel Mug" Wan Quan

例中之“**盛**”为动词。根据译文中其所在的句子结构，“盛”与“热”并列，二者以动名词的形式作为介词“for”之宾语。

盆（3）、（有）益（1）：会意字，由“水”在“皿”上会意，表示“皿”中满溢出来水的意思。[9]

在我工作的时候，我总是写了几十个字，就到院中去看看，浇浇这棵，搬搬那**盆**，然后回到屋中再写一点，然后再出去，如此循环，把脑力劳动与体力劳动结合到一起，有**益**身心，胜于吃药。

《养花》老舍

I often leave off sedentary work after writing a few dozen words and go to courtyard to take a look at the flowers, watering them and moving about the ***potted*** ones. Then I'll return to my room to write a bit more. I'll go through the same back and forth process again and again, thus combining mental with manual labor. This is a better way to ***keep*** me ***fit*** in mind and body than taking medicine.[15]

"On Growing Flowers" Lao She

以上 3 例“**盆**”字的译文中，前两例取决于其前的定语“炭”（盆 **brazier**）和“面”（盆 **basin**），从“浇浇这棵，搬搬那**盆**”可以看出，第三个“盆”是“花盆”（**pot**），故此，虽同一个汉语“盆”字，其译文因语境不同而各异。

(有)益(2)

我们每天有许多零碎的时间于不知不觉中浪费掉了，我们若能养成一种利用闲暇的习惯，一遇空闲，无论其为多么短暂，都利用其做一点**有益**身心之事，则积少成多终必有成。

《养成好习惯》梁实秋

Every day we are unconsciously wasting many odd moments. We should acquire the habits of utilizing leisure time, and snatch every odd moment to do whatever is ***beneficial*** to our body and mind. That will enable us to achieve good results little by little. [15]

"Cultivating Good Habits" Liang Shiqiu

益（1）“有**益**身心，胜于吃药”之“益”偏重于身体的健康，译文选用“**fit**”（healthy and strong）与原文之意相符。益（2）“一遇空闲，无论其为多么短暂，都利用其做一点有**益**身心之事，则积少成多终必有成”之“益”译为“**beneficial**”（improving a situation; having a helpful or useful effect），表达出了原文“益”（好处）之意。

盈：会意字，由皿、夃会意[9]。“夃”：秦地人把到集市出卖、多得利叫作夃。

有一次，在东单小市上，在一个只有几件售品的地摊上，我发现了一只纯白的瑞典茶缸。这正是我所需要的。可是地摊女主人的索价超过我的购买力。我希望她降低售价，她竟眼泪**盈**眶；这时我才发觉她是一个知识分子模样的青年妇女。她解释说家有病人等钱吃药，所卖的是自己家用的东西。我马上尽我所有付了款价。

《搪瓷茶缸》万全

Once, while roaming about a small market in Dongdan, I came across a pure white Swedish enamel mug at a roadside stall displaying only a handful of articles for sale. That was just what I needed. But the price asked by the woman owner of the stall was too high for me. When I bargained, I noticed tears ***brimming*** in her eyes. And then I also realized that she was sort of an educated young woman. She said what she had for sale was her personal belongings because she was badly in need of money to pay for the medical care of someone at home. Thereupon, I gave her all the money I had with me for the mug. [15]

"The Enamel Mug" Wan Quan

五、六画

竹

用“**竹**”组合的字，同竹器制品有关。例字中除“**竹**”外，其余皆为形声字：上形下声。

笠

千山鸟飞绝， O'er thousands of hills and mountains no birds are in flight,
万径人踪灭。 On thousands of paths and roads no person's traces are in sight.
孤舟蓑**笠**翁， In a solitary boat an old man wearing a wide-rimmed bamboo ***hat*** and a straw cloak,
独钓寒江雪。 Is fishing on the snow-permeated river icy-cold. [13]

《江雪》 "Fishing on the Snow-Permeated River"
（唐）柳宗元 (The Tang Dynasty) Liu Zongyuan

笙

行云去后遥山暝， The floating clouds blown off, dim is the distant hill;
已放**笙**歌池院静。 ***Flute***-songs are hushed, deserted gardens quiet.
中庭月色正清明， Steeped in pure moonlight, the middle court is still;
无数杨花过无影。 Without a shadow, the willow-downs run riot. [1]

《玉楼春·乙卯吴興寒食》 Tune: Spring in Jade Pavilion, "Written on Cold Food Day, 1075"
（宋）张先 (The Song Dynasty) Zhang Xian

竽

齐宣王使人吹**竽**，必三百人。
南郭处士请为王吹竽。宣王悦之，廪食以数百人。
宣王死，湣王立，好一一听之。
处士逃。

《韩非子》（战国）韩非

When Prince Xuan of Qi called for ***reed pipe*** music, he would have three hundred men playing at the same time. Then a scholar named Nanguo asked for a place in the orchestra, and the prince, taking a fancy to him, gave him a salary large enough to feed several hundred men.

After Prince Xuan's death, however, Prince Min came to the throne, and he liked sole performances.

There upon the scholar fled. [14]

"Han Fei Zi" (The Warring States Period) Han Fei

簇

又有医者，自称善外科。一裨将阵回，中流失，深入膜内，延使治。
乃持并州剪，剪去矢管，跪而请谢。
裨将曰："**簇**在膜内者，须亟治。"
医曰："此内科事，不意并责我。"

《雪涛小书》（明）江盈科

A surgeon once boasted about his ability. A soldier, returning from battle with an arrow penetrating his leg, came to him for treatment.

The surgeon took a pair of sharp scissors and cut off the stem of the arrow close to the flesh, then asked for pay.

"But you haven't taken out ***the head of the arrow***," complained the soldier.

"That's an internal matter. That's a physician's business, not mine," was the reply. [14]

"Stories by Xue Tao" (The Ming Dynasty) Jiang Yingke

笼

丘之小不能一亩，可以**笼**而有之。

《永州八记》（唐）柳宗元

The knoll was less than a quarter of an acre—so compact that it looked as if it could be ***wrapped*** up in a sleeve. [8]

"Eight Travel Journals on the State of Yong: Ⅲ. The Knoll to the West of Tarn Gumu"
(The Tang Dynasty) Liu Zongyuan

"**笼**"之译文"**wrapped**"体现出其被动含义。

篱

恰离了绿水青山那答，	Having just left green hills and water blue,
早来到竹**篱**茅舍人家。	I come to thatched cots with ***fence*** of bamboo.
野花路畔开，	By the roadside wild flowers blow;
村酒槽头榨。	In the trough I see home brew flow. [5]
《沉醉东风 · 闲居》	Tune: Intoxicated in East Wind, "Rural Life"
（元）卢挚	(The Yuan Dynasty) Lu Zhi

簪

献赋十年犹未遇，	I' ve submitted written statements to the emperor for ten years yet I haven't seen a prospect bright.
羞将白发对华**簪**。	So I' m very ashamed to face your gorgeous ***hair-pin*** with my hair white.[13]

《赠阙下裴舍人》

"To High-Ranking Official Pei Who Works in the Royal Palace"

（唐）钱起 （The Tang Dynasty） Qian Qi

竹：象形字。

1. 荷风送香气， Carrying the lotus scent the breeze blows by,
   竹露滴清响。 With a clear sound, the dewdrops drip from the ***bamboos*** nearby.[13]

   《夏日南亭怀辛大》

   "Missing Xin the First in the South Pavilion on a Summer Night"

   （唐）孟浩然 （The Tang Dynasty） Meng Haoran

2. 柳堤， Willowy shores,
   竹溪， ***Bamboo***-lined stream,
   日影筛金翠。 The sun sieves green and golden shades as in a dream.
   杖藜徐步近钓矶， Cane in hand, slowly I go to the fishing place
   看鸥鹭闲游戏。 To watch at leisure
   Gulls and herons play with pleasure.[5]

   《朝天子》 Tune: Skyward Song,

   （元）张养浩 （The Yuan Dynasty） Zhang Yanghao

两例之"**竹**"在原文中均为名词，分别作"露"和"溪"的定语。**例 1**"**竹**露滴清响"中，竹之露珠滴下之声既然可以被听到，则说明此声非一竹一滴之所为，译文使用复数"**bamboos**"可充分体现原文所含之义。**例 2** 之"**竹**"在译文中与"lined"构成合成形容词，作"溪"的定语。在合成形容词中的名词一般是单数形式，译文为"**bamboo**"。

耳

用"**耳**"组成的字，与耳朵、声音或外形像"耳"的东西有关。例字中除"**取**、**耳**"外，其他为形声字，其中，"**闻**"为内形外声，其他为左形右声。

闻

闻恶不可就恶，恐为谗夫泄怒；闻善不可即亲，恐引奸人进身。

《菜根谭》（明）洪应明

When you ***hear*** that someone has done evil, do not detest him in a hurry, lest that an enemy of his should frame a case against him. Likewise, when you hear that someone has done good, do not take a liking to him immediately, lest that it might be a trick used by the treacherous to promote himself. [6]

"The Roots of Wisdom" (The Ming Dynasty) Hong Yingming

"闻"之意为"听见"，故译文取"**hear**"。

聆

《水经》云："彭蠡之口有石钟山焉。"……至唐李渤始访其踪迹，得双石于潭上，扣而***聆***之，南声函胡，北音清越，桴止响腾，余韵徐歇。

《石钟山记》（宋）苏轼

The Book of Water says, "Standing at the mouth of Lake Pengli is Mount Rock Bell" ...Yet, this explanation remained unchallenged until the Tang Dynasty, when Li Bo explored this place and found two rocks by the lake. He beat them with a drumstick and ***listened*** to them. The one on the south sounded deep and low, while the one on he north loud and clear. When he stopped beating them, the sound lingered and gradually died away. [8]

"Mount Rock Bell" (The Song Dynasty) Su Shi

"***聆***"之意为"听"，故译为"**listen**"。

聪

推让而不自疑，莫若舜之二十二臣，舜亦不疑而皆用之；然而后世不诮舜为二十二人朋党所欺，而称舜为**聪**明之圣者，以能辨君子与小人也。

《朋党论》（宋）欧阳修

We can also concluded that no one has ever exceeded the twenty-two officials in the time of Shun in complimenting, recommending and trusting one another, whom Shun had never hesitated in employing. Later generations have never considered Shun to be ever deceived by the twenty-two, but instead thought him a ***wise*** sage who could distinguish the noble from the ignoble. [8]

"On Coterie" (The Song Dynasty) Ouyang Xiu

聊

绿竹入幽径， The green bamboo groves shelter the secluded path winding,

青萝拂行衣。 The hanging green vines touch our clothing.
欢言得所憩， Gladly I say I get a place for rest,
美酒***聊***共挥。 Then ***toasts*** are proposed one after another between the host Husi and I, the guest. [13]

《下终南山过斛斯山人宿置酒》

"Descending from the Zhongnan Mountain, Visiting the Hermit Husi, Staying Overnight and Being Entertained with Wine"

（唐）李白 (The Tang Dynasty) Li Bai

"***聊***"之意为"闲谈"。此处之"聊"意译为"**toasts**"间接地体现出诗句"美酒***聊***共挥"中"聊"之含义："toast"之意为"为…举杯祝酒"，"祝酒"自然要说祝酒词，则"聊"之意即在其中。

取：会意字，由"又"（手）、由"耳"会意。《周礼》说："被捕获的野兽割取左耳。"

1. 青，***取***之于蓝，而青于蓝；冰，水为之，而寒于水。

《劝学篇》（战国）荀子

Indigo ***derives*** from woad, yet is bluer than woad. Ice comes from water, yet is colder than water. [12]

"On Learning" (The Warring States Period) Xun Zi

2. 且夫天地之间，物各有主。苟非吾之所有，虽一毫而莫***取***。惟江上之清风，与山间之明月，耳得之而为声，目遇之而成色，取之无尽，用之不竭，是造物者无尽藏也，而吾与子之所共适。

《前赤壁赋》（宋）苏轼

All things under heaven have their separate owners. If a thing does not belong to me, not even a mite of it should be ***taken*** as mine. Only the refreshing breeze on the river and the bright moon over the hills, which generate in our ears a pleasant sound and in our eyes a dreamy color, are inexhaustible and can be freely enjoyed. They are an immeasurable treasure granted to us by our Creator for our common happiness. [12]

"Boating at the Red Cliff" (The Song Dynasty) Su Shi

通篇译文之主语皆非"吾"，体现出英语的客体思维方式。此"取"译为"**taken**"，乃盖其所在句的被动形式使然。

耳：象形字。

枕席而卧，则清泠之状与目谋，潛潛之声与***耳***谋，悠然而虚者与神谋，渊然而静者与心谋。

《永州八记》（唐）柳宗元

Spreading out our bamboo mats and setting up our pillows, we lay down. What pleased our eyes was the cooling scenery; what caressed our ***ears***, the gurgling sound; what transcended our spirit, the illimitable void; and what harmonized with our hearts, the profound tranquility. [8]

"Eight Travel Journals on the State of Yong"
(The Tang Dynasty) Liu Zongyuan

页

用"***页***"组合的字与头有关。例字中除"***烦***"外，其余为形声字：右形左声。

额

陈侯立身何坦荡，	Standing in society, you're broad-minded and never worried,
虬须虎眉仍大***额***。	It's just like you have a dragon beard, tiger's brows and a big ***forehead***. [13]
《送陈章甫》 （唐）李颀	"Seeing Off Chen Zhangfu" (The Tang Dynasty) Li Qi

顾（顧）

1. 停杯投箸不能食，	I push aside my cup and chopsticks because I can't eat or drink,
拔剑四***顾***心茫然。	Then I draw out my sword and ***look*** around without knowing what to think. [13]
《行路难》 （唐）李白	"Hard Is the Way" (The Tang Dynasty) Li Bai
2. 三***顾***频烦天下计，	To get the state power Liu Bei thrice ***called on*** Zhuge Liang for the plan,
两朝开济老臣心。	The prime minister devotedly served the two reigns on end. [13]
《蜀相》 （唐）杜甫	"The Prime Minister of Shu" (The Tang Dynasty) Du Fu
3. 相看白刃血纷纷，	The warriors see each other's swords all covered with bloodstain,
死节从来岂***顾***勋？	Only thinking of dying for the loyalty to the emperor, how would they ***care for*** personal gain? [13]

《燕歌行》　"Song of the Northern Frontiers"

（唐）高适　(The Tang Dynasty) Gao Shi

例1中"拔剑四***顾***心茫然"之"顾"意"看"，译文取"**look**"（to turn one's eyes in a particular direction）。**例2**中"三***顾***频烦天下计"之"顾"是三国时期刘备三顾茅庐访聘诸葛亮之事，此"顾"意"邀请、恭请"，译文取"**called on**"（to formally invite）。**例3**中"死节从来岂***顾***勋"之"顾"意"在意、关心、在乎"，译为"**care for**"（mind, care about）此三例之译文均贴切原文之意。

颈

宋人有耕田者。田中有株。兔走触株，折***颈***而死。因释其耒而守株，冀复得兔。

—兔不可复得，而身为宋国笑。

《韩非子》（战国）韩非

There was a peasant in the state of Song. One day a hare dashed up, knocked against a tree in his field, broke its ***neck*** and fell dead. Then the peasant put down his hoe and waited by the tree for another hare to turn up. No more appeared, however, but he became the laughing-stock of the state. [14]

"Han Fei Zi" (The Warring States Period) Han Fei

颜

晓月过残垒，　You'll pass the ruined barracks under the daybreak moonlight,

繁星宿故关。　You'll take a lodging at the old passes under the starlight.

寒禽与衰草，　Only the birds in the cold weather and the grasses that have fallen into decay,

处处伴愁***颜***。　Will accompany your worried ***look*** all the way. [13]

《贼平后送人北归》　"Seeing Off a Friend Who Returns to the North After the Suppression of the An-Si Armed Rebellion"

（唐）司空曙　(The Tang Dynasty) Sikong Shu

额

少年十五二十时，　At the age of fifteen to twenty he was young, when

步行夺得胡马骑。　He was like Li Guang who once seized a horse on foot from a

	riding Hunnis horseman.
射杀山中白**额**虎，	And like Zhou Chu who once killed a whit-***forehead*** tiger in a mountain,
肯数邺下黄须儿。	And he looked on the yellow-beard Cao Zhang as very common. [13]

《老将行》　　“Song of an Old General”

（唐）王维　　（The Tang Dynasty）Wang Wei

颔颐

古者世称大手笔，	“In ancient times those who wrote such articles were regarded as great masters,
此事不系于职司。	So this kind of job cannot be entrusted with the ordinary writers.
当仁自古有不让，	There have been the saying ‘not to yield the practice of benevolence to others’ since the ancient times”
言讫屡**颔**天子**颐**。	Hearing Han Yu's remarks the emperor ***nodded*** several times. [13]

《韩碑》　　“The Han Yu Stele”

（唐）李商隐　　（The Tang Dynasty）Li Shangyin

烦：会意字，由“页”、由“火”会意[9]。

1. 本以高难饱，	High up in the tree it's of course difficult for the cicada to eat its fill,
徒劳恨费声。	So in vain it sings its complaints with a trill.
五更疏欲断，	At dawn its singing diminishes till it dies away,
一树碧无情。	But the green tree it's in remains as indifferent as it may.
薄宦梗犹泛，	A low-ranking official, I'm still like a twig that on water floats here and there,
故园芜已平。	And my family garden has been overgrown with weeds everywhere.
烦君最相警，	***Thank*** the cicada for giving me a warning,
我亦举家清。	My family and I will remain as poor and clean as it has been. [13]

《蝉》　　“The Cicada”

（唐）李商隐　　（The Tang Dynasty）Li Shangyin

2. 家有一坐头，绝低矮，迂公每坐，必取瓦片支其四足。后不胜**烦**，忽思得策，呼侍者，移置楼上坐。

及坐好，低为故，乃曰：“人言楼高，浪得名耳。”

《雅谑》

Yu Gong had a very low stool. When he wanted to sit on it, he always placed bricks under each leg. Later he found it very ***troublesome*** and hit upon an idea. He ordered a servant to take it upstairs. But when he sat on it again, he found it just as low.

“Well, people say it's higher upstairs, but I don't find it so!” he said.

“Ya Nue”

例 1 中“***烦***君最相警”之“烦”意“烦劳”，引申为“感激”，译为“**thank**”（to tell sb that you are grateful for sth），间接地体现出原文所含之意。**例 2** 中“不胜***烦***”之“烦”意“烦恼”，即译文“**troublesome**”（causing trouble, pain, etc. over a long period of time）之意。

虫

由“***虫***”组合的字一般与微小的活物相关。例字皆为形声字，其中，“***蛩***、***蠹***”为下形上声，其他为左形右声。

蛩

风飘飘，雨潇潇，	Wind and rain, wind and rain,
便做陈抟睡不着。	The slumbering immortal is sleepless.
懊恼伤怀抱，	Sorrow bothers me so much.
扑簌簌泪点抛。	As my tears run down my cheeks.
秋蝉儿噪罢寒**蛩**儿叫，	Cicadas droning, ***cricket*** chirping;
淅零零细雨打芭蕉。	Like raindrops on the palm leaves,
	My tears dripping.[10]
《大德歌 · 秋》	Tune: Song of Great Virtue, “Autumn Tastes”
（元）关汉卿	（The Yuan Dynasty）Guan Hanqing

蛛

更能消几番风雨，	How much more can Spring bear of wind and rain?
匆匆春又归去。	Too hastily, I fear, 'twill leave again.

惜春长怕花开早，	Lovers of Spring would fear to see the flowers red
何况落红无数。	Budding too soon and fallen petals too wide spread.
春且住，	O Spring, please stay!
见说道、	I've heard it said that sweet grass far away
天涯芳草无归路。	Would stop you from seeing your backward way.
怨春不语。	But I've not heard
算只有殷勤、	Spring say a word,
画檐**蛛**网，	Only the busy ***spiders*** weave
尽日惹飞絮。	Webs all day by the painted eave
	To keep the willow-down from taking leave. [1]

《摸鱼儿》 Tune: Groping for Fish

（宋）辛弃疾 (The Song Dynasty) Xin Qiji

蛟

洞庭连天九嶷高，	The Dongting Lake is so vast as to link the sky and Mount Jiuyi soars, where,
蛟龙出没猩鼯号。	The flood ***dragon*** haunt, the gorillas howl and the flying squirrels cry in the air. [13]

《八月十五日夜赠张功曹》

"To Official Zhang on the Night of the 15th the Eighth Moon"

（唐）韩愈 (The Tang Dynasty) Han Yu

蝼蚁

苦心岂免容***蝼蚁***，	Bitter in its core, it can't avoid being harmed by ***mole crickets***,
香叶曾经宿鸾凤。	Having fragrant leaves, it was once nestled by the phoenix. [13]

《古柏行》 "Song of the Old Cypress"

（唐）杜甫 (The Tang Dynasty) Du Fu

蝉、螳螂

园中有树，其上有***蝉***。

蝉方奋翼悲鸣，欲饮清露，不知***螳螂***之在其后，曲其颈，欲攫而食之。

螳螂方欲食蝉，而不知黄雀在后，举其颈，欲啄而食之也。

黄雀方欲食螳螂，不知童子挟弹丸在下，迎而欲弹之。

《说苑》（汉）刘向

There is a tree in the garden, and on it there is a ***cicada***. This cicada perches up there, chirping away and drinking the dew, not knowing that there is a ***praying mantis*** behind it. And the praying mantis leans forward, raising its forelegs to catch the cicada, not knowing that there is a sparrow beside it. The sparrow, again, cranes its neck to peck at the praying mantis, not knowing that there is someone with a catapult waiting below.[14]

"The Garden of Anecdotes" (The Han Dynasty) Liu Xiang

蛾

立身不高一步立，如尘里振衣，泥中濯足，如何超达？处事不退一步处，如飞**蛾**投烛，羝羊触藩，如何安乐？

《菜根谭》（明）洪应明

If a man cannot stand on a higher plane in his pursuit, it is similar to dusting his clothes in the dust and washing his feet in the muddy water. How can he rise above the general run of people? If a man does not know how to make compromises in social intercourse, he would resemble a ***moth*** darting into flame or a ram rushing against fences. How can he rest his life on peace and ease?[6]

"Stand on a higher plane in pursuit and for the sake of security, learn how to compromise."

"The Roots of Wisdom" (The Ming Dynasty) Hong Yingming

羽

用"***羽***"组合的字，与鸟、羽毛、鸟飞的姿态有关。例字中除"***羽***"外，其余皆为形声字，其中，"**翠**"：上形下声；"**翕，翳**"：下形上声。其余为右形左声。

翠、翕

青树**翠**蔓，蒙络摇缀，参差披拂。潭中鱼可百许头，皆若空游无所依。日光下彻，影布石上，佁然不动；俶尔远逝，往来**翕**忽，似与游者相乐。

《永州八记》（唐）柳宗元

The trees were laden with ***jade-green*** leaves and creeping vines, which, in a drooping and swinging manner, looked clustered and tangled. The pond was teeming with a hundred fish or more, and the water was so limpid that they looked as if they were floating in the transparent air. The sunlight cast their shadows onto the boulder bed, and for a moment, they stayed motionless before they abruptly swam away. Then they ***darted*** back and forth as if they were teasing the visitors. [8]

"Eight Travel Journals on the State of Yong"

(The Tang Dynasty) Liu Zongyuan

"**翕**"之本意为"闭合、收拢"。在"俶尔远逝，往来**翕**忽"中，"翕忽"之意是急速、轻快敏捷的样子。译文没有直接体现"翕"之本意，而是通过"**darted**"（猛冲、突进、飞奔）表达出"翕忽"中所含之"翕"：森林雀类在丛林间快速穿梭，为减少体力消耗，飞行中间歇性地合拢双翼（close their wings）。

翳

已而夕阳在山，人影散乱，太守归而宾客从也。树林阴**翳**，鸣声上下，游人去而禽鸟乐也。然而禽鸟知山林之乐，而不知人之乐；人知从太守游而乐，而不知太守之乐其乐也。醉能同其乐，醒能述其文者，太守也。

《醉翁亭记》（宋）欧阳修

Soon the glowing sun sinks toward the hills, slanting and scattering the human shadows. The Governor starts to leave, followed by his guests. The verdant woods are ***shaded***, and the birds, rioting. The retreat of the humans brings cheer to fowl and birds. Yet, the fowl and birds only know the happiness obtained from the hills and woods, but do not understand the human's happiness, and the guests only know the happiness of accompanying the Governor, but not that their Governor enjoys his own enjoyments, that is, when drunk, enjoying his guests, and when sober, enjoying writing down his prose. This is the type of Governor he is! [8]

"The Pavilion of an Old Drunkard" (The Song Dynasty) Ouyang Xiu

例中"**翳**"为动词，意"遮蔽、掩盖"。"树林阴**翳**"即树林里浓荫遮蔽，译文"**shaded**，"以过去分词的形式表达出原文中所潜在的被动之意。

翎

鹫**翎**金仆姑，	His arrow named Jinpugu is tufted with the hawk's ***feather***,
燕尾锈蝥弧。	His pennon named Maohu has a ribbon shaped like a swallow-tail.
独立扬新令，	Standing bolt upright the general issues a new order,
千营共一呼。	The warriors of all the battalions with one voice shout hail. [13]
《塞下曲》	"Song of Frontiers"

（唐）卢纶　　（The Tang Dynasty）Lu Lun

翩

1. ***翩翩***野舟，　A ***floating*** boat,
泛泛沙鸥。　A gull carefree,
登临不尽古今愁，　I climb the height with endless sorrow old and new,
白云去留。　White clouds linger with me.
凤凰台上青山旧，　From Phoenix Tower I find the changeless hills blue;
秋千墙里垂杨瘦，　Beside the swing within the wall
琵琶亭畔野花秋。　The weeping willow slender grows;
长江自流。　Before the pavilion late autumn flowers fall,
　But heedless, the endless river still flows. [5]

《醉太平·怀古》　Tune: Drunk in Time of Peace, "Thinking of the Past"
（元）张可久　　（The Yuan Dynasty）Zhang Kejiu

2. ***翩翩***堂前燕，　***Flitting***, flitting, the swallows before the hall;
冬藏夏来见。　In winter they vanish, in summer they return;
兄弟两三人，　Yet I, with two brothers of my own,
流宕在他县。　Am still a wanderer in a strange land. [4]

《燕歌行》　"Homesick"
（汉）　（The Han Dynasty）

"***翩翩***"形容轻快地跳舞或动物飞舞。**例 1** 之"翩翩"修饰"野舟"。因是"野舟"，无人管理，任其漂浮于水上，其译文取"**floating**"（to move slowly on water）意在表达：随波逐流，上下浮动似鸟之翻飞。**例 2** 中之"翩翩"修饰"堂前燕"，燕子在堂前上下翻飞起舞；译文"**flitting**"（to move lightly and quickly from one place or thing to another）与其对应，意在表达"掠过，轻快地从一处飞至另一处"。

综合型思维方式通过重叠词"翩翩"的使用，更生动地体现出飞舞中的燕子之轻疾与自如；分析型思维则通过词形变化所构成的现在分词 floating 与 flitting 来体现动作的进行。

翅

时将半夜，四顾寂寥。适有孤鹤，横江东来。***翅***如车轮，玄裳缟衣，戛然长鸣，掠予舟而西也。

《后赤壁赋》（宋）苏轼

It was approaching midnight, and looking around, I saw that everything had subsided into quiescence. It was right at this moment that a lonely crane came flying across the river from the east. Its ***wings*** were as large as the wheels of a horse-cart. With an abrupt, long warbling, this white-feathered but black-tailed bird flapped over my boat and went west. [8]

"My Second Visit to the Red Cliff" (The Song Dynasty) Su Shi

原文"***翅***"的单数与其译文"**wings**"的复数即不同思维方式的体现。

翔

至春和景明，波澜不惊，上下天光，一碧万顷；沙鸥***翔***集，锦鳞游泳；岸芷汀兰，郁郁青青。而或长烟一空，皓月千里，浮光跃金，静影沉璧，渔歌互答，此乐何极！

《岳阳楼记》（宋）范仲淹

As for the days when spring weather is mild and sunny, nature is lit with a bright smile, and the waves being halcyon, the sky and the lake are tinged with the same hue, making up an infinitely huge canvas of light blue, on which white gulls are ***hovering*** in bevies and fish shimmering with silvery scales. And the lake shores adorned with irises and sandbars dotted with orchids are all enshrouded in a sweet and lush green. Sometimes the broad firmament is clear of all haze, a bright moon shines over the vast lake gleaming with a golden glow, and the moon' s reflection in the watery mirror looks like a sunken jade. And then the fishermen' s songs are heard to be echoing one another. What an unbounded joy! [12]

"Yueyang Tower" (The Song Dynasty) Fan Zhongyan

汉语"正在飞"之意的表达是通过"翔"之词义"盘旋地飞，飞"，此即词汇手段的运用；英语则需通过语法形式来体现动作的进行，故其译文为现在分词形式的"**hovering**"。

羽：象形字。

有鹦鹉飞集他山，山中禽兽辄相贵重，鹦鹉自念，虽乐不可久也。便去。

后数日，山中大火。鹦鹉遥见，便入水濡***羽***，飞而洒之。天神言："汝虽有志，意何足云也？"对曰："虽知不能，然尝侨居是山，禽兽行善，皆为兄弟，不忍见耳。”

天神嘉感，即为灭火。

《太平广记选》（宋）李昉等

There was once a parrot living on a mountain. He was well respected by his fellow birds and beasts. Though that seemed an ideal place to inhabit, the parrot thought he should not be stuck there all his life, so he flew away.

A few days later, a terrible fire broke out on the mountain. Seeing this from afar, the parrot dipped his ***wings*** in a water hole and flew over to drench the fire. God said, "Determined as you might be, what use will your efforts come to?"

"I know this is of little use," answered the parrot, "but as I once lived there as a member of a congenial brotherhood, I can't watch them suffer unmoved."

God was so impressed that He extinguished the fire. [3]

"The Selections from Records of the Taiping Era"
(The Song Dynasty) Li Fang *et al.*

“***羽***”之意除“羽毛”外，鸟类或昆虫的翅膀也可称“羽”，如“振羽”，此处之“羽”的译文为“**wings**”，与原文之意相符。

舟

用“***舟***”组成的字一般与“船”相关。例字中除“***舟***”外，其余为形声字：左形右声。

舫

落帆逗淮镇，　I let down the sail so as to stay at Xuyi county seat,
停***舫***临孤驿。　Then I moor my ***boat*** near a solitary post house I meet.
浩浩风起波，　The mighty wind is raising waves white,
冥冥日沉夕。　The sun has set and dusk has cast down dim light. [13]
《夕次盱眙县》　"Mooring at Xuyi County at Dusk"
（唐）韦应物　(The Tang Dynasty) Wei Yingwu

舴艋

龙头***舴艋***吴儿兢，　The Southerners in dragon-***boats*** contest in speed,
笋柱秋千游女并。　Fair maidens on the bamboo seat swing to and fro.
芳洲拾翠暮忘归，　And picking flowers, the women linger in the mead;
秀野踏青来不定。　Treading the green field, townspeople come and go. [1]

《玉楼春·乙卯吴興寒食》

Tune: Spring in Jade Pavilion, "Written on Cold Food Day, 1075"

（宋）张先 (The Song Dynasty) Zhang Xian

艖

雪纷华，舞梨花，	Snow flakes dancing, like pear blossoms,
再不见烟村四五家。	Block the view of a distant village,
密洒堪图画，	Which is worth drawing a picture.
看疏林噪晚鸦。	What I see is a crow in the woods.
黄芦掩映清江下，	Brook flows slowly behind the Weeds,
斜缆着钓鱼***艖***。	And my ***boat*** moors slant. [10]

《大德歌·冬》 Tune: Song of Great Virtue, "A Winter Scene"

（元）关汉卿 (The Yuan Dynasty) Guan Hanqing

航

夕阳下，酒旆闲，	Twilight was playing with the streamer hanging in front of the wine shop.
两三***航***未曾着岸。	A fishing ***boat*** was making efforts towards the shore,
落花水香茅舍晚，	Flowers falling by the cottages at dusk
断桥头卖鱼人散。	Before the fishmongers dispersed by the bridge and then went home. [10]

《寿阳曲· 园浦归帆》

Tune: Song of Long-lived Sun, "Fisherman's Evening"

（元）马致远 (The Yuan Dynasty) Ma Zhiyuan

原文中"***航***"的书面用语之义为"船"，故有此译。

舸、舰

1. 闾阎扑地，钟鸣鼎食之家；***舸舰***迷津，青雀黄龙之舳。

《滕王阁序》（唐）王勃

The land is paved with houses—homes of rich and the noble. The ferry is crowded with *boats*—***ships*** decorated with blue birds and yellow dragons. [12]

"The Tower of Prince Teng" (The Tang Dynasty) Wang Bo

2. 倏尔黄烟四起，人物略不相睹，水爆轰震，声如崩山；烟消波静，则一***舸***无迹，仅有"敌船"为火所焚，随波而逝。

《观潮》（宋）周密

Then a sudden burst of yellow smoke caused the men to be almost entirely invisible, and a shell exploded with an earsplitting crashing sound like that of a landslide. When the smoke dissipated and the waves calmed down, not even a single ***ship*** could be seen. Only the mock hostile craft was found to be burning and vanishing with the currents. [12]

"Viewing Tidal Waves" (The Song Dynasty) Zhou Mi

例2文中所示乃军事演习，此处之"***舸***"意在"舰"，故译为"**ship**"。

舟：象形字。

怨不在大，可谓惟人；载***舟***覆舟，所宜深慎。

《谏太宗十思书》(唐)魏征

Disaffection need not be great. It is the people that are formidable. They are like water which is able to bear a ***boat*** or overturn a boat. This indeed warrants your profound discretion. [12]

"Ten Points of Deliberation Recommended to Emperor Taizong"
(The Tang Dynasty) Wei Zheng

羊

"羊"本意为"吉祥"。由"羊"组合的字往往与"羊"或寓意美好、吉祥的字相关。例字中，除"**美**、**羌**、**羊**"外，"***群***"为形声字，右形左声。

群

几乎每次都是这样，先走到老龙潭，看着被晚风吹皱的湖水，有时也比赛投几颗石子，看谁比谁投的远，还要看一个个倒映在水里的人影，一***群***群的肥鸭，一缕缕的炊烟……然后，慢慢走回来。

《黄昏》谢冰莹

Usually, we would first to the Lao Long Lake to take a look at its water rippling in the evening breeze. Sometimes we competed with each other in playing ducks and drakes while our reflections were mirrored in the water, fat ducks swimming in ***flocks***, wisps of cooking smoke curling up from chimney... Then we would walk back home leisurely. [15]

"Dusk" Xie Bingying

原文"***群***"无词形变化，其复数含义通过词汇手段来表达："一***群***群"；译文则通过名词的复数形式来体现：**flocks**。

美：会意字，由羊、由大会意。

1. 我喜欢看秋风里满山的芒。在山坡上，在水边上，白的那样凄凉，**美**而孤独。

《我喜欢》张晓风

I love to watch the ***pretty*** but forlorn Chinese silvergrass, of a dreary white, growing against the autumn wind all over the hills——on the slopes, by the waterside. [15]

"I Love..." Zhang Xiaofeng

2. 我还喜欢看书，特别是在夜晚。在书籍里面，我不能自抑地要喜爱那些泛黄的线装书，握着它就觉得握着一脉优美的传统，那涩黯的纸面蕴含着一种古典的**美**。历史的兴亡、人物的迭代本是这样虚幻，唯有书中的智慧永远长存。

《我喜欢》张晓风

I also love reading books, especially at night. I cherish a deep love for thread-bound Chinese books yellowed with age. They show me our most brilliant traditions as well as a kind of classical ***beauty***. While the rise and fall of a nation and the vicissitudes of life are all vanity, the wisdom contained in books is everlasting. [15]

"I Love..." Zhang Xiaofeng

例 1 中"美"之所指乃"芒"。"芒"是某些禾本植物种子壳上的细刺。译文"**pretty**"（pleasing by delicacy or grace）与其对应，体现出"芒"之精致、小巧。**例 2** 中"美"之所指乃"古典的美"，其译文取"**beauty**"（the quality of being pleasing to the senses or to the mind），体现出此"美"之令人赏心悦目、给人以精神层次上的享受。

羌：会意字，由人、由羊会意[9]：羌，西戎牧羊人也。

羌笛何须怨杨柳，	There is no need for the ***Qiang*** flute to turn the song Willow Tree into the resentful sound,
春风不度玉门关。	For at the Yumen Pass no spring breeze is ever found. [13]
《出塞》	"Out of the Frontiers"
（唐）王之涣	(The Tang Dynasty) Wang Zhihuan

"**羌**"为我国古代民族，原住在以今青海为中心，南至四川，北接新疆的一带地区，东汉时移居今甘肃一带。因其属专有名词，故音译，由汉语拼音"**Qiang**"转写。

羊：象形字。

我们使用的是商品，还是包装？而负担那些庞大的包装费用的，羊毛出在**羊**身上，还是我们这些顾客，而华美绝伦的包装，商品取出后，不过是一堆垃圾。

《论包装》季羡林

The commodity or the package, which do you need? After all, the wool still comes from the ***sheep***'s back as the saying goes. It is customers like us that will have to bear all the heavy expenses for packaging. And the flashy package, when emptied of its contents, will be nothing but a garbage heap. [15]

"On Packaging" Ji Xianlin

米

"**米**"意为米粟的籽实。由"米"组合的字多指粒状可吃的食物或其引申含义。例字中，除"**米**"外，其余为形声字：均左形右声。

精

人类是变得越来越**精**呢？还是越来越蠢？

答案好像是明摆着的：越来越精。

《论包装》季羡林

Are human beings getting increasingly ***intelligent*** or stupid?

The following answer seems beyond dispute: They are getting more and more intelligent. [15]

"On Packaging" Ji Xianlin

此处"**精**"的翻译在于其上下文"人类是变得越来越精呢？还是越来越蠢？"：与"蠢"相对应之"精"意在"聪明"，译文"**intelligent**"与其对应。

粗（且 ju）

1. 这里有不同的颜色：紫色的茄子、白色的萝卜、红色的西红柿、绿色的小白菜，纷然杂陈，交光互影。这里又有各种不同的线条：大冬瓜又圆又**粗**，豆荚又细又长，白菜的叶子又扁又宽。就这样，不同的颜色，不同的线条，紧密地摆在一起，于纷杂中见统一。

《上海菜市场》季羡林

Take for example the vegetable stall with its display of colors: purple eggplants, white radishes, red tomatoes, greenish cabbages. It also displayed various shapes:

round ***clumsy*** wax gourds, long narrow bean pods, flat wide cabbage leaves. Hence, different colors and lines merged into an organic whole showing diversity in unity. [15]

"The Shanghai Food market" Ji Xianlin

2. 我虽爱买书，而对于书却不甚爱惜。读书的时候，常在书上把我所认为最要紧的处所标出。线装书大概用笔加圈，洋装书竟用红铅笔划***粗***粗的线。经我看过的书，统体干净的很少。

《我之于书》夏丏尊

Much as I love books, I take little care of them. In doing my reading, I often mark out what I regard as important in a book. If it is a thread-bound Chinese book, I use a writing brush to draw small circles as markings. Otherwise, I use a red pencil to draw ***heavy*** underlines. Consequently, the books I have read are rarely clean. [15]

"Books and I" Xia Mianzun

3. 据我***粗***略的统计，有的商品在大包装中仅占空间十分之一，二十分之一，甚至五十分之一。……我不禁要问：我们使用的是商品，还是包装？

《论包装》季羡林

According to my ***rough*** statistics, some commodities take up only one tenth, one twentieth or even one fiftieth of the space in the huge package. ... I cannot but ask, "The commodity or the package, which do you need?" [15]

"On Packaging" Ji Xianlin

4. 检查其他行李，我绝无意见。但是，在哈尔滨买的一把***粗***糙的铁皮壶，却成了被检查的首要对象。这里敲敲，那里敲敲，薄薄的一层铁皮决藏不下一颗炸弹的，然而他们却敲打不止。

《容忍》季羡林

I had no objection to the check-up of my belongings except when a ***crudely***-made tinplate kettle that I had bought at Harbin became something very fishy to them. The kettle was certainly too flimsy for holding a hidden bomb, but they barked up the wrong tree and kept clanking it repeatedly here and there. [15]

"Patience" Ji Xianlin

以上各例"***粗***"的译文体现出其在文中所含之意。**例 1** 中"大冬瓜又圆又***粗***"之"粗"意在"横剖面大"，故译为"**clumsy**"（difficult to handle or manage especially because of shape）。**例 2** 中"用红铅笔划***粗***粗的线"之"粗"意在"长条东西直径较大"，"**heavy**"（not delicate）与其对应。**例 3** 中"据我***粗***略的统计"之"粗"意在"不精确、大略"，译文"**rough**"（not exact, not including all details）即其意。**例 4** 中“一把**粗**糙的铁皮壶”之“粗”意在“（质料）不精细、不光滑”，“**crudely**”（in an unskilled manner）可表此意。

粉

当时，我正在揉面，我举起了沾着白**粉**的手，温和地摸摸他的头发，慢慢地说：“傻子，我不会死的，因为还得给你做饺子呢！”

《不死鸟》三毛

I was then kneading dough. Raising my hand caked with white ***flour*** to caress his hair with tenderness, I said unhurriedly, “O silly, I'm not going to die, I have to live on to make *jiaozi* for you![15]”

“The surviving Bird” San Mao

粮

它走向前来，拿粉红色的舌头舔我的手背，用鼻子拱我口袋。我拿出干**粮**招待它。它吃完干粮，转身卧倒在地，示意请我骑到背上。我犹豫了一下，终于骑上去。此时夕阳西去，夜幕缓缓升起。我忐忑不安，不知是悲是喜？

《过戈壁》哲中

As it (camel) moved close to me, it stuck out its pink tongue to lick the back of my hand and dug its snout into my pocket. I gave it a feed of the ***food*** I had brought with me for the journey. After eating, it turned to lie on the ground, motioning me to ride on it. I did accordingly after some hesitation. The sun was setting in the west and night was falling. I felt uneasy, not knowing if I was sad or happy.[15]

“Crossing the Gobi Desert” Zhe Zhong

粒

“长妈妈”懂得许多莫名其妙的道理，还有许多规矩，这一切都是孩子们所不理解的。譬如说，人死了，不说死掉，而说“老掉了”；……饭**粒**子落在地上，必须捡起来，最好是吃下去。

《幼年鲁迅》王士菁

“Mama Chang” was so full of mysterious lore and had so many rulers of behaviour that the children sometimes found her quite puzzling. For instance, if someone died, you should not say he was dead but “he has passed away.” ... If a ***grain*** of rice fell to the ground, you should pick it up, and the best thing was to eat it.[15]

“When Lu Xun Was a Child” Wang Shijing

米：象形字。

1. 带着一元票子和一张当票，我快快地走，走起路来感到很爽快，默认自已是很有钱的人。菜市，**米**店我都去过，臂上抱了很多东西，感到非常愿意抱这些东西，手冻得很疼，觉得这是应该，对于手一点也不感到可惜，本来手就应该给我服务，好像冻掉了也不可惜。

《当铺》萧红

Armed with a one-dollar note and a pawn ticket, I, unhappy as I was, walked with a light step and felt like one of the rich. I visited the food market and the ***grain*** shop. I did not tire of carrying an armful of purchases. My hands ached with cold, but this was as it should be. I felt no pity for then. It was their bounden duty to wait on me——even at the cost of suffering frostbite. [15]

"The Pawnshop" Xiao Hong

2. 立在厨房门内的孩子们的母亲向门外的沙地上撒了一握**米**粒出来。
母鸡们咯咯咯地叫了起来，鸡雏们也啁啁地争食起来了。

《夕暮》郭沫若

The kids' mother, standing by the kitchen door, sprinkled a handful of ***rice*** onto the sandy ground in the open.

At the clucking of the hens, the chicks scrambled for the feed, chirping. [15]

"Dusk" Guo Moruo

"**米**"乃谷类或其他植物的籽实去了皮的名称，如小米、稻米、大米。**例1**中"**米**店"之"米"作为"店"的定语，即对店里不同谷物的通称，译为"**grain**"（the small hard seeds of food plants such as wheat, rice, etc.）与原文之意相符。**例2**之"米"乃泛指喂鸡之所用，故译文取"**rice**"（short, narrow white or brown grain on wet land in hot countries as food）。

六、七画

足

由"***足***"组成的字一般与脚或腿的动作相关。例字皆为形声字：左形右声。

踟蹰

1. 峰峦如聚，	Peaks like brows knit,
波涛如怒，	Angry waves spit.
山河表里潼关路。	With mountain and river far and near,
望西都，	On the road to Tong Pass I appear.
意***踟蹰***。	Gazing on Western Capital,

伤心秦汉经行处，
宫阙万间都做了土。

I ***hesitate***, alas!
To see the place where ancient warriors did pass
The ancient palaces, hall on hall,
Are turned to dust, one and all. [5]

《山坡羊 · 潼关怀古》
Tune: Sheep on the Slope, "Thinking of the Past on My Way to Tong Pass"
（元）张养浩 (The Yuan Dynasty) Zhang Yanghao

2. 使君从南来，
五马立***踟蹰***。
使君遣使往，
问是谁家姝。

From the south comes a lordling
In carriage with five horses;
Surprised, ***halts*** and sends one
To make an inquiry,
"Who is that beauty,
And who are her kin?"[4]

《陌上桑》 "By the Roadside Mulberry"
（汉） (The Han Dynasty)

3. 小巷的动人之处就是它的悠闲。无论谁，只要你到巷里去***踟蹰***一会儿，你的心情就会如巷尾不波的古井，那是一种和平的静穆，而不是阴森和肃杀。它闹中取静，别有天地，仍是人间。它可能是一条现代的乌衣巷，家家有自己的一本哀乐账，一部兴衰史，可是重门叠户，讳莫如深，夕阳影里，野花闲草，燕子低飞，寻觅归家。只是一片澄明如水的气氛，净化一切，笼罩一切，使人忘忧。

《巷》柯灵

The charm of the lane lies in its absolute serenity. No matter who you are, if you ***loiter*** around in the lane for a while, your mind will experience unruffled as the ancient well at the end of the lane. There you will experience a kind of peaceful calmness rather than gloomy sternness. There reigns peace and quiet in the midst of noisy bustle. It is a world of its own on earth. It may be a modern version of Wuyixiang, a special residential area of nobility in the Jin Dynasty southeast of today's Nanking, where each family, secluded behind closed doors, has its own covered-up story of joys and sorrows, and rise and decline. When the sun is setting, swallows will fly low over wild flowers and grass on their way to their nests. The all-pervading and all-purifying atmosphere of water-like placidness makes one forget all cares and worries. [15]

"The Lane" Ke Ling

“***踟蹰***”本意为“心里迟疑，要走不走的样子”。**例 1**“望西都，意***踟蹰***”中 的“西都”指长安（现在的西安）。作者看到眼前的长安，追忆其当年之繁华，不禁思绪万千。“踟蹰”此处指陷入思索，徘徊不定，故译为“**hesitate**”。**例 2**“使君从南来，五马立***踟蹰***”之“踟蹰”着意于“徘徊不前”，故其译文取“**halts**”即表此意。译文之所以在 halt 之后+s，因其主语并非“五马”，而是五马所拉之人：使君。明显的词形变化是分析型思维方式的体现。**例 3**之“踟蹰”着意于“随便走左、散步”，故译为“**loiter**”与其意对应。

踏

曲栏杆碾玉亭白，	The balustrade winds round the bower of carved jade,
小树粉蝶翅，	Over young trees butterflies flit about.
苍苔点绿胎，	The ground dotted with green moss looks like deer skin.
踏碎青鞋。	Let us ***tread*** on it till our shoes are worn out. [5]

《水仙子 · 梅边即事》 Tune：Song of Daffodils，“Drinking by Mume Trees”

（元）张可久 （The Yuan Dynasty）Zhang Kejiu

踪

不恨此花飞尽，	I do not grieve the willow catkins flown away，
恨西园落红难缀。	But that in Western Garden fallen red
晓来雨过，	Can't be restored. When dawns the day
遗***踪***何在？	And rain is o'er，we cannot find their ***traces***
一池萍碎。	But in a pond with duckweeds overspread. [1]

《水龙吟 · 次韵章质夫杨花词》

Tune：Water Dragon Chant，“After Zhang Zhifu's lyric on willow catkins， using the same rhyming words”

（宋）苏轼 （The Song Dynasty）Su Shi

趾

金陵为明之留都，社稷百官皆在；而又当太平盛时，人易为乐。其士女之问桃叶渡、游雨花台者，***趾***相错也。

《马伶传》（清）侯方域

...Nanjing was the subsidiary capital in the Ming Dynasty. As it was a time of peace and prosperity，and there was a great assemblage of high officials of the State，people were prone to pleasure-seeking. Thus the ladies making trips to Taoyedu and Yuhuatai followed upon the ***heels*** of one another. [12]

"Actor Ma"（The Qing Dynasty）Hou Fangyu

此处"***趾***"的译文取"**heels**"与"follow"的使用相关：跟在某人后面所能触碰到的自然是脚跟，而非脚趾。这里"**heels**"与上之"**traces**"的复数形式乃分析型思维使然。

蹲

余常于土墙凹凸处，花台小草丛杂处，***蹲***其身，使与台齐；定神细视，以丛草为林，以虫蚁为兽，以土砾凸者为丘，凹者为壑，神游其中，怡然自得。

《童趣》（清）沈复

I often ***squatted*** at the spots where there were concavities or convexities on the mud walls or did so over the clusters of grass on the flower-bed, with my eyes level with the latter. I looked with great attention, taking the clustered grass for forests, the insects and the ants for beasts, the convex parts of the mud wall for mountains and the concave ones for valleys. With my mind wandering among them, I felt much satisfied. [12]

"Childish Fun"（The Qing Dynasty）Shen Fu

文章题目中"童趣"之"童"字体现出汉语是通过词汇手段来表达其语法形式："童"中含"过去"之意。"蹲"之译文"**squatted**"则是通过词形变化（动词+ed）来体现动作发生在过去。

踞

江流有声，断岸千尺；山高月小，水落石出。曾日月之几何，而江山不可复识矣！予乃摄衣而上，履巉岩，披蒙茸，***踞***虎豹，登虬龙，攀栖鹘之危巢，俯冯夷之幽宫。

《后赤壁赋》（宋）苏轼

The rolling river was humming; the cragged bank towered a thousand feet high; the lofty mountains dwarfed the moon; the ebbing water exposed the rocks. What great changes had taken place within such a short time span since my last visit here—the place was already beyond my recognition! Tucking up my gown, I went ashore. I trod on the precipitous cliffs, wound through the wanton weeds, ***crouched*** on rocks shaped like tigers and leopards, climbed up tree trunks twisted like dragons, crept up to get to the perilously-perched falcon-aerie, and gazed down at the secluded palace of Fengyi, the river god. [8]

"My Second Visit to the Red Cliff"（The Song Dynasty）Su Shi

"***踞***"之原文与译文"**crouched**"体现出汉、英不同的思维方式在时态表达上的不同（同上例之"蹲"）。

跣、践

石渠之事既穷，上由桥西北下土山之阴，民又桥焉。其水之大，倍石渠三之一，亘石为底，达于两涯。若床若堂，若陈筵席，若限阃奥。水平布其上，流若织文，响若操琴。揭***跣***而往，折竹扫陈叶，排腐木，可罗胡床十八九居之。交络之流，触激之音，皆在床下；翠羽之木，龙鳞之石，均荫其上。古之人其有乐乎此耶？后之来者有能追予之***践***履耶？得意之日，与石渠同。

《永州八记》（唐）柳宗元

After exploring the rock flume, I descended the northern slope of an earthen hill from the northwest side of the plank bridge and came across another plank bridge being thrown there by the local folks. Water here was about one-third more voluminous than that in the rock flume. Its bed was formed with rocks from end to end, some of them resembling couches, parlor floors, banquet dishware, and some simply boudoirs. The water was ripping like a piece of silk and sounded like a piece of harp music. After ***taking off*** my ***shoes*** and rolling up my clothes, I waded into it, and with a bamboo rod snapped off from a bamboo tree, I swept off the fallen leaves and rotten wood and cleared off a space big enough to hold about twenty reclining chairs. Rioting under the imagined chairs would be curling ripples and lapping sounds and casting onto them would be shades from bluish-green feather-like trees and dragon-scale-like rocks. Who among the ancients had experienced a pleasure such as mine here, and will any of our descendents follow my trail to ***set*** his ***foot*** here? I was elated at discovering this gorge as I was when I found the flume. [8]

"Eight Travel Journals on the State of Yong"

(The Tang Dynasty) Liu Zongyuan

酉

“***酉***”的本意为“成熟”。“酉”代表八月，这时黍成熟，可以酿制醇酒。酉表示秋季闭着的门，万物已进入门内，酉上的“一”是闭门的象征[9]。由“酉”组合的字往往与酒相关。例字中，除“***酒***、***醉***”外，其余为形声字：左形右声。

醒

1. 所以心如槁木不如工愁多感，迷蒙的醒不如热的梦，一口苦水胜于一盏白汤，一场痛哭胜于哀乐两忘。但这里并不是说愉快乐观是要不得的，清健的***醒***是不须求的，甜汤是罪恶的，狂笑是魔道的。这里只说有味总比淡漠远胜罢了。

《没有秋虫的地方》叶圣陶

Therefore, being sentimental is better than apathetic, having a warm dream is better than becoming a living corpse, drinking a bitter cup is better than a cup of insipid water, having a good cry is better than being insensitive to both sorrow and happiness. This does not mean, however, that happiness and optimism are no good, healthy ***wakefulness*** is undesirable, sweets of life are evil and hearty laughter is vicious. What I mean here is that susceptibility is always preferable to insensibility. [15]

"A Place Without Autumn Insects" Ye Shengtao

2. 她这梦也应到了***醒***觉的时候了！人生就是一场梦么？……

十年深刻的印象，遗留于她现在的生活中的，只是矫强的性质了— 她依旧是喜欢看那整齐的步伐，听那悲壮的军号，但与其说她是喜欢看，喜欢听，不如说她是怕看，怕听罢。

横刀跃马，和执笔沉思的她，原都是一个人，然而时代将这些事隔开了……

童年！只是一个深刻的梦么？

《梦》冰心

Soon it was about time for her to ***wake*** up from the dream! After all, life is a dream, isn't it? ...

Now what the ten unforgettable years has left her is a strong character. She is still fond of watching soldiers march in stepand hearing the solemn and stirring call of a bugle. Nay, that's not what she is so much fond as afraid of watching.

Whether, wielding a sword on a galloping horse or holding a pen in deep thought, she is the same person. Only time has made all the difference...

Childhood! It's an indelible dream, isn't it?[15]

"Dreamlike Childhood" Bing Xin

酷

再往南行入西班牙，气候就变得干暖。马德里在高台地的中央，七月的午间并不闷热，入夜甚至得穿毛衣。我在南部安达露西亚地区及阳光海岸（Costa del Sol）开车，一路又干又热，枯黄的草原，干燥的石堆，大地像一块烙饼，摊在***酷***蓝的天穹之下，路旁的草丛常因干燥而起火，势颇惊人。可是那是干热，并不令人出汗，和台湾的湿闷不同。

《西欧的夏天》余光中

Down is Spain, the climate is arid and warm. Madrid is located in the center of a plateau. Its noontime temperature in June is not sultry, and you have to wear a woolen sweater towards the evening. In Southern Spain, when driving in the Andalucia region and along the Costa del Sol, I found everything dry and hot. The grass was turning yellow and the rocks were dry. The earth was like a pancake roasting under the ***deep*** blue firmament. Alarmingly, the roadside grass often started burning by itself. Unlike Taiwan which is humid, Southern Spain is hot and dry and so people there don't sweat at all.[15]

"Summer in Western Europe" Yu Guangzhong

此处以"deep"作为"酷"的译文，表现出"酷"意所含之程度的"深"和"极"。

酒：会意字，由水、由酉会意。《说文解字》中对"酒"的解释：酒，就也，所以就人性之善恶。[酒，迁就，是用来迁就（助长）人性的善良和丑恶的饮料。][9]

吃饭的时候，我饮了***酒***，用祖父的酒杯饮的。饭后我跑到后园玫瑰树下去卧倒，园中飞着蜂子和蝴蝶，绿草的清凉的气味，这都和十年前一样。可是十年前死了妈妈，妈妈死后我仍是在园中扑蝴蝶；这回祖父死去，我却饮了酒。

《祖父死了的时候》萧红

At lunch, I drank ***wine*** using grandpa's cup. After lunch, I lay under the rose bush in the back garden where, like when mother died ten years before, bees and butterflies were flying and the air was filled with the refreshing scent of green grass. After mother's death, I had continued to dash at butterflies in the back garden. Now after grandpa's death, I drank wine.[15]

"When Grandpa Died" Xiao Hong

醉：由酉、由卒会意。《说文解字》中对"醉"的解释：醉，卒也。卒其度量，不至于乱也。一曰：溃也。（醉，尽量。使其酒量满尽，而不达到昏乱的地步。另一文说，是溃乱。）[9]

在那种苦痛的心情之下，我却绝不愿意流露丝毫给对方知道；和他通了一年多的信，从没有把我爱他、思念他的情感流露过。我天天写日记和白话诗，有时偷偷地买了烧酒来喝个烂***醉***，有时想约几个同性朋友，住到深山古庙里修行去。她们都不知道我的秘密，唉！多么圣洁的值得回忆的初恋啊！

《初恋》谢冰莹

I managed, however, to refrain from revealing to him my troubled state of mind. For over a year when I exchanged correspondence with him I never let him know how much I loved and thought fondly of him. Every day I wrote an entry in my diary as well as some free verse in vernacular Chinese. Sometimes I got dead ***drunk*** with the strong liquor I had bought on the sly. Sometimes I even thought of asking some friends of the same sex to go with me to an ancient temple in the remote mountains to become Buddhist nuns. They of course had no idea of what had happened to me. Oh, first love, how unblemished and unforgettable it is![15]

"First Love" —Fragments from My Diary Xie Bingying

原文中，"***醉***"为动词，喝醉状态的表达依靠的是词汇手段："喝个烂醉"；译文中"醉"的体现则是通过过去分词"**drunk**"。

走

"***走***"的本意为"跑"。由"走"组合的字往往表示人、动物、交通工具等的向前移动。例字中，除"***走***"外，其余为形声字：左形右声。

趁： 右半部读 zhen。

1. 诸位毕业同学：你们现在要离开母校了，我没有什么礼物送给你们，只好送你们一句话罢。

这一句话是："不要抛弃学问。"以前的功课也许有一大部分是为了这张毕业文凭，不得已而做的，从今以后，你们可以依自己的心愿去自由研究了。***趁***现在年富力强的时候，努力做一种专门学问。少年是一去不复返的，等到精力衰时，要做学问也来不及了。即为吃饭计，学问决不会辜负人的。吃饭而不求学问，三年五年之后，你们都要被后来少年淘汰掉的。到那时再想做点学问来补救，恐怕已太晚了。

《不要抛弃学问》胡适

Dear Students of the Graduating Class,

As you are leaving your alma mater, I have nothing to offer you as a gift except a word of advice.

My advice is, "Never give up the pursuit of learning." You have perhaps finished your college courses mostly for obtaining the diploma, or, in other words, out of sheer necessity. However, from now on you are free to follow your own bent in the choice of studies. ***While*** you are in the prime of life, why not devote yourselves to a special field of study? Youth will soon be gone never to return. And it will be too late for you to go into scholarship when in your declining years. Knowledge will do you a good turn even as a means of subsistence. If you give up studies while holding a job, you will in a couple of years have had yourselves replaced by younger people. It will then be too late to remedy the situation by picking up studies again. [15]

"Never Give up the Pursuit of Learning" Hu Shi

2. 绿叶阴浓，	Green leaves casting deep shade
遍池亭水阁，	Over pavilions and bowers by the pool
偏***趁***凉多。	***Bring*** a delightful cool.
海榴初绽，	The pomegranates in early flower
朵朵蹙红罗。	Look like frowning red brocade. [5]

《小圣乐 · 骤雨打新荷》

Tune: Minor Sacred Music, "Sudden Shower Beating on New Lotus Leaves"

（元）元好问　　(The Yuan Dynasty) Yuan Haowen

例 1 中原文之“趁”为介词，其意：利用（时间、机会）。译文中用连词“**while**”来对应“趁”是取其本意（during the time that sth is happening）。**例 2** 之“趁”为动词，其意：“拥有”。根据英文遣词造句的语法要求，译文将前三行换成一个完整的逻辑语句：主语为 leaves，“趁”充当句子的谓语，其译文“**bring**”（provide）体现出了此“趁”之意。

赶

父亲常常为着贪婪而失掉了人性。他对待仆人，对待自己的儿女，以及对待我的祖父都是同样的吝啬而疏远，甚至于无情。

有一次，为着房屋租金的事情，父亲把房客的全套的马车***赶***了过来。房客的家属们哭着诉说着，向我的祖父跪了下来，于是祖父把两匹棕色的马从车上解下来还了回去。

《永远的憧憬和追求》萧红

Father, driven by avarice, often became very unfeeling. He would treat his servants, his own children and even my grandpa alike with meanness and indifference, not to say with ruthlessness.

Once, due to a dispute over house rent, he took away by force a tenant's horse-drawn cart and ***drove*** it home. The tenant's family came to see grandpa and dropping to their knees, tearfully related their troubles. Grandpa unharnessed the two chestnut horses and returned them to the tenant. [15]

"My Everlasting Dream and Pursuit" Xiao Hong

思维方式的不同表现在：原文中“赶”的过去时态通过语篇中“有一次”来体现；译文中则是通过动词的过去时态（**drove**）来表达。

趣

1. 花开不并百花丛，　It does not appear among other flowers when blooming,

独立疏篱**趣**未穷。　Alone on a flimsy fence, it gives ***delight*** without bound.
宁可枝头抱香死，　Close to the branch it would rather die sweet and cling,
何曾吹落北风中。　Than be carried down by the north wind to the ground. [17]
《画菊》　"Chrysanthemum in a Painting"
（宋）郑思肖　(The Song Dynasty) Zheng Sixiao

2. 车尘马足富者**趣**，　The rich may ***love*** their dust-raising carriages and bowers;
酒盏花枝贫者缘。　The poor only enjoy their cup of wine and flowers. [22]
《桃花庵歌》　"Song of Peach Blossom Cottage"
（明）唐寅　(The Ming Dynasty) Tang Yin

例1“花开不并百花丛，独立疏篱**趣**未穷”之意：这花不像别的花那样在百花丛中绽放，而是独自开在稀疏的篱笆旁，且意趣/乐趣无穷。这里“趣”含“乐趣、意趣”之意，译为“**delight**”（a feeling of great pleasure）在一定程度上表达了诗中所含之意。**例2**诗中之“趣”为动词，其意通“趋”。这两句诗的意思是富人所感兴趣的是车与马，而与贫者结缘的是花和酒，“趣”在这里之意为“感兴趣”，意译为“**love**”，符合原文之意。

起

1. 身高殊不觉，　Atop the peak I feel not high;
四顾乃无峰。　Looking around, I find no crest.
但有浮云度，　I only see clouds floating by
时时一荡胸。　Now and then purify my breast.
地沉星尽没，　Beyond dark earth stars sink awake;
天跃日初熔。　The sun leaps up like molten gold.
半勺洞庭水，　From half the spoon of Dongting Lake
秋寒欲**起**龙。　Dragon would ***rise*** in autumn cold. [22]
《晨登衡岳祝融峰》
"At Dawn Atop the Highest Peak of the Southern Mountain"
（清）谭嗣同　(The Qing Dynasty) Tan Sitong

2. 翻译就像一座桥，桥两端，气候悬殊，风光迥异。两端之间，原隔着险峻的山谷，湍急的溪流。两旁的人，各忙各的，世代相传，
分别发展出一套不同的习俗风尚以及语言文化来。
有一天，这不同文化习俗的人，忽然想起要跟对岸打个招呼，怎么办？要渡

过峡谷，不得不起一座桥，谁来***起***桥？

《一座长桥》金圣华

Translation is like a bridge with a very different climate and landscape at either end of it. Under the bridge, there lies a valley between steep mountains with a rapid stream flowing through it. Before the bridge is built, people on either side of the valley have for generations made no contact with those on the other. Hence, there have developed two different customs and habits, and two different languages and cultures.

One day, people of the two sides, each with a different culture and custom, suddenly desire to communicate with each other. What can they do? A bridge of course has to be built in order to cross the valley. But who is to ***build*** it?[15]

"A Long Bridge" Jin Shenghua

例中之“起”指能（举足）站立。《段注》“起本发步之称，引申之，训为立，又引申之凡始事、凡兴作之称。”**例1**“***起***龙”之意为“使龙腾飞”，译文“**rise**”即含《段注》之意。**例2**之“起”所含乃其引申之意，这里“起”之宾语是“桥”，译为“**build**”与其对应。

趋：“刍”读 chu。

予在患难中，间以诗记所遭，今存其本，不忍废，道中手自抄录。……脱京口，***趋***真州、扬州、高邮、泰州、通州，为一卷。

《指南录后序》（宋）文天祥

During my tribulations, I now and then put them down in poems. I kept the manuscript and could not bear to discard it. So I copied it all along my journey. ... The part dealing with my leaving Jingkou ***for*** Zhenzhou, Yangzhou, Gaoyou, Taizhou, Tongzhou belongs to the third volume.[12]

"Epilogue to the Zhinan Collection" (The Song Dynasty) Wen Tianxiang

原文中“***趋***”为动词，意“奔赴、趋向”。译文中为符合译语语言规范，转换为介词“for”。

走：会意字，由夭、止二字会意[9]。小篆体“走”的上、下两部分分别为“夭、止”，其意为“腿脚弯曲”。

1. 使人生圆滑进行的微妙的要素，莫如“渐”；造物主骗人的手段，也莫如“渐”。在不知不觉之中，天真烂漫的孩子“渐渐”变成野心勃勃的青年；慷慨豪爽的青年“渐渐”变成冷酷的成人；血气旺盛的成人“渐渐”变成顽固的老头子。因为其变更是渐进的，一年一年地，一月一月地，一日一日地，一时一时地，一分一分地，一秒一秒地渐进，犹如从斜度极缓的长远的山坡上***走***下来，使人不察其递降的痕迹，不见其各阶段的境界，而似乎觉得常在同样的地位，恒久不变，又无时不有生的意趣与价值，于是人生就被确实肯定，而圆滑进行了。

《渐》丰子恺

The subtle factor that makes life endurable is "gradualness" . It is by this "gradualness" that the Creator deceives all humans. Through the process of imperceptible gradual change, innocent kids become ambitious youths, chivalrous youths become unfeeling grownups, aggressive grownups become mulish old fogeys. Since the change takes place by slow degrees——year by year, moth by month, day by day, hour by hour, minute by minute, second by second, you feel as if you were permanently your same old self always seeing much fun and meaning in life, like one, ***walking*** a long, long way down an extremely gentle mountain slope, hardly perceives its degree of incline or notices the altered scenes as he moves along. You thus take a positive view of life and find it endurable. [15]

"Gradualness" Feng Zikai

2. 过去的日子如轻烟，被微风吹散了，如薄雾，被初阳蒸融了；我留着些什么痕迹呢？我何曾留着像游丝样的痕迹呢？我赤裸裸来到这世界，转眼间也将赤裸裸的回去罢？但不能平的，为什么偏要白白**走**这一遭啊？

《匆匆》朱自清

The bygone days, like wisps of smoke, have been dispersed by gentle winds, and, like thin mists, have been evaporated by the rising sun. What traces have I left behind? No, nothing, not even gossamer-like traces. I have come to this world stark naked, and in the twinkling of an eye, I am to go back as stark naked as ever. However, I am taking it very much to heart: why should I be made to ***pass through*** this world for nothing at all?[15]

"Transient Days" Zhu Ziqing

3. 在白蝴蝶危难时我怜悯它，可是当它真的自由翱翔而去时我又感到如此失落、怅惘，"唉！人啊人……"我默默伫望了一阵，转身向青草地**走**去。

《白蝴蝶之恋》刘白羽

I had taken pity on the white butterfly when it was in adversity. But now, as it was soaring freely way up into the sky, I experienced a feeling of loss and sadness. "Oh, how mentally fragile man is! ... " I sighed. I stood watching numbly for a long time, and then turned to ***stroll*** away on the meadow. [15]

"A White Butterfly" Liu Baiyu

4. 双峰的驼背上，每匹都驮着两麻袋煤。我在想，麻袋里面是“南山高木”呢？还是“乌金墨玉”？我常常看见顺城街煤栈的白墙上，写着这样几个大黑字。但是拉骆驼的说，他们从门头沟来，是一步一步**走**来的。

《冬阳 · 童年 · 骆驼队》林海音

The camels had each two sacks of coal on their two-humped backs. I was curious about the sacks of “top-grade coal dust from Southern Mountain” or “black gold and inky jade”, as I often saw in ads splashed in large black Chinese characters over the white wall of the coal storehouse near the city wall. But the camel driver said he had ***trekked*** with the camels all the way from Mentougou”, step by step. [15]

“Winter Sun · Childhood · Caravan” Lin Haiyin

5. 老师教给我，要学骆驼，沉得住气的动物。看它从不肯急，慢慢的**走**，慢慢的嚼，总会走到的，总会吃饱的。也许它天生是该慢慢的，偶然躲避车子跑两步，姿势很难看。

《冬阳 · 童年 · 骆驼队》林海音

As my teacher told me, I should learn from the camel——an animal so calm and steady and so patient. It ***moves*** slowly, but never fails to reach the destination of its journey; it chews its food slowly, but never fails to get its fill. Maybe it is slow by nature. Occasionally it will take a few quickened steps to dodge a car, but in a very awkward manner though. [15]

“Winter Sun · Childhood · Caravan” Lin Haiyin

6. 宝剑直千金，	My sword is worth its weight in gold, no less
被服丽且鲜。	Is worth my fashionable riding dress.
斗鸡东郊道，	On eastern pathway I would watch cocks fight;
走马长楸间。	I ***run*** my steed between the poplars white. [21]
《名都篇》	“Song of the Capital”
（三国）曹植	(Three Kingdoms Period) Cao Zhi

所处语境不同，例字之译文自然各异。**例 1** 之“走”着意于一般的步行，译文取“**walking**”，此其一；其二，分析型思维方式的体现。**例 2** 的“走”着意于“经历”，译文取“**pass through**”(to experience)。**例 3**“走”之意含“漫无目的，走走停停”，译为“**stroll**”(to walk somewhere in a slow relaxed way)。**例 4** 中，从“一步一步”可以看出这个“走”中含有“长途跋涉，旅程艰辛”之意，译文取“**trek**”(to make a long, difficult journey especially in the mountains)。**例 5** 之“看它（骆驼）从不肯急，慢慢的**走**”中，“走”着意于一般的向前移动，

译作“**move**”。**例 6**：“走”作为书面上的文言词语，其意为“跑；奔”。“**走**马”即“使马跑起来”，译文选取“**run**”。以上 6 例之译文均体现出其在所处语境中的含意。

豸

“**豸**”意为“有着长长脊骨的猛兽”。用“豸”构成的字一般与动物相关。例字均为形声字，左形右声。

豹

蛇蚖蜈蚣豺狼虎**豹**，虫之最毒者也，然天既生之，我何得而杀之。若必欲尽杀，天地又何必生。

《潍县署中与舍弟墨第二书》（节录）（清）郑燮

Snakes and centipedes, tigers, ***leopards*** and wolves are most dangerous animals. But since Heaven has given birth to them, what right have we to take their lives? If they were all meant to be killed then why in the first place did Heaven give them life?[19]

"Second Letter to Brother Mo, from the Magistrate's Residence at Weihsien"
(The Qing Dynasty) Zheng Xie

貔

行军司马智且勇，	His aide-de-camp was courageous and resourceful,
十四万众犹虎**貔**。	Like tigers and ***panthers*** were his one hundred and forty thousand warriors all.[13]
《韩碑》	"The Han Yu Stele"
（唐）李商隐	(The Tang Dynasty) Li Shangyin

豺

豺狼在邑龙在野，	I say, "The dragon is in opposition while the ***jackals*** and wolves are in office,
王孙善保千金躯。	You must take good care of your body priceless. …"[13]
《哀王孙》	"Feeling Sad About a Prince"
（唐）杜甫	(The Tang Dynasty) Du Fu

貂

老夫聊发少年狂，	Rejuvenated, I my fiery zeal display:

左牵黄，	On left hand leash, a yellow hound,
右擎苍，	On right hand wrist, a falcon gray.
锦帽**貂**裘，	A thousand silk-capped, ***sable***-coated horsemen sweep
千骑卷平岗。	Across the rising ground
为报倾城随太守，	And hillocks steep.
亲射虎，看孙郎。	Townspeople pour from out the city gate
	To watch the tiger-hunting magistrate.[1]

《江城子·密州出猎》 Tune: A Riverside Town, "Hunting at Mizhou"

（宋）苏轼 (The Song Dynasty) Su Shi

貊（同"貉"）：原意为"北方与豸兽共处的种族"。

1. 溥博渊泉，而时出之。溥博如天，渊泉如渊。见而民莫不敬，言而民莫不信，行而民莫不说，是以声名洋溢乎中国，施及蛮**貊**。

《中庸》（战国）子思

(The virtue of the greatest sage) is broad and profound and shown from time to time. It manifests itself like the vast sky and deep waters. No men who see him would fail to show their reverence; no men who listen to him would refuse to believe him; no men who see his behaviors would show their displeasure. Thus his reputation reaches far and wide across the central land, and expands to the ***outlying tribal areas***.[23]

"Doctrine of the Mean" (The Warring States Period) Zi Si

2. 故不登高山，不知天之高也；不临深溪，不知地之厚也；不闻先生遗言，不知学问之大也。干、越、夷、**貉**之子，生而同声，长而异俗，教使之然也。

《劝学篇》（战国）荀子

Without standing on a high mountain, one can hardly know the height of the sky. Without overlooking a deep gulley, one can hardly know the thickness of the earth. Without grasping the legated teachings of our deceased kings, one can never know the greatness of their learnings. The children of the tribes of Gan, Yue, Yi, ***Mo*** are born with the same voice, yet differ in customs. It is due to education.[12]

"On Learning" (The Warring States Period) Xun Zi

"**貉**"在译文中没有与其意义相同的对等词语，此即文化差异所带来的词汇空缺所致。译文"The children of the tribes of Gan, Yue, Yi, Mo are born with the same voice, yet differ in customs."中的"the tribes"(a group of people of the same race, and with the same customs, language, religion, etc., living in a particular area and often led by a CHIEF）说明了“Gan, Yue, Yi, Mo”为少数民族部落，故此，音译“貉”为“**Mo**”以及对“貉”的解释（“**the tribes**”），有助于解决翻译中的困难，同时还尽量保留了中国独特的文化意象。

【译法点滴】 文化差异对翻译的影响：词汇空缺及其译法——音译+释义

音译是翻译方法中的一种，但对有些民族文化内涵非常丰富的词语，翻译时还需加以注释。音译+注释的方法有助于保留中国独特的文化意象，并方便译语读者对原语独特文化的了解。如对阴、阳两字的翻译：在《汉英词典》中“阴”、“阳”两字分别注释为：In Chinese philosophy, medicine, etc. **yin**, the feminine or negative principle in nature; **yang**, the masculine or positive principle in nature. 再如“道”，在《美国韦氏大学词典》中音译为“**Tao**”，其释义为“the unconditional and unknowable source and guiding principle of all reality as conceived by Taoists.”

七、八画

雨

由“***雨***”组成的字大都与雨及其相似物有关。例字均为形声字：上形下声。

霭

白云廻望合， Look back, and all is hidden in white clouds,
青**霭**入看无。 Enter the azure ***mist***, to find it vanished.[2]
《终南山》 “The Zhongnan Mountains”
（唐）王维 （The Tang Dynasty）Wang Wei

露

露从今夜白， From tonight on ***dew*** begins to turn white,
月是故乡明。 The moon seen at my hometown is more bright.[13]
《月夜忆舍弟》 “Thinking of My Younger Brothers on a Moonlight Night”
（唐）杜甫 （The Tang Dynasty）Du Fu

雾

日出**雾**露余， Though the sun has risen the dew and ***mist*** are there yet,
青松如膏沐。 As if covered by grease, the green pines look all wet.[13]
《晨诣超师院读禅经》 “Coming to Monk Chao's Temple in the Morning

to Read the Buddhist Scriptures"

（唐）柳宗元 （The Tang Dynasty）Liu Zongyuan

霁

长桥卧波，未云何龙？复道行空，不**霁**何虹？高低冥迷，不知西东。

《阿房宫赋》（唐）杜牧

A long bridge arched over the waves——no clouds, why there emerged a dragon? A colorful band was seen in the sky——no ***sun after rain***, why there appeared a rainbow?[12]

"Efang Palace"（The Tang Dynasty）Du Mu

霞

落**霞**与孤鹜齐飞，秋水共长天一色。

《滕王阁序》（唐）王勃

Setting ***clouds*** are flying together with a solitary wild bird, and autumnal waters share the same hue with the broad sky.[12]

"The Tower of Prince Teng"（The Tang Dynasty）Wang Bo

此处之"**霞**"指日落时出现的彩色云，译文取"**clouds**"，贴切原文之意。

霄

反己者，触事皆成药石；尤人者，动念即是矛戈。一以辟众善之路，一以浚诸恶之源，相去**霄**壤矣。

《菜根谭》（明）洪应明

One able to count everything he comes into contact with as a curing medicine does so by often reflecting on himself. And one liable to hurt others with his invasive thoughts which act like dagger-axes and spears does so by always laying blames upon others. Of the two fashions, one can be called a path leading to universal good and another a source breeding various evils. They are as different as ***heaven*** and earth.[6]

"The Roots of Wisdom"（The Ming Dynasty）Hong Yingming

这里的"霄"之意为"天空"。其所在之上下文"相去**霄**壤"，即天壤之别，故译为"**heaven**"。

霜

王皓性迂缓。曾从齐文宣北伐，乘一赤马，平旦蒙**霜**，遂不复识，自言失马。须臾，日出，马体霜尽，依然系在前。方云："我马尚在。"

《北史》（唐）李延寿

Wang Hao was a slow-witted man. Once he accompanied the emperor of Qi to battle riding on a chestnut horse. During the night, it turned very cold. When morning came, the horse was coated with ***sleet***. When he went out he could not find his horse, so he ordered a search for it, but in vain.

When the sun rose, the sleet melted and the horse reappeared.

"Oh, it was here all the time!" he said. [14]

"History of the Northern Dynasties"
(The Tang Dynasty) Li Yanshou

霏

若夫日出而林**霏**开，云归而岩穴暝，晦明变化者，山间之朝暮也。

《醉翁亭记》（宋）欧阳修

The sun rises, the ***fog*** in the forests dissipates, and the stone caves become obscured as clouds are vanishing—the shift of light to darkness marks the passage of time from dawn till dusk. [12]

"The Arbour of the Drunken Greybeard"
(The Song Dynasty) Ouyang Xiu

"**霏**"用作形容词时，往往用来修饰雨、雪、烟、云、雾气等：烟雨霏微，形容雾气、细雨等弥漫的样子。根据上下文，此处之"霏"为名词，其意：弥漫的云气，译文选用"**fog**"，盖日出雾散。

鱼

由"**鱼**"组成的字往往与水中动物相关。例字中，除"**鱼**"外，其他为形声字：左形右声。

鲜

水果摊子更是琳琅满目。肥大的水蜜桃、大个儿西瓜、又黄又圆的香瓜、白嫩的**鲜**藕，摆在一起，竞妍斗艳。

《上海菜市场》季羡林

Arrayed side by side were juicy honey peaches, plump watermelons, yellow round muskmelons, ***fresh*** tender lotus roots, vying with each other to be the most beautiful. [15]

"The Shanghai FoodMarket" Ji Xianlin

鲤（鱼）

卖鱼的摊子上，活鱼在水里游泳，十几斤重的大**鲤鱼**躺在案板上。

《上海菜市场》季羡林

At fish stalls, live fish were swimming in the water and big ***carps*** weighing more than five kilos each were lying on chopping boards. [15]

"The Shanghai FoodMarket" Ji Xianlin

鱼：象形字。

话说回来，一个人的健康，要从生理、心理、适应能力这三方面来决定。我能活到现在，大概是总结了过去几十年的经验教训，卸下了思想包袱，不生气、不悲观。我这个人还有一个好处，就是求知欲强，趣味广泛。上至天下大事，下至草木**鱼**虫，我都有兴趣爱好。

《无题》夏衍

Three things, however, have much to do with one's health, namely, physiology, psychology and adaptability. That I've lived to this age is probably due to my effort to sum up my personal experience of the past decades and draw a lesson from it. I've never been weighed down by cares. I never get angry or become pessimistic. Another strong point of mine is that I'm always thirsting for knowledge and have many-sided interests. My interests range over a wide field, from major events at home and abroad to plants and trees, and ***fish*** and worms. [15]

"No Title" Xia Yan

八、九画

革

"**革**"之意为去了毛并加过功的兽皮。其引申义为"改变、除去"。用"革"构成的字往往与皮革相关。例字中"**革**"为象形字，其余均为形声字，左形右声。

革：象形字。

1. 西装、**革**履、领带，这种包装在西方已定型几百年，并早已成为全世界公认的正式服饰，而且居然在不断更新的时装流变中岿然不动。

《再说包装》(节录) 吴冠中

The Western-style suit with ***leather*** shoes and necktie to go with it is a kind of packaging that has taken shape in the West ever since several hundred years ago. It has long become universally accepted formal wear and even survived the vicissitudes of garment style intact. [15]

"More on Packaging" (Excerpt) Wu Guanzhong

2. 倾耳聆波澜，　I give ear to the surging billows,
举目眺岖嵚。　And feast my eyes on craggy hills,
初景**革**绪风，　In early spring ***no*** cold winds blow;
新阳改故阴。　The new sun dispels shadows old. [21]
《登池上楼》　"On Poolside Tower"
（东晋）谢灵运　(The Eastern Jin Dynasty) Xie Lingyun

以上两例之"革"在原文中的含义不同，故其译文有所区别。**例 1** 之"革"为名词，"皮革"之意，直译为"**leather**"。**例 2** 之"革"为动词，"革除"之意，意译为"**no**"，与所在诗句的结构及对押韵相关。

鞭

1. 深山曲路见桃花，　On winding hillside road peach blossoms come in sight,
马上匆匆日欲斜。　But I must hurry, for the sun sheds slanting ray.
可奈玉**鞭**留不住，　How could I with my ***whip*** of jade retain daylight!
又衔春恨到天涯。　With vernal grief at heart I must go on my way. [22]
《偶见》　"A Roadside View"
（明）徐祯卿　(The Ming Dynasty) Xu Zhenqing

2. 我看不见那个小孩的脸，不知道他脸上的表情，但是从他刚才的话里，我知道对于他另外有一个世界存在。没有家，没有爱，没有温暖，只有一根生活的**鞭**子在赶他。

《一个车夫》巴金

I couldn't read his countenance without seeing his face. However, judging from what he had said, he was evidently living in a world of his own—bereft of home, love or warmth, and flogged by the ***scourge*** of life. [15]

"A Rickshaw Boy" Ba Jin

3. 子曰"道不同不相为谋"，亦各从其志也。故曰"富贵如可求，虽执**鞭**之士，吾亦为之。如不可求，从吾所好"。岁寒，然后知松柏之后凋。举世混沌，清士乃见，岂以其重若彼，其轻若此哉？

《伯夷列传》（汉）司马迁

Confucius says, "People who do not believe in the same things cannot do business with one another," by which he means that all one can do will be just to follow his own convictions. That is why Confucius says of himself, "I would even be willing to be ***a carriage driver*** if I knew that by so doing I could get rich by my own effort. Since I cannot be sure, I will do what I like to do." Again he says, "When winter comes, then one finds out that the pines and cypresses stand the cold best." A pure-hearted man stands out in a world of general corruption. He knows what he values most, and disregards the rest.[20]

"Life of Poyi" (The Han Dynasty) Sima Qian

例 1 中，"可奈玉***鞭***留不住"之"鞭"即策马扬鞭之"鞭"，译文选"**whip**"，即可用于打人也可用来抽打动物。**例 2** 中，"只有一根生活的***鞭***子在赶他"之"鞭"并非指作抽打之用的鞭子，而是指生活之艰辛如同鞭子一般，这是一个暗喻，"**scourge**"（a person or thing that causes trouble or suffering）与其意对应。**例 3** 中没有明确的译文与之对应，而是将"鞭"之意隐含于"**a carriage driver**"（马车夫）之中。赶马车之人手里往往都会有一根用作赶马的鞭子，所以，例 3 之"鞭"属意译。

鞍

1. 不意金吾子　Who would have thought a captain of the guard
娉婷过我庐。　Would drop in and pay me his high regard!
银***鞍***何煜爚，　His silver ***saddle*** has a dazzling sheen;
翠盖空踟蹰。　His carriage waits with a canopy green.[21]
《羽林郎》　"Captain of the Guard"
（汉）辛延年　(The Han Dynasty) Xin Yannian

2. 画船儿载不起离愁，　Our parting grief outweighs your painted boat,
人到西陵，　I'll still at Ferry West,
恨满东州。　Your sorrow eastward flows.
懒上归***鞍***，　On my ***steed*** I won't ride,
慵开泪眼，　Nor open tearful eyes.
怕倚层楼。　I fear to lean on rails of tower high.[21]
《折桂令·西陵送别》
Tune: Plucking Laurel Branch, "Farewell at the West Ferry"
（元）张可久　(The Yuan Dynasty) Zhang Kejiu

3. 关山虽胜路难堪，　Hard is the way along mighty mountains and streams;
才上征***鞍***又解骖。　I have just mounted my ***horse*** and dismount it now.
十丈黄尘千尺雪，　Yellow sand rises high and fathomless snow seems.
可知俱不似江南。　How can this be compared with Southern shore! O how![22]
《阻雪》　"Stopped by Snow on My Northward Way"
（清）吴伟业　(The Qing Dynasty) Wu Weiye

例 1 之译文"**saddle**"为直译。**例 2**"懒上归***鞍***"之"鞍"指"马"。根据词中之意，要"上"的自然是"马"，不会只是坐在"鞍"上。因诗句中并未直接提及"马"，译文选用"**steed**"（坐骑）较为委婉含蓄。**例 3** 的译文选取"**horse**"，考虑到诗句中的"骖"（古代驾在车前两侧的马），故此，直接用"horse"作为其"鞍"的意译文。

靸

箭徑酸风射眼，　On Arrow Lane the eyes were hurt in chilly air,
腻水染花腥。　And rouged water stained with fallen flowers sweet.
时***靸***双鸳响，　Leaves fall on hollow ground,
廊叶秋声。　'Tis Autumn's sound,
　It seems as if I heard the lady's ***slipper***ed feet.[1]

《八声甘州 · 陪庾幕诸公游灵岩》
Tune: Eight Beats of a Ganzhou Song, "Visiting the Star Cliff with My Friends"
（宋）吴文英　(The Song Dynasty) Wu Wenying

靰

当流赤足蹋涧石，　I stand on the stone in the brook bare-footed,
水声激激风吹衣。　The water rushes noisily and the wind blows my garmert.
人生如此自可乐，　Such a life is of course full of pleasures,
岂必局促为人***靰***。　Why must we be ***controlled and fettered*** by others![13]

《山石》　"A Trip to the Temple"
（唐）韩愈　(The Tang Dynasty) Han Yu

"靰"意为"马缰绳"。根据上下文，诗句"岂必局促为人***靰***"的意思是：何必受到约束，宛若被套上马缰。这里"靰"暗喻"约束"，译文选取"***controlled and fettered***"。

音

用"***音***"构成的字往往与"声"、"乐"相关，也可引申为"消息"。例字中"***韶***"为形声字，左形右声，其余为会意字。

韶

朝飞暮卷，云霞翠轩，　From morning to evening, twilights flying
雨丝风片，烟波画船一锦屏　Over the pavilion by the rippled pond,

人忒看的这**韶**光贱！ A drizzle carried by a breeze puzzles the boat
In a distance—a misty view.
Youthful hour is felt so cheap
By one who is locked in the room![10]

《原来姹紫嫣红开遍》 "So Many Colors Splendid"
(明) 汤显祖 (The Ming Dynasty) Tang Xianzu

音：会意字。音，言语的声音。从心底产生，受口腔节制的，叫音。由"言"含"一"表示。林义光《文源》："一以示音在言中。"[9]

1. 丞相祠堂何处寻， Where would I find the Prince Minister's shrine?
锦官城外柏森森。 Somewhere outside Jinguan, in a dense cypress glade
映阶碧草自春色， Where the grass covered steps don the color of spring
隔叶黄鹂空好**音**。 And the orioles' fine ***songs*** go unheard.[2]
《蜀相》 "The Shu Prime Minister"
(唐) 杜甫 (The Tang Dynasty) Du Fu

2. 少小离乡老大回， To leave home very young and to return very old,
乡**音**无改鬓毛衰。 With ***accent*** unchanged, but hair grown thin.
儿童相见不相识， They see but know me not,
the smiling children who inquire:
笑问客从何处来。 "And from where do you come, Honored Guest?"[2]
《回乡偶书》
"Impromptu Lines Composed upon Returning to My Native Place"
(唐) 贺知章 (The Tang Dynasty) He Zhizhang

3. 玉容寂寞泪阑干， Her lovely face was covered with tears streaming,
梨花一枝春带雨。 Which was like a spray of pear blossoms with the raindrops in spring.
含情凝睇谢君王， Gazing with deep affection at the envoy she asked him to thank the emperor
一别**音**容两渺茫。 Saying "Since we parted we haven't known the ***voice*** and look of each other..."[13]

《长恨歌》 "Song of Everlasting Remorse"
(唐) 白居易 (The Tang Dynasty) Bai Juyi

4. 山光悦鸟性，	The beautiful scenery on the hill makes the birds happily fly and sing,
潭影空人心。	The reflection of the people in the deep pond rids their minds of all the selifish considerations clean.
万籁此俱寂，	All the sounds of nature are hushed here,
惟闻钟磬**音**。	Only the ***chime*** of the temple bell and percussion is heard clear.[13]

《破山寺后禅院》

"A Visit to the Buddhist Abode in the Back of the Poshan Temple"

（唐）常建　　(The Tang Dynasty) Chang Jian

5. 乐游园上清秋节，	All's merry on Clear Autumn Day,
咸阳古道**音**尘绝。	But she receives no ***word*** from ancient northwest way.
音尘绝，	And now o'er ancient northwest way
西风残照，	The sun declines, the west wind falls
汉家陵阙。	O'er royal tombs and palace walls.[1]

《忆秦娥》　　Tune: Dream of a Maid of Honor

（唐）李白　　(The Tang Dynasty) Li Bai

例 1"好**音**"的"音"着意于黄鹂的声音好听，如歌声一般，译文"**songs**"含有"好听"之意。**例 2** 因是"乡**音**"，说话时自然带有故乡的"口音、腔调"，"**accent**"（a way of pronouncing the words of a language that shows which country or eara a person comes from）即"暗"。**例 3**"**音**容"指人的容貌与说话的声音，故此"音"与"**voice**"对应。**例 4**"钟磬**音**"之"音"乃"钟、铃"之声，"**chime**"（a ringing sound, especially one that is made by a bell）即可体现此"音"。**例 5**"咸阳古道**音**尘绝"的意思是：通往咸阳古路上的音信早已断绝。此处之"音"意在"信息"，其译文取"**word**"（a piece of information or news）即含信息之意。

章：会意字，由"音"、由"十"会意。音乐一曲完了叫一章。十是十进位的末尾数（末尾数意终了，即一章）[9]。

1. 孟子曰："观水有术，必观其澜。日月有明，容光必照焉。流水之为物也，不盈科不行；君子之志于道也，不成**章**不达。"

《孟子》

Mencius said, "There is an art of watching waters. It is to watch its surging waves. The sun and the moon give out their radiance, shining through even narrow gaps. Flowing water is a thing that does not run forward until it has filled the hollows in its course. A man who has aimed to seek the truth cannot have a broader perceptive unless he has scaled a certain ***height***. "[24]

"Mencius"

2. 至诚无息。不息则久，久则征，征则悠远，悠远则博厚，博厚则高明。博厚，所以载物也；高明，所以覆物也；悠久，所以成物也。薄厚配地，高明配天，永久无疆。如此者，不见而**章**，不动而变，无为而成。

《中庸》（战国）子思

Sincerity to its utmost extent will never end. It never ends so it will last long. It lasts long so it will manifest itself. It manifests itself so it will reach far and wide. It reaches far and wide so it will be rich and weighty. It is rich and weighty so it will be lofty and brilliant. It is rich and weighty so it sustains all things. It is lofty and brilliant so it covers all things. It lasts long and reaches far and wide so it will allow all things to grow. It is rich and weighty like the earth, and lofty and brilliant like the sky, lasting long without limit. With all this, it becomes ***prominent*** even before it manifests itself, it changes even before it takes action, and it accomplishes something without doing anything. [23]

"Doctrine of the Mean" (The Warring States Period) Zi Si

3. 君子知之，故不以形体之有无为生死；而以志气之消长为生死。吾今日形体无恙，而志气已竭，斯为死矣；吾志气配乎道义，发乎文**章**，且与天地同流，而奚有于形体乎？故简策所载古圣贤人，虽死已久矣，而其辉光如日星之灿然，盖其人至今存也。

《直立说》（清）张士元

A gentleman is aware of this fact. He therefore does not regard life and death as depending upon the existence or nonexistence of bodily form, but rather upon the growth or decay of his spirit of life. When a man is perfectly well in his body but his vital spirit is gone, he may well be regarded as dead. If, however, one's life spirit is developed to find expression in principles of truth and justice or in ***literature***, it becomes the a part of the great stream of life of this universe. He is then freed from this dependence on a material body. [19]

"Thought on Self-Reliance" (The Qing Dynasty) Zhang Shiyuan

4. 迢迢牵牛星，　Far, far away the Cowherd Star;
皎皎河汉女。　Bright, bright riverside Weaving Maid.
纤纤擢素手，　Slender, slender her fingers are;
扎扎弄机杼。　Clack, clack her shuttle's tune is played.
终日不成**章**，　She weaves all day, no ***web*** is done;
泣涕零如雨。　Like rain her tears drip one by one. [21]
《迢迢牵牛星》　"Far, Far Away the Cowherd Star"
（汉）无名氏　(The Han Dynasty) Anonymous

例 1 中"成**章**"之"章"的本意："乐竟为一章"，由此引申，指事物达到一定阶段或有一定规模。"君子之志于道也，不成**章**不达。"的意思是：君子立志追求真理，不达到一定的高度，就不能说达到目的（通达）了。此处"章"之译文取"**height**"(the point when sth is at its best or strongest)，意在表达"到达一定高度"。**例 2**"不见而**章**"之意为即使不表现也会自己彰显。据此，此"章"之译文取"**prominent**"(easily seen)，以体现"彰显"之意。**例 3**"吾志气配乎道义，发乎文**章**，且与天地同流，而奚有于形体乎?"的意思：我的志气能够和道义配合，通过文章表达出来，那生命就会与天地同寿，还顾及什么形体呢? 这里，"发乎文**章**"之"章"指的是通过文章将自己的志气表达出来，"**literature**"（文学作品）即表此"章"。**例 4**"终日不成**章**"之"章"指的是织布机所织出的一块布料。译文取"**web**"而不用"cloth"，押韵是需要考虑的一个因素："done"与"one"。

意：会意字，心之音为意。

1. 古之欲明明德于天下者，先治其国；欲治其国者，先齐其家；欲齐其家者，先修其身；欲修其身者，先正其心；欲正其心者，先诚其**意**；欲诚其意者，先致其知；致知在格物。

《大学》（春秋）曾子

Those in ancient times who wished to extend their moral excellence all over the land would first govern their states rightly; in order to govern their states rightly they would first manage their families well; in order to manage their families well they would first cultivate themselves; in order to cultivate themselves they would first rectify their mind; in order to rectify their mind they would would first form sincerity in ***thought***; in order to form sincerity in thought they first acquire knowledge; in order to acquire knowledge they would first make researches on the way of things. Knowledge can be acquired only when researches are made into the way of things. [23]

"Great Learning" (The Spring and Autumn Period) Zeng Zi

2. 挂绝壁枯松倒倚，	The frowning cliff thrusts out a bending ancient pine;
落残霞孤鹜齐飞。	With lonely swan fly rainbow clouds on the decline.
四围不尽山，	Surrounded by endless hill on hill,
一望无穷水。	On boundless water I gaze my fill.
数西风满天秋**意**。	The western breeze spreads autumn ***air*** in wide, wide skies. [5]
《沉醉东风 · 秋景》	Tune: Intoxicated in East Wind, "Autumn"
（元）卢挚	(The Yuan Dynasty) Lu Zhi

3. 峰峦如聚，波涛如怒，	Peaks stand high, waves rise high.
山河表里潼关路。	The Tongguan Pass guards the gate of capital,
望西都，**意**踟蹰。	Chang'an, I see you, in low ***spirit***, oh well.
伤心秦汉经行处，	The Qin and Han dynasties had taken place here,
宫阙万间都做了土。	Before their palaces were reduced to dust. [10]
《山坡羊 · 潼关怀古》	Tune: Sheep on the Slope, "Pondering on History from Tongguan Pass"
（元）张养浩	(Yuan Dynasty) Zhang Yanghao

4. 石鼓之歌止于此，	My song of the stone drums is here ended,
呜呼吾**意**其蹉跎！	Alas, my ***suggestions***, I'm afraid, will not result in a bit. [13]
《石鼓歌》	"Song of the Stone Drums"
（唐）韩愈	(The Tang Dynasty) Han Yu

例 1“欲正其心者，先诚其**意**”的意思是：要想端正自己的心志，就要先使自己的意念真诚，这里“意”之译文选“**thought**”，取其“mind, idea”之意。**例 2**“秋**意**”即指秋天的情景、印象。译为“**air**”（the particular feeling or impression that is given by sb/sth），取其“impression”之意。**例 3**“望西都，**意**踟蹰”之意是：遥望古都长安，思绪此起彼伏。从后两句“伤心秦汉经行处，宫阙万间都做了土”可以看出作者面对繁华过后的废墟所感到的伤心和悲凉。此处，译文选用“**spirit**”，其意在“a state of mind or mood”。**例 4**“石鼓歌”是一首呼吁朝廷抢救保护文物、重视古文化的诗。诗人感慨石鼓文物的废弃，力荐当局保护石鼓而不得采纳，故此，诗的最后一句是“呜呼吾**意**其蹉跎”，其意思是：我的想法恐怕是白费心思。此处“意”是“想法”。这里的“意”通过诗中所提之建议表述出来，译文“**suggestions**”可达此意。

九、十一画

鹿

用“***鹿***”构成的字多与鹿属或鹿形的动物相关。例字中，除“***鹿***”外，其余为形声字，其中，“***麝***”为上形下声，其余左形右声。

鹿：象形字。

迸泉飒飒飞木末，　The sound is like the erupting fountain falling down on the tops of trees rustling,

野***鹿***呦呦走堂下。　And it's also like a wild ***deer*** walking past the hall crying.[13]

《听董大弹胡笳弄兼寄语房给事》

"Listen to Dong the First Playing the Tunes of the Reed Pipe on the Zither and Presenting This Poem to Prime Fang Guan"

（唐）李颀　(The Tang Dynasty) Li Qi

麟：左形右声

叹凤嗟身否，　Seeing no phoenix you lamented o'er your bad luck in your day,

伤***麟***怨道穷。　Seeing a caught ***kylin*** you complained your doctrines couldn't make way.[13]

《经路祭孔子而叹之》　"Pasting the State Lu and Offering a Sacrifice to and Sighing o'er Confucius"

（唐）李隆基　(The Tang Dynasty) Li Longji

麒麟：左形右声

1. 玉京群帝集北斗，　Around the Plough the immortals in the sky gather on and on,
   或骑***麒麟***翳凤凰。　Some of them ride on the ***kylins***, some on the phoenixes when they come along.[13]

   《寄韩谏议注》　"To Adviser Han Zhu"

   （唐）杜甫　(The Tang Dynasty) Du Fu

2. 绣罗衣裳照暮春，　Their silk clothes shine with the beautiful scenery in the late spring,
   蹙金孔雀银***麒麟***。　On them are the patterns of peacocks embroidered with gold line and of ***unicorns*** with silver line.[13]

《丽人行》 "Song of the Beauties"
（唐）杜甫 （The Tang Dynasty）Du Fu

麝： 上形下声

蜡照半笼金翡翠，The candle-light illuminates half of my quilt with an embroidered golden kingfisher on it,

麝熏微度绣芙蓉。The smell of ***musk*** comes into my lotus bed-curtain bit by bit. [13]

《无题》 "A Poem Without a Title"
（唐）李商隐 （The Tang Dynasty）Li Shangyin

麻

用"**麻**"构成的字多与麻类植物及其纤维或织物相关。例字中，除"**麻**"外，余者皆为形声字，下形上声。

麻： 会意字，由"广（意为'屋'）"、由"林"会意，是人们刮制的植物，在敞屋之下。

1. 移家虽带郭，Though his new house is near the town's outer wall,
野径入桑**麻**。Yet the path in the wild leads to a stretch of mulberry and ***hemp*** tall.
近种篱边菊，Near the fence he has planted some chrysanthemum,
秋来未著花。Which, though autumn has come, haven't come into bloom. [13]

《寻陆鸿渐不遇》 "Visiting Lu Hongjian without Meeting Him"
（唐）僧皎然 （The Tang Dynasty）Seng Jiaoran

2. 我们挤到人丛中了，母亲牢牢地跟在我的后面。一个拿着棍子的歪眼的查房，向我们装出了不耐烦的脸相。别的一个，**麻**脸的，凶恶的家伙，睁着狗一般的黄眼睛，请示似地，向账房先生看了一眼，便冲到大肚子的战栗的身子旁边，狠狠地一脚—

《长江轮上》叶紫

I elbowed my way through the crowd, followed closely by mother. A squint-eyed steward, stick in hand, eyed us with an assumed air of impatience. Another steward, with a ferocious ***pock***-marked face and wide-open dog-like yellow eyes, after giving a wink to the accountant as if requesting his instructions, dashed to the shivering pregnant woman and gave her a hard kick. [15]

"On a Yangtse River Steamer" Ye Zi

以上两例“**麻**”所表达的意思不同。**例 1** 中“桑**麻**”之“麻”是指一种草本植物，可用来织布、制绳索。译文“**hemp**”（a plant which is used for making rope and fabric）即此“麻”之意。**例 2** 中“**麻**脸”之“麻”指脸上的凹陷疤痕，往往因天花所致。所以，译文选取“**pock**”[Pit：a mark left on the surface of the skin by some disease，such as chickempox（水痘）] 与此“麻”之意相符。

摩

1. 牧童敲火牛砺角，　As a result the cowboys stroke them for fire and the oxen rubbed their horns there,
谁复著手为**摩**挲。　Who would again ***touch*** them with loving care?[13]
《石鼓歌》　“Song of the Stone Drum”
（唐）韩愈　（The Tang Dynasty）Han Yu

2. 自入南口，或容十骑，或容两骑，或容一骑。蒙古自北来，鞭橐驼，与余**摩**臂行，时时橐驼冲余骑颠，余亦挝蒙古帽，堕于橐驼前，蒙古大笑。

《说居庸关》（清）龚自珍

All the way from Nankou, the path was wide enough to allow the passage of ten horses, two horses, or a single horse. Some Mongols, who came from the north, whipped their camels and ***rubbed*** shoulders with me. Now and them a camel would rush at my horse and once made it tumble. I also beat the Mongol on the hat, which dropped before the camel. The Mongol laughed heartily.[12]

“Juyong Pass”（The Qing Dynasty）Gong Zizhen

3. 突兀压神州，　It towers so high as if it controls the sacred lands,
峥嵘如鬼工。　It' s so magnificent as if it' s built by the god' s hands.
四角碍白日，　The four angles of the eaves block the sunlight in the high,
七层**摩**苍穹。　The seventh story of the pagoda ***reaches*** into the blue sky.[13]
《与高适薛据登慈恩寺浮图》
“Ascending the Pagoda in the Temple of Benevolence and Grace Together with Gao Shi and Xue Ju”
（唐）岑参　（The Tang Dynasty）Cen Shen

4. 拔地**摩**天独立高，　The earth bursts forth to ***scrape*** the sky; lofty appears;
莲峰涌出海东涛。　The Lotus Peak upsurging from the Eastern Sea.
两千五百年前雪，　The snow has lasted o' ver two thousand five hundred years;

一白茫茫积未消。	Its boundless white has purified a myriad li.[22]
《日本杂事诗》	"Mount Fuji in Japan"
（清）黄遵宪	(The Qing Dynasty) Huang Zunxian

得太公《阴符》之谋，伏而诵之，简练以为揣摩。读书欲睡，引锥自刺其股，血流至足。……期年，揣摩成，曰："此真可以说当世之君矣。"

于是乃**摩**燕乌集阙，见说赵王于华屋之下，抵掌而谈。赵王大悦，封为武安君，受相印。

《战国策·秦策》（汉）刘向

As he came upon *the Book of Stratety* written by Jiang Taigong, he began to be immersed in reading it. He tried to master the content of the book by using the method of selecting, assimilating the essentials and figuring things out. The moment he was going to doze off, he would prick his thigh with an awl, causing the blood to stream down his leg. …

One year was gone and he worked out his arguments. He said, "They will surely convince the contemporary sovereigns."

Then he ***went past*** the fort of Yanwuji to solicit the support of the King of Zhao in his magnificent palace. He talked with the King in great intimacy, making him much pleased. So he was honored with the title of Lord of Wu'an and granted the Premier's seal.[12]

"Warring States Records" (The Han Dynasty) Liu Xiang

"**摩**"之意为"擦、蹭、接触"。**例1**"谁复著手为**摩**挲"之"摩挲"意"用手抚摩"，这里"摩"有"接触"之意，译为"**touch**"。**例2**"与余**摩**臂行"之"摩"意"擦"，译文"**rubbed**"即"摩擦"之"擦"。**例3**"七层**摩**苍穹"之"摩"意"挨近"，译为"**reaches**"，取其"到达，抵达"之意。**例4**"拔地**摩**天独立高"之"摩"有"摩擦"之意。"**scrape**"（to rub sth accidentally so that it gets damaged or hurt）意在形容其高：高耸直入云端以致天空都被其擦伤。**例5**"于是乃**摩**燕乌集阙"之"摩"意"走近"，译文取"**went past**"即含此意，"Past"之意为：on or to the other side of sth。例1与例2为直译，例3~例5为意译。

磨

1. 剑阁峥嵘而崔嵬，	The Sword Gate Pass is so steep and high, that if it's guarded by one,
一夫当关，万夫莫开。	It would never be broken through by ten thousand men.

所守或亲匪，	If the guards are not loyal to the court,
化为狼与豺。	They would become wolves and jackals on the spot.
朝避猛虎，夕避长蛇，	Thus the tourists have to avoid these fierce tigers at daybreak and these long snakes at dusk,
磨牙吮血，杀人如麻。	They ***grind*** their teeth and suck blood and kill people like cutting the hemp fast.
锦城虽云乐，	Though Chengdu might be a merry-making place for you,
不如早还家。	Yet you tourists may as well early homeward go. [13]
《蜀道难》	"Hard Is the Road to Shu"
（唐）李白	(The Tang Dynasty) Li Bai

2. 折戟沉沙铁未销，	A piece of broken halberd is not yet rotten though it is buried in the sand,
自将***磨***洗认前朝。	Taking it out, ***rubbing*** and washing it. I identify it to be a relic of the Red Cliff War.
东风不与周郎便，	If the east wind hadn't given General Zhou Yu a helping hand,
铜雀春深锁二乔。	The sisters Qiao would have been locked in the enchanting spring within the Copper Bird Terrace wall. [13]
《赤壁》	"The Red Cliff"
（唐）杜牧	(The Tang Dynasty) Du Mu

3. 此时月如镜新***磨***，山复整妆，湖复颒面，……

《西湖七月半》（明）张岱

This time the moon looks as if it were a mirror newly ***polished***, and the hills newly clad, the lake newly washed. [12]

"The West Lake in the Middle of the Seventh Month"

(The Ming Dynasty) Zhang Dai

4. 咬定青山不放松，	Upright stands the bamboo amid green mountains steep,
立根原在破岩中。	Its toothlike root in broken rock is planted deep.
千***磨***万击还坚韧，	It's strong and firm though ***struck*** and beaten without rest,
任尔东西南北风。	Careless of the wind from north or south; east or west. [22]
《竹石》	《Bamboo in the Rocks》
（清）郑燮	(The Qing Dynasty) Zheng Xie

例 1~例 3 之“***磨***”均为直译。**例 1**“***磨***牙”之意为牙齿相互摩擦出声的现象。此“磨”译为“**grind**”(to rub together, or to make hard objects rub together, often producing an unpleasant noise),意在表达出牙齿之间的摩擦和同时伴有的声响。**例 2**“自将***磨***洗认前朝”之“磨”含“打磨”之意,“**rub**”(to move your hand, or sth such as a cloth, backwards and forwards over a surface while pressing firmly)与其对应。**例 3**“此时月如镜新***磨***”之“磨”的意思为“擦亮、磨光”,译为“**polish**”(to make sth smooth and shiny by rubbing it with a piece of fabric, often with polish on it)。**例 4** 之“磨”在此处意为“磨炼、折磨”,意译为“**struck**”(to hit sb/sth hard or with force),间接地表达了“千磨万击”的“磨”之意。此译文以过去分词的形式表现出其被动的含义。

麾

1\. 清时有味是无能, In time of peace it's my incompetence to live a leisurely life,
闲爱孤云静爱僧。 I love the solitary cloud that is leisurely floating and the calm-minded monk who leads a peaceful life.
欲把一***麾***江海去, With an official ***banner*** in my hand I'm leaving for Wuxing today,
乐游原上望昭陵。 Yet I want to ascend the Recreational Plain to gaze afar at the Zhao Mausoleum before going my way. [13]

《将赴吴兴登乐游原》 "Ascending the Recreational Plain Before Leaving for Wuxing"

(唐)杜牧 (The Tang Dynasty) Du Mu

2\. 曹操遣权书曰:“近者奉辞伐罪,旌***麾***南指,刘琮束手。今治水军八十万,方与将军会猎于吴。”权以示群下,莫不响震失色。

《赤壁之战》(宋)司马光

Caocao dispatched a letter to Sun Quan, saying, "Recently I have been engaged in a punitive expedition by order of the Emperor. Soon after I had ***led*** my troops to the south, Liu Cong surrendered. As I have levied a water-borne army of eight hundred thousand strong, I am ready to have a hunting party with Your Highness in your land of Wu." Sun showed the letter to his subjects and they were all shocked and turned pale. [12]

"The War at the Red Cliff" (The Song Dynasty) Sima Guang

3\. 鲁字亮侪,奇男子也。田文镜督河南严,提、镇、司、道以下,受署惟谨，无游目视者。鲁效力**麾**下。

《书鲁亮侪》（清）袁枚

Lu Zhiyu, alias Lu Liangchai, was a man of unusual character. When Tian Wenjing was governor of Henan, he was strict with the conduct of government affairs. His subordinates all obeyed his commands with great deference, and listened to him with undivided attention. Lu worked under his ***leadership***.[12]

"Lu Liangchai" (The Qing Dynasty) Yuan Mei

"**麾**"之意为1. 名词：古代指挥军队的旗子；2. 动词：指挥（军队）。**例1**中，"欲把一**麾**江海去"之"麾"意为：指挥军队用的旗帜，这里表示吴兴刺史身份的旌旗。故译为"**banner**"。**例2**中，"旌**麾**南指"之"麾"意"指挥、指引"。这里译文通过"**led**"（引领）表达出"指挥"之意。**例3**中之"**麾**下"指将帅的部下，亦即在其所指挥的军旗之下，受其领导，故译文选取"**leadership**"。

靡

《诗》曰："奏假无言，时**靡**有争。"

《中庸》（战国）子思

The Book of Poetry says: "Quality pray in splendid music, and let there be ***no*** murmuring."[23]

"Doctrine of the Mean" (The Warring States Period) Zi Si

糜

行行日已远。	Each day go farther off our forces;
人马同时饥。	Our men are hungry as their horses.
担囊行取薪，	Pack on shoulder, we snatch firewood
斧冰持作**糜**。	And chop ice to boil as our ***food***.[21]
《苦寒行》	"Song of the Cold Endured"
（汉）曹操	(The Han Dynasty) Cao Cao

"糜"本意为"粥"。译文选取"**food**"，考虑到了语境及押韵（firew<u>ood</u>→<u>food</u>）。

十、十二画

黑

用"**黑**"构成的字多与颜色、时间、光线有关。例字中，除"**黑**、**墨**"

外，余者为形声字，其中，“黛”，下形上声；“黯”，左形右声。

黑： 会意字。小篆字形，上面是古“囱”字，即烟囱，下面是“炎”（火）字，表示焚烧出烟之盛。合起来表示烟火熏黑之意。

1. 月**黑**雁飞高，	The moon is ***dark***, the wild geese flying high.
单于夜遁逃。	The Hun chieftain flees into the night.
欲将轻骑逐，	The commander would give chase with mounted men;
大雪满弓刀。	A heavy snow covers their bows, their swords. [2]
《塞下曲六首》	"A Song of the Border"
（唐）卢纶	(The Tang Dynasty) Lu Lun

2. 满地黄花堆积，	The ground is covered with yellow flowers
憔悴损，	Faded and fallen in showers.
如今有谁堪摘？	Who will pick them up now?
守着窗儿，	Sitting alone at the window, how
独自怎生得**黑**！	Could I but quicken
	The pace of ***darkness*** which won't thicken? [1]
《声声慢》	"Slow, Slow Tune"
（宋）李清照	(The Song Dynasty) Li Qingzhao

3. 今有人于此，少见**黑**曰**黑**，多见**黑**曰白，则以此人不知白**黑**之辨矣；少尝苦曰苦，多尝苦曰甘，则此人不知甘苦之辨矣。

《非攻》（战国）墨子

If a man calls something which is a little ***black*** "***black***," but calls deep ***black*** "white," then it may be said of him that he does not know the difference between ***black*** and white. If a man tastes something slightly bitter and calls it "bitter," but calls what is very bitter "sweet," he, too, may be said not to know the difference between sweetness and bitterness. [20]

"Against Wars of Aggression" (The Warring States Period) Motse

例 1 之“黑”为形容词，表示光线之暗，故译为“**dark**”（with no or very little light, especially because it is night）。**例 2** 之“黑”含意“天黑”，仍有“光线暗淡”之意。考虑到其所在译语的句子结构，通过词形变化（dark+ness），从原文中的形容词转换为译语中的名词“**darkness**”。**例 3** 之“黑”侧重在“颜色”，“**black**”即黑色。

墨：会意字，由“土”、由“黑”会意[9]。

1. 我家洗砚池边树，　Beside our ancestor's inky pool grows a tree;
朵朵花开淡**墨**痕。　Each and every flower bears the pale ***inky*** trace.
不要人夸颜色好，　It needs no one to praise its color in high glee,
只留清气满乾坤。　For it will leave on earth but its uncommon grace.[17]
《墨菊》　"Mume Blossoms Painted in Black Ink"
（元）王冕　(The Yuan Dynasty) Wang Mian

2. 纸笔**墨**砚，吾家所有，宜不时散给诸众同学。每见贫家之子，寡妇之儿，求十数钱，买川连纸钉仿字簿，而十日不得见，当察其故而无意中与之。

《潍县寄舍弟墨第三书》（清）郑燮

We have plenty of writing brush and ***ink*** and paper at our home and should distribute them to the school children. I have often observed how a son of a poor widow tried for ten days to get money for buying writing paper to make a writing pad and failed. We should keep an eye on such a boy and give it to him unintentionally.[19]

"Third Letter to Brother Mo from Weihsien"
(The Qing Dynasty) Zheng Xie

黛：形声字，下形上声。

1. 孔明庙前有老柏，　In front of Kongming Temple, there is a cypress old,
柯如青铜根如石。　Its trunk looks like green copper and its root a stone bold.
霜皮溜雨四十围，　It's as thick as forty arm-spans and on its frost-like bark rain slides,
黛色参天二千尺。　Being two thousand feet tall, its ***dark green*** twigs tower to the skies.[13]
《古柏行》　"Song of the Old Cypress"
（唐）杜甫　(The Tang Dynasty) Du Fu

2. 风向日暮吹芳芷，　At twilight, the fragrance laden breeze begins to blow;
月落山深哭杜鹃。　As the moon sets, from the mountain depths a cuckoo cries.
犹似含颦望巡狩，　The maidens seem to knit their brows to view his majesty's arrival,
九嶷如**黛**隔湘川。　While across the Xiang, the Nine Peaked mount grows ***greener*** still.[2]
《黄陵廟》　"Huangling Temple"
（唐）李群玉　(The Tang Dynasty) Li Qunyu

3. 翠冷松云徑，　Roadside pines in cold emerald dye,
嫣然眉**黛**冷。　***Black*** brow overshadows smilling eye. [5]
《一枝花 · 湖上归》　Tune: A Spring of Flowers, "Return from the Lake"
（元）张可久　(The Yuan Dynasty) Zhang Kejiu

"**黛**"可以用来表示深绿色、浅蓝色、靛蓝色或黑色。以上三例"黛"的翻译均为直译。**例1**"**黛**色参天二千尺"中的"黛"是指高耸在空中古柏树枝的颜色，故译为深绿"**dark green**"。**例2**"九嶷如**黛**隔湘川"中的九嶷山又名苍梧山，位于湖南省南部，宁远县境内。山中秦松汉柏高耸入云，香杉修竹茂密苍翠。前人有诗云："万里辞黄屋，千秋寄碧岭"，故此，这里"黛"的译文选取"**greener**"。**例3**"嫣然眉**黛**冷"中的"黛"指眉的颜色，故译文用"**Black**"。

黯：形声字，左形右声。

1. 秋风飒飒撼梧桐，　Autumn's wind shakes the parasol.
秋雨潇潇响翠竹，　Autumn's rain moistures the bamboo.
秋云**黯黯**迷烟树。　Autumn's cloud ***darkens*** the village.
三般儿一样苦，　All the three images are bare symbols,
苦得人魂魄全无。　And bitter tastes of human life. [10]
《水仙子 · 相思》　Tune: Song of Daffodils, "Lovesickness"
（元）刘庭信　(The Yuan Dynasty) Liu Tingxin

2. 饮马渡秋水，　When the warriors water their horses and cross the Tao River,
水寒风似刀。　Cutting is the wind and icy in the water.
平沙日未没，　O'er the vast stretch of sands, the sun has not yet set,
黯黯见临洮。　A ***dim*** view of Lintao they already get. [13]
《塞下曲》　"Song of the Frontiers"
（唐）王昌龄　(The Tang Dynasty) Wang Changling

3. 去年花里逢君别，　I met and parted with you amid the flowers last year,
今日花开又一年。　Today the flowers come into bloom again in a new year.
世事茫茫难自料，　The worldly affairs are so fast changing that I can't foresee them in any way,
春愁**黯黯**独成眠。　So ***deeply*** worried in spring, I drowse alone from day to day. [13]
《寄李儋元锡》　"To Li Dan"
（唐）韦应物　(The Tang Dynasty) Wei Yingwu

4. 紞如三鼓，	A leaf falls in the night so deep,
铿然一叶，	Then drums beat thrice with a ring so loud
黯黯梦云惊断。	That ***gloomy***, I awake from my dream of the Cloud.
夜茫茫，	Under the boundless pall of night,
重寻无处，	Nowhere again can she be found
觉来小园行遍。	Though I've searched o'er all the small garden's ground. [1]
《永遇乐》	Tune: Joy of Eternal Union
（宋）苏轼	(The Song Dynasty) Su Shi

“**黯**”为形容词。**例 1**“黯”之意侧重在光线昏暗，其译文“**darkens**”涉及到了词类转换：考虑到与第一、二句译文结构的一致性，“黯黯”从原文中的形容词“dark”转换为译文中的动词“**darkens**”。**例 2** 之“黯黯”的意思是：影影绰绰，模糊不清，译文“**dim**”（where you cannot see well because there is not much light）即表此意。**例 3**“黯黯”之意为“浓重”，借此表达出作者愁绪满怀，意译为“**deeply**”，体现程度。**例 4**“**黯黯**梦云惊断”之意为梦中惊醒，觉得黯然心伤。“黯黯”此处表示沮丧忧愁貌，“**gloomy**”（sad and without hope）与原文之意相符。

第三部分　非独体字部首偏旁

一、一画

一

“一”，最初，万物形成之始，道建立了一。[9]用“一”构成的字，往往有“初始、为首”等含义。例字皆非形声字。

天：会意字，由“一”、“大”会意。巅顶，最高而无以上加的部位[9]。

1. 春者，**天**之本怀；秋者，天之别调。

《幽梦影》（节录）（清）张潮

Spring is the natural disposition of ***Heaven*** (***the creator***); autumn is one of its varying moods. [19]

“Quiet Dream Shadows” (Nature)
(The Qing Dynasty) Zhang Chao

2. 后辈轻薄前辈者，往往促算。何者？彼既残老，**天**岂以贱者赠之。

《安得长者言》（节录）（明）陈继儒

The unbalanced youth who are critical of the older people often die young. This is natural. Since they are critical of the old, why should ***God*** let them grow old?[19]

“Wish I Had Heard It from an Elder”
(The Ming Dynasty) Zhang Jiru

3. 凡折花须择枝，…… 取俯仰高下，疏密斜正，各具意态，全得画家折枝花景，方有**天**趣。

《瓶花谱》（明）张谦德

In cutting flowers, choose the twig for its bend and posture, … In putting them in the vase, see that they bend or turn up, or incline or stand straight, in a harmonious grouping and height, so that each seems to say something, such as the postures chosen by artists for painting. Thus their ***natural*** beauty may be preserved. [19]

“Cutt Flowers and Vases”
(The Ming Dynasty) Zhang Qiande

4. 若将富贵比贫者，　If you compare the poor with the rich low and high,
一在平地一在**天**；　You'll find the one on earth, the other in the ***sky***.
若将贫贱比车马，　If you compare the poor with the carriage and steed,
他得驱驰我得闲。　The poor have leisure while the rich gallop with speed.[22]
《桃花庵歌》　"Song of Peach Blossom Cottage"
（唐）唐寅　(The Tang Dynasty) Tang Yin

5. 十年前此晓霜**天**，　Can I forget ten years ago this frosty ***day***;
惊破晨钟梦亦仙。　The morning bells broke my dream, my wife passed away?
一断藕丝无续处，　When the lotus root snaps, it can't be joined again;
寒风落叶洒新阡。　The chilly wind blows dead leaves o'er her graveside lane.[22]
《悼亡四首》　"Elegy on My Deceased Wife"
（明）王夫之　(The Ming Dynasty) Wang Fuzhi

例1和例2之"天"的译文体现出不同的民族心理所渗透的文化内涵。**例1"Heaven"**为直译，保留了原语中的文化内涵：中国是一个佛教较为盛行的国家，在佛教文化观念中的"天"具有主宰万物的能力。**例2"God"**为意译，将原文中的佛教文化观念转换成西方基督教文化观念，便于译语读者理解。例3、4和5的译文主要考虑到上下文语境。**例3**中的"瓶花"，着意于其应各具意态，给人以浑然天成之感。故此，以"**natural**"对应"天"。**例4**"一在平地一在**天**"："地"(earth)与"天"对应，故"天"在此译为"**sky**"(the space above the earth that you can see when you look up ...)。**例5**"十年前此晓霜**天**"中的"晓"意为"天刚亮"，含"白天"之意，故译文选用"**day**"。

【译法点滴】 文化差异对翻译的影响：民族心理的差异及其译法——直译、意译

民族心理是指在一定的社会历史条件下构成一个民族的人们通过共同的感觉、知觉、思维情绪、思想感情、性格特征等心理活动表现出的对客观事物的反映。民族心理渗透着该民族的共同文化传统。不同的社会制度、自然环境、宗教信仰、民情风俗、思维方式和语言表达习惯等必然会在词汇的语义上刻上各自的民族文化烙印，使其隐含着不同的民族文化内涵。在跨文化交际中，不同的民族文化所导致的不同的民族心理会给语际翻译带来一定程度的障碍和困难，因此，在翻译方法的选择和运用上所考虑的不仅仅是语言的转换，同时要兼顾到文化的沟通与交流。

上面例1和例2中两个"天"字的翻译分别采用直译和意译的方法体现出不

同民族心理所具有的文化内涵。中国是一个佛教较为盛行的国家，在佛教文化观念中的“天”具有主宰万物的能力。**例 1** 中的“天”直译为“**Heaven**”，遵循了忠于原作的原则，同时也起到了向西方移植中国佛教文化的作用。基督教认为“上帝”是自然界的主宰。**例 2** 之“天”意译为“**God**”，考虑了译语读者的宗教背景和民族心理，便于读者理解。此两例“天”的译法理据充分、各有千秋。

云：象形字。两横划表示天上横向的云层，弯钩表示卷状的云团[11]。

1. **云**之为物，或崔巍如山，或潋滟如水，或如人，或如兽，或如鸟毳，或如鱼鳞。故天下万物皆可画，唯云不能画。世所画云，亦强名耳。

《幽梦影》(节录)(清) 张潮

The ***cloud*** is ever-changeful, sometimes piled up like high cliffs, sometimes translucent like water, and sometimes it resembles human beings or beasts or fish or insects. That is why clouds are most difficult to paint. The so-called paintings of clouds that I have seen are sheer tours de force.

“Quiet Dream Shadows” (Nature)
(The Qing Dynasty) Zhang Chao

2. 作画如蒸**云**，度空触石，一任渺弥，遮露晦明，不可预定，要不失天成之致，乃为合作。学画如洗石，荡尽浮沙浊土，则灵窍自呈，秀色自现。二者于当境时卓竖真宰，于释用时深加观力，方有入路耳。

《紫桃轩杂缀》(节录)(明) 李日华

Let your painting develop like floating ***clouds***, sailing into space and going around rocks, spreading out here and obstructing the sunlight there, with complete spontaneity. That is the way to achieve an effect of nature. Then it will hold. Practicing calligraphy is like washing pebbles. When the dirt on the surface is washed off, the colors and brilliance of the pebbles reveal themselves naturally. In both cases, the vitality comes from careful observation in spare time and high concentration and mastery at the time the brush touches the paper. [19]

“Purple Peach Hall Miscellany” (The Ming Dynasty) Li Rihua

3. 韶华休笑本无根：	Do not jeer at me as rootless,
好风凭借力，	But lend me strength, good wind,
送我上青**云**。	To soar up to the azure ***sky*** at last. [17]
《临江仙》	Tune: Linjiangxian
(清) 曹雪芹	(The Qing Dynasty) Cao Xunqin

例 2“蒸云”之“蒸”的意思是 1. 动词，其意“气体上升”；2. 形容词，表示“众多”。据此，“云”的译文使用复数形式“**clouds**”，体现出“白云朵朵”之意。**例 3** 所写是“风筝”。放风筝时，借助风力，使其升入空中，此处之“云”对应“**sky**”为意译。

吏：会意字，由“一”、由“史”会意。一：言其执法如一；史：“史”借作“人”字用，表示执法的官员。[9]

1. 人各有能力，不可强。有其宝而怀之，快也；无其才而试之，妄也。子试观今之为**吏**者，或以盗贼招尤，或以逋逃获谴，或以讼狱而谪，或以钱榖而免。其罣乎吏者，盖不胜其夥也。

《七疗》(清) 张潮

People are made differently; some have talent and some have not. I shan't pretend that I have any administrative ability, and even if I had, I wouldn't make it my ambition. Look at what happened to so many ***officials***. Some got into trouble because of permitting bandits or because of the escape of convicts. Some were dismissed on account of faulty administration of justice and some because of accounts in money or grains. And many are subjected to official criticism of one kind or another. [19]

"The Seven Remedies" (The Qing Dynasty) Zhang Chao

2. 少小虽非投笔**吏**，	Though, when young, I didn't give up pen for sword as ***Ban Chao*** did,
论功还欲请长缨。	Yet to serve our country, I now beg to go to the frontiers to achieve deeds of merit. [13]
《望蓟门》 (唐) 祖咏	"Looking at Jimen in the Distance" (The Tang Dynasty) Zu Yong

例 1、例 2 中的“吏”为直译。**例 2** 中的“投笔**吏**”源于东汉班超投笔从戎的典故。班超为西域的回归、促进民族融合，做出了巨大贡献，官至西域都护，封定远侯。这一文化信息在译语中没有与其相对应的词语，因此，在整句诗的译文中，单字“吏”则意译为“**Ban Chao**”。

夏：会意字，由“頁”、由“夊”会意[9]。夏时称中原地区的人为夏人，以别于周边地区的不同民族。“頁”，表示头；“夊”，表示两只脚。

春水满四泽，	Spring water overbrims the streams;
夏云多奇峰。	***Summer*** cloud fancy peaks outshines;
秋月杨明辉，	The autumn moon sheds brilliant beams;

冬岭秀寒松。 On winter cliffs stand cold-proof pines. [21]

《神情诗》 "Spirit of the Four Seasons"

（东晋）顾恺之 (The Eastern Jin Dynasty) Gu Kaizhi

画：象形字。

1. 夜静云帆月影低， The shadow of my cloudlike sail hangs low at moonrise.
   载我在潇湘***画***里。 My boat seems to float in the ***picture*** of two streams. [5]
   《沉醉东风 · 秋景》 Tune: Intoxicated in East Wind, "Autumn"
   （元）卢挚 (The Yuan Dynasty) Lu Zhi

2. 碧水青山曲径遐， A long, long winding path leads to green hill and rill;
   薜萝门巷足烟霞。 Ivy leaves and rainbow clouds veil your cottage still.
   寻诗人去留僧舍， Gone for poetic verve, in temple cell you stay;
   卖***画***钱来付酒家。 With money earned by ***pictures*** sold, for wine you pay. [22]
   《赠曹雪芹》 "To Cao Xueqin"
   （清）敦敏 (The Qing Dynasty) Dun Min

3. 月如牙， The new moon rose, casting
   早庭前疏影印窗纱。 The image of a plum in blossom
   逃禅老笔应难***画***， onto the window screen.
   别样清佳。 The master painter could not ***depict*** its grace. [10]
   《殿前欢 · 梅花》 Tune: Joy Before Palace, "Plum Blossom"
   （元）景元启 (The Yuan Dynasty) Jing Yuanqi

4. ***画***船儿载不起离愁， Our parting grief outweighs your ***painted*** boat.
   人到西陵， I'm still at Ferry West,
   恨满东州。 Your sorrow eastward flows. [22]
   《折桂令 · 西陵送别》
   Tune: Plucking Laurel Branch, "Farewell at the West Ferry"
   （元）张可久 (The Yuan Dynasty) Zhang Kejiu

例4中的"画"为"涂有彩绘"之意，译为"**painted**"，表达出"船"之涂。

丨

"丨"表示上下通彻。例字皆非形声字。

中：会意字，是指“丨”纳入“口”中的意思[9]。

1. 冰雪林**中**著此身，	You look so pure ***in*** the forest of ice and snow;
不同桃李混芳尘。	With peach and plum blossoms for splendor you won't vie.
忽然一夜清香发，	Suddenly one night your fragrance begins to flow,
散做乾坤万里春。	It will spread out and turn into spring far and nigh. [17]
《白梅》	"The White Mume Blossoms"
（元）王冕	(The Yuan Dynasty) Wang Mian

2. 长安豪贵惜春残，	Nobles in the Capital treasure the late spring;
争赏街西紫牡丹。	All go to appreciate pink peonies in west Chang'an.
别有玉盘承露冷，	Yet Mr. Pei's bedewed blooming peonies jade white,
无人起就月**中**看。	Totally neglected, shines alone ***under*** the moonlight. [17]
《裴给事宅白牡丹》	"The White Peony in Mr. Pei's Yard"
（唐）裴潾	(The Tang Dynasty) Pei Lin

例2之“月**中**看”即借月色观赏（在月光之下观看），“中”在此对应“**under**”为意译。

曲：象形字。甲骨文和金文“曲”都像曲尺，本意是“弯曲”[11]。

1. 霜溪***曲曲***转旌旗，	Our banners undulate along the ***winding*** stream
几许沙鸥睡未知。	Without disturbing the riverside birds from their dream.
笳鼓声高寒吹起，	Suddenly we beat drums and blow our bugles shrill
深山惊杀老阇梨。	To startle even the deaf old monk beyond the hill. [22]
《晓征》	"March at Dawn"
（明）戚继光	(The Ming Dynasty) Qi Jiguang

2. 上有弦歌声，	Music from there comes to my ear,
音响一何悲！	Its sound so sad, it tune so drear.
谁能为此***曲***？	Who could compose such doleful ***song***
无乃杞梁妻。	But one whose secret grief's life-long?
清商随风发，	Sad music rise with the breeze;
中***曲***正徘徊。	The middle ***tune*** wafts ill at ease. [21]
《西北有高楼》	"In Northwest There's a Tower Proud"
（汉）无名氏	(The Han Dynasty) Anonymous

3. 我欲竟此***曲***。　I try to finish this ***refrain***,

此曲悲且长。 So sad that I put it apart;
弃置勿重陈， So long I won't sing it again,
重陈令心伤！ For fear lest it should break my heart. [21]
《扶风歌》 "Riding the Wind"
（西晋）刘琨 (The Western Jin Dynasty) Liu Kun

4. 辕条上都是马， In the shafs steed on steed,
套顶上不见驴 In harness there's no ass.
黄罗伞柄天生**曲**。A ***crooked*** pole supports a yellow canopy. [5]
《四煞》 Tune: Last Stanza But Four
（元）睢景臣 (The Yuan Dynasty) Ju Jingchen

5. 木落雁南渡， The tree leaves falling, the wild geese southward fly,
北风江上寒。 The north wind brings about coldness on the Yangtze River.
我家襄水**曲**， The ***bend*** of the Xiang River my home stands by,
遥隔楚云端。 It's very far and veiled by the Chu Clouds all over. [13]
《早寒有怀》 "Thoughts on the Early Cold Weather"
（唐）孟浩然 (The Tang Dynasty) Meng Haoran

6. 岭树重遮千里目， The dense trees on the mountains prevent me from having distant views,
江流**曲**似九回肠。 My pent-up feeling of sadness is like the Liu River ***zigzag*** flows. [13]
《登柳州城楼寄漳汀封连四州刺史》
"A Poem to the Four Friends Demoted to Zhangzhou, Tingzhou, Fengzhou and Lianzhou after Ascending the Gate Tower of Liuzhou"
（唐）柳宗元 (The Tang Dynasty) Liu Zongyuan

7. 羹是手调才有味， I relished no rich soup but prepared by her hand;
语无心**曲**不同商。 Our ***talk*** from heart to heart gave nothing but delight.
如何二十多年事， How could the twenty years we passed in southern land
只抵春宵一梦长。 Last not so long as happy dreams of vernal night? [22]
《哭聪娘》 "Elegy on My Wise Mistress"
（清）袁枚 (The Qing Dynasty) Yuan Mei

8. 花迎剑佩星初落， The flowers greet the officials with the swords when stars begin to disappear in the sky,

柳拂旌旗露未干。	The flags are touched by the willows with dew not yet dry.
独有凤凰池上客，	It's only you who work at the Phoenix Pool nearby,
阳春一***曲***和皆难。	To whose high-level ***poem*** it is hard for all the others to reply. [13]
《和贾至舍人早朝大明宫之作》	"Replying to Jia Zhi's Poem An Early Levee at Daming Palace"
（唐）岑参	(The Tang Dynasty) Cen Shen

9. 少陵野老吞声哭，	I, an old and poor man from the Shao Mausoleum, gulp down my sobs on my way,
春日潜行曲江***曲***。	When I stealthily walk along the most ***deserted place*** of Qu River on a spring day. [13]
《哀江头》	"Feeling Sad at the Side of the Qu River"
（唐）杜甫	(The Tang Dynasty) Du Fu

10. ***曲***能有诚，诚则形，形则著，著则明，明则动，动则变，变则化。唯天下之至诚为能化。

《中庸》（战国）子思

Being devoted to some specific aspects they can also become sincere. When they are sincere they will surely have their sincerity shown. When they have their sincerity shown it will grow prominent. When it grows prominent it will be carried forward. When it is carried forward it will affect others. When it affects others it will bring about changes. When it brings about changes it will be able to help nourish everything. It is only the most sincere people who can help nourish every on the earth. [23]

"Doctrine of the Mean"

(The Warring States Period) Zi Si

以上**例 1～例 6** 中的"曲"为直译，**例 7～例 10** 为意译。根据上下文语境：**例 7**"语无心***曲***不同商"之"心曲"意"心声"（发自内心深处的话语），"**talk**"即"话语"。**例 8** 的题目"和贾至舍人早朝大明宫之作"显示出"阳春一***曲***和皆难"之"曲"是"诗"、而非"歌"，"**poem**"与诗中之意相符。**例 9** 之"曲"作为名词，含意"偏僻之处"。诗的作者杜甫曾在少陵附近居住过，故自称"少陵野老"。因当时的长安是在叛军的控制之下，其"吞声"和"潜行"都有不敢声张之意，所以，此"曲"必是曲江的偏僻之处，即"**deserted place**"（空寂无人的所在）。**例 10**"***曲***能有诚"：老子讲"曲则全"，用曲，用曲线容易完成一个圆圈到达圆满。把转一个弯，最后还是直道，到达这个诚。就是方法问题。译文“**Being devoted to some specific aspects**”含有此“曲”之意。

丿

“丿”向左拉长的样子。例字皆非形声字。

川：象形字。

1. 嗟乎！镜非辞照，真性在不照之间；***川***无舍流，静因有不流之体。然则屡照足以疲镜，长流足以损***川***，推移之际，微乎其难测也。

《秋醒词序》（清）王闿运

The thought comes to me that the essence of a mirror, while permitting reflections, is independent of them, and that of a ***river***, while it flows continuously, is something which stays in its place. But the continuous reflections and the continuous flow do something to the mirror and the ***river*** respectively, although the changes in the course of time are hardly perceptible at the moment. [19]

"Preface to Autumn Awake Poems"
(The Qing Dynasty) Wang Kaiyun

2. 百***川***东到海，	A hundred ***streams*** flow eastwards to the sea.
何时复西归！	When to return to the west can they be free?
少壮不努力，	If one does not make good use of his youth,
老大徒伤悲。	In vain will he pass his old age in ruth. [21]
《长歌行》	"A Slow Song"
（汉）	(The Han Dynasty)

3. 远游越山***川***，	I got far across hill and ***rill***;
山川修且广。	Mountains and streams stretch far and wide.
振策陟崇丘，	I whip my horse to climb the hill;
安辔遵平莽。	I rein up along countryside. [21]
《赴洛道中作二首（其二）》	"On My Way to Luoyang (II) "
（西晋）陆机	(The Western Jin Dynasty) Lu Ji

以上3例“川”的译文分别为 river、stream 和 rill。这三个英文“川”的不同在于：A river is a large stream of water that discharges into the ocean, a lake or another stream. A rill is a tiny stream. 在用法上，Stream and river can be used figuratively and literally. They may refer to a continuous flow of anything, as well as to a flow of water. 故此，用于说理，**例1**之“川”译为“**river**”与原文意思更为贴切。**例2**之“川”是“百川”Stream is the most general word in the group。**例3**“远游

越山**川**”中此“山”的译文“hill”是小山，与其相对的“川”，译为“**rill**”（小川）即含原文之意。此外，hill→rill押韵。

千：会意字。“千”，十个百，由“十”、由“人”（小篆体的“白”字由“人”字包含着“二”字构成；“百”，十个十，十个百为一贯。）会意[9]。

1. 凡物莫不有死，草木鸟兽昆虫，有朝生而暮死者，有春夏生而秋冬死者，有十年百年**千**年而死者，虽有迟速，相去曾几何时？

《自立说》（清）张士元

All things in this universe die. Among the plants, birds, beasts, and insects, some are born in the morning and die at eve, some have a life span of a year, and some last ten, or hundred, or a ***thousand*** years. But they all die . The difference is merely one of length of time. [19]

“Thought on Self-Reliance”（The Qing Dynasty）Zhang Shihyuan

2. 爆竹声声一岁除，
春风送暖入屠苏。
千门万户曈曈日，
总把新桃换旧符。

The sound of firecrackers ushers in a new spring,
People in the warm wind drink the wine they themselves brew.
Thousands of families are bathed in the sun rising,
They always change the old peach wood charms for the new. [17]

《元日》
（宋）王安石

“First Day of the First LunarMonth”
（The Song Dynasty）Wang Anshi

3. **千**山鸟飞绝，
万径人踪灭。
孤舟蓑笠翁，
独钓寒江雪。

A hundred mountains and no bird,
A thousand paths without a footprint;
A little boat, a bamboo cloak,
An old man fishing in the cold river-snow[27].

《江雪》
（唐）柳宗元

“River Snow”
（The Tang Dynasty）Liu Zongyuan

4. 一节复一节，
千枝攒万叶；
我自不开花，
免撩蜂与蝶。

I'm made up of one section on another,
On ***lots*** of my branches countless leaves cluster.
I never bloom by nature, as you see,
To attract no butterfly and no bee. [17]

《竹》
（清）郑板桥

“Bamboo”
（The Qing Dynasty）Zheng Banqiao

5. 遥看一处攒云树，　Looking afar he sees a stretch of mist-covered trees,
近入**千**家散花竹。　Walking near he sees ***many*** houses scatter in the bamboos and flowers. [13]

《桃源行》　"Song of the Peach-Flower Land"
（唐）王维　(The Tang Dynasty) Wang Wei

6. 万事可忘记，难忘者名心一段；**千**般易读，未读者美酒三杯。

《幽梦影》（节录）（清）张潮

One can forget everything except the thought of fame, and learn to be cool toward ***everything*** except three cups of wine. [19]

"Quiet Dream Shadows" (Human Life)
(The Qing Dynasty) Zhang Chao

7. 假使梦能自主，虽**千**里无难命驾，可不羡长房之缩地；…… 五岳可以卧游，可不俟婚嫁之尽毕。

《幽梦影》（节录）（清）张潮

That one might control one's dreams! Then one could go ***anywhere*** one likes, ... and set out on a world trip without waiting for the sons and daughters to be married off first.

"Quiet Dream Shadows" (Human Life)
(The Qing Dynasty) Zhang Chao

在以上的7例中，**例1**、**例2**中之"千"的译文为"**thousand（s）**"，保留了原文中的"千"，是谓直译。**例3**之"千"在译文中为"**a hundred**"，改动了原文中的数字，是为改译。**例4～例7**中，"千"的译文分别为"**lots**"、"**many**"、"**everything**"和"**anywhere**"，舍弃了数字，为意译。

【译法点滴】　数字语义的模糊性及其翻译：直译、改译、意译

在民间语言和文学作品中，数字往往只是一个泛化的虚数，通常与修辞中的"比喻"、"夸张"有关，不表示确切的数量概念，如"万古流芳"，"千里送鹅毛"等等。在特定的语境中，模糊数字的语义外延，给人以更大的思索和想象空间，使译者能够更进一步的发挥和进行再创造。

汉语和英语中用得较多的数字分别是"十"、"千"、"万"和"ten"、"thousand"、"million"。汉语中较常用的"万"，在英语中却用得较少，"万"的译文往往是"thousands"或"ten thousand"，如：1. "仍怜故乡水，**万**里送行舟"（李白，"渡荆门送别"）的译文：I shall love the waters from my hometown, which carry my ship for ***ten thousand*** li and on. [13]；2. "雨中春树**万**人家"（王维，"奉和圣制从蓬莱向兴庆阁道中留春雨中春望之作应制"）的译文：In the rain the green trees and ***thousands*** of houses are scattered about[13]；3. “**万**里云罗一雁飞”（李商隐，“春雨”）的译文：Oh，just turn to the wild goose flying in the ***ten-thousand***-li clouds of whorl.[13]

翻译时，以民族性、通俗性及形象性为基本原则，根据对上下文语境的理解，可采用直译（保留数字）、改译（变动数字）和意译（舍弃数字）的方法，如上面七例“千”的译文所示。

久：象形字，意为“从后面支拒着”，像人的两腿后面有抵拒的东西[9]。

1. 天地之道，博也，厚也，高也，明也，悠也，**久**也。

《中庸》（战国）子思

The way of Heaven and Earth is broad，rich，lofty，brilliant，far-reaching and ***permanent***.[23]

"Doctrine of the Mean"

(The Warring States Period) Zi Si

2. 立分**久**暂，暂可无倚，久当思傍。亭亭独立之事，但可偶一为之，旦旦如是，则筋骨皆悬而脚跟如砥，有血脉胶凝之患矣。

《随时即景就事行乐之法》（节录）（清）李渔

Stand straight，but do not do it ***for long***. Otherwise，all leg muscles will become stiff and circulation will be blocked up.[19]

"The Arts of Sleeping，Walking，Sitting and Standing"（The Qing Dynasty）Li Yu

3. 春未绿，鬓先丝，	Spring is not yet green，
人间别**久**不成悲。	My hair gray has been；
谁叫岁岁红莲夜，	***Long*** absence should have worn out our grief clean，
两处沉吟各自知。	Then why are we made each in silence to cry
	When the yearly Lantern Festival draws night?[17]

《鹧鸪天·元夕有所梦》

Tune：The Partridge Sky，"A Dream on the Eve of the Lantern Festival"

（宋）姜夔　　(The Song Dynasty) Jiang Kui

丹：象形字。像采丹井，一像朱砂的形，故引申为“红色”。

1. 门人黄章甫索书，余因戏为评古次第云：“晋、唐墨迹第一，五代、宋图画第二，隋、唐、宋古帖第三，苏、黄、蔡、米手迹第四，……汉、秦以前彝鼎***丹***翠焕发着第十一，……

《紫桃轩杂缀》（节录）（明）李日华

My disciple Huang Changfu asked me for a handwritten script，and I wrote the following grading of antiques in their order of value：

1. Calligraphy of Chin and Tang.
2. Paintings of Wutai and Earlier Song.
3. Ancient rubbings (prints from inscriptions) of Sui, Tang, and Song.
4. Calligraphy of Su Tango, Huang Tighten, Mi Fey, and Tsai Shying ....

11. Bronze vessels before Han and Tsin, with brilliant greens and ***reds*** .... [19]

"From Purple Peach Hall Miscellany" (The Ming Dynasty) Li Rihua

2. 青天有月来几时，	When did the moon first come to be?
我今停杯一问之。	Just now I've set my wine aside to ask.
人攀明月不可得，	Unreached by anyone, accompanying everyone,
月行却与人相随。	A flying mirror brightness over ***crimson*** palace gates,
皎如飞镜临**丹**阙，	Her purest light shines forth when azure mists have been dispersed. [2]
绿烟灭尽清辉发。	How is it that what disappears in clouds at dawn.
但见宵从海上来，	Is seen arising only over the sea at dusk? [2]
宁知晓向云间没。	
《把酒问月》	"Inquiring of the Moon, Winecup in Hand"
（唐）李白	(The Tang Dynasty) Li Bai

例 2 之"丹"修饰"阙"（帝王所居之所），皇宫围墙朱红色（深红）为多，故译为"**crimson**"。

丘：象形字。

1. 有地上之山水，有画上之山水，有梦中之山水，有胸中之山水。地上者，妙在**丘**壑深邃；画上者，妙在笔墨淋漓；梦中者，妙在景象变幻；胸中者，妙在位置自如。

《幽梦影》（节录）（清）张潮

There are hills and waters on the earth, in paintings, in dreams, and in one's imagination. The beauty of such ***hills*** and waters on the earth is in their grace and variety; that in paintings, richness of ink and freedom of the brush; that in dreams, their changefulness; and that in one's imagination, good composition. [19]

"Quiet Dream Shadows" (Human Life)
(The Qing Dynasty) Zhang Chao

2. 贤愚千载知是谁，Who was right when right and wrong through the ages are

	mixed toghther?
满眼蓬蒿共一***丘***。	They all had to sink into ***graves*** covered with wormwood all over. [17]
《清明》	"Qing Ming"
（宋）黄庭坚	(The Song Dynasty) Huang Tingjian

例 2 的题目"清明"已点明此诗的内容与祭扫有关。作者眼中所见皆荒坟野草。"共一***丘***"即无论谁，其下场都是："荒冢一堆草没了"。所以，诗的上下文语境很清楚地显示出此处之"丘"乃"坟墓"，非"山丘"，其译文为"**graves**"即原文之意。

秉：会意字。从小篆体的"秉"可以看出，由"又"（手）持握着"禾"表意。

1. 关公大义，二嫂同居；***秉***烛达旦，终夜观书。

《关公秉烛》（三国）

As the incarnation of justice, Guan Yu camp overnight in order to protect the safety of his brother's wife, ***holding*** candles in the night guard at the barracks of Cao.

"Guan Gong Holding Candle" (Three Kingdoms Period)

2. 宿昔***秉***良弓，	Since then he's learned to ***draw*** the strongest bow
楛矢何参差。	And shoot arrows of hard wood high and low.
控弦破左的，	He bends the string and hits the target at left,
右发摧月氏。	And at destroying that at right he's deft. [21]
《白马篇》	"Song of the White Horse"
（三国）曹植	(Three Kindoms Period) Cao Zhi

3. 古人***秉***烛夜游，良有以也。

《春夜宴桃李园序》（唐）李白

The ancients made nocturnal promenades ***by*** candle light ——it was only too sensible!

"A Spring Night Feast in the Peach-Plum Garden" (The Tang Dynasty) Li Bai

4. "《诗》：'天生蒸民，有物有则。民之***秉***彝，好是铭德。'孔子曰：'为此诗者，其知道乎！故有物必有则；民之***秉***彝也，故好是铭德。'"

《孟子》

"The Book of Poetry says: 'Heaven lets there be men, and lets each thing have its rule. Men ***uphold*** regular rules, so they incline to moral goodness,' Confucius said, 'The composer of this poem knew indeed the way of things! To one thing there ought to be one rule attached, and when men ***uphold*** the rules, they will incline to moral goodness.' "[24] 《Mencius》

"秉"之意为（1）拿着，握着；（2）掌握，主持。**例 1** "***秉***烛"之"秉"即拿着，译文"**holding**"（having sth in the hand）所表达的即是此"秉"之意。现在分词的使用表示伴随情况，乃分析性思维的体现。**例 2** "秉"之译文"**draw**"为意译。根据上下文所示：此处之"秉"非"拿着"或"握着"，而是"拉"弓放箭 —"楛矢何参差"、"控弦"、"右发"皆是放箭之举。**例** 3 译文中的谓语动词是"made"，出于对译文句子结构的考虑，"秉"需从原文的动词转换为译文中的介词"**by**"，以符合译语的语言规范。**例 4** 中"***秉***彝"之意是"持执常道"。"秉"意"执"；"彝"意"法度，常规"。据"秉"此处之意，译为"**uphold**"（to support sth that you think is right, fair, etc. and make sure that it continues to exist）。

后（後）： 会意字，由"彳、幺、夂（古文终字）"会意，其意为"走在后面，落在后面"。

前不见古人，	Before me, unseen are the ancients,
后不见来者。	***Behind*** me, unseen those to come.
念天地之悠悠，	Thinking of this infinite universe
独怆然而涕下。	Alone, in my sorrow, I shed tears.[2]
《登幽州台歌》	"Upon Ascending the Parapet at Youzhou"
（唐）陈子昂	(The Tang Dynasty) Chen Ziang

由于英、汉民族对于时间坐标不同的思维方式（中国人是面向着过去来区分时间的先后，英美人是面向着未来来区分时间的先后），因此，在时间先后的表达上表现出了一定的差异：汉语用"前"指过去，用"后"指未来，而英语中用"back"指过去的时间，用"forward"指未来的时间。原文诗中第一句"前不见古人"之"前"指的是过去，译文通过"before"来指过去而没有造成误解，在于"the ancients"；第二句"**后**不见来者"的译文"behind"指的是"未来"，在于后面的"those to come"。

【译法点滴】 顺向思维与逆向思维

由于民族的不同，其观察某些事物或现象的角度及思维方式也不同，由此构成了我们所谓的"顺向思维"与"逆向思维"。在语言上的表现可能是使用不同、甚至相反的形式来描述同一事物或现象。如在方位词的表达上，汉语习惯的顺序是"东西南北/东南西北"，而英语则是"north, south, east, and west"（人们认知策略的不同：汉、英语都是以东西为基点，不同的是说汉语的人认知过程一般是参照点先于目标，而说英语的人一般是目标先于参照点。汉语的"东西南北/东南西北”的方位表达习惯都是将“东”置于首位，反映出参照点先于目标的规律。）。在时间的先后上，中国人是面向着过去来区分时间的先后，所以汉语用“前”指过去，用“后”指未来，而英美人是面向着未来来区分时间的先后，因此英语中用“back”指过去，用“forward”指未来。在实际付款的比例上也表现出不同的视角倾向：汉语着眼于打折后；英语则着眼于所打的折扣。汉语中的“九折”，英语则用“ten percent discount”来表达，两者视角完全相反。凡此种种，皆源于不同的思维着眼点，因此，在翻译的过程中，务必要考虑到英语的表达习惯，不要造成误解。

咬定青山不放松，	Upright stands the bamboo amid green mountains steep,
立根原在破岩中。	Its toothlike root in broken rock is planted deep.
千磨万击还坚劲，	It's strong and firm though struck and beaten without rest,
任尔东西南北风。	Careless of the wind from north or south; east or west.[21]
《竹石》	“Bamboo in the Rocks”
（清）郑燮	(The Qing Dynasty) Zheng Xie

原文“东西南北”体现出汉语的表达习惯。根据英美人在方位上的思维习惯，其译文则为 north or south; east or west。

二、二画

亻

用“亻”构成的字多与人的类别、品德、动作、行为等有关。例字中除“***休***、***众***、***信***、***仰***”外，余者皆为形声字，由左形右声构成。

催

葡萄美酒夜光杯，	They are about to drink
欲饮琵琶马上**催**。	The finest wine from Evening Radiance cups,
醉卧沙场君莫笑，	When the sudden sounding of the pipa ***urges*** them forth.
	Don't scorn them,
古来征战几人回。	They who drunken fall upon the battlefield:
	In ancient days or now, how many return who go to war?[2]
《凉州词》	“Liangzhou Lines”
（唐）王翰	(The Tang Dynasty) Wang Han

偎

游女带花**偎**伴笑，	Perfumed maidens ***leaning*** on each other make fun,

争窈窕，	Vying to be the fairest one,
竞折团荷遮晚照。	They take round lotus leaves to shun The setting sun. [1]
《南乡子》	Tune: Song of a Southern Country
（唐）李珣	(The Tang Dynasty) Li Xun

倦

天涯***倦***客，	A ***tired*** wanderer far from home
山中归路，	Vainly through mountains and hills may roam,
望断故园心眼。	His native land from view is gone. [1]
《永遇乐》	Tune: Joy of Eternal Union
（宋）苏轼	(The Song Dynasty) Su Shi

何

1. 山中***何***事？	***What*** can I do in the mountain?
松花酿酒，	With leaves of pine
春水煎茶。	I'll brew my tea with vernal water from the fountain. [5]
《人月圆·山中书事》	Tune: Men and Moon, "Written in the Mountain"
（元）张可久	Zhang Kejiu

2. 透疏帘风摇杨柳阴，	On window screen the breeze sways shadows of willow trees;
泻长空月转梧桐影。	In wide sky the moon round casts plane's shade on the ground.
冷雕盘香销金兽火，	On chiseled plate of gold incense is burned and cold;
咽铜龙漏滴玉壶冰。	The bronze dragon sobs when icy waterclock throbs.
何处银筝？	From ***where*** comes the zither song? [5]
《一枝花·秋夜闻筝》	Tune: A Spring of Flowers, "The Zither Heard on an Autumn Night"
（元）班惟志	(The Yuan Dynasty) Ban Weizhi

3. 今有人，日攘邻人之鸡者。
或告之曰："是非君子之道。"
曰："请损之，月攘一鸡。以待来年，然后已。"
如知其非义，斯速已矣，***何***待来年？

《孟子》

There was a man who used to steal a chicken from his neighbors every day.

"It is wrong to steal," someone told him.

"I'll cut down on it," promised the chicken thief. "I shall steal one chicken a month from now on, and stop altogether next year."

Since he knew he was wrong, he ought to have stopped at once. ***Why*** wait for another year?[14]

"Mencius"

以上 3 例之"何"的译文"**what**，**where**，**why**"分别取决于其后所修饰的"事、处、待"。

僮仆

乱山残雪夜，	At night when the remnant snow covers the hills and the mountains here and there,
孤独异乡人。	By a solitary candle sit I, a man from a land elsewhere.
渐与骨肉远，	I'm away from my kinsfolk farther and farther,
转於**僮仆**亲。	So to my ***houseboy*** I've become closer and closer.[13]
《除夜有怀》	"Thoughts on a New Year's Eve"
（唐）崔涂	(The Tang Dynasty) Cui Tu

侠

从来幽并客，	From the ancient times, the frontier guards from You and Bing prefectures,
皆共沙尘老。	Have remained on the battle-fields till their old age approaches.
莫学游**侠**儿，	You people never imitate the ***knight***-hood,
矜夸紫骝好。	Who boast of their horses good.[13]
《塞上曲》	"Song of the Frontiers"
（唐）王昌龄	(The Tang Dynasty) Wang Changling

此处"**knight**"为"侠"的引申义。

伪

恋爱人人都会，可不见得人人都懂，世俗大半以性欲**伪**充恋爱，以游戏的态度处置恋爱，于是我们时刻可以看到因恋爱而不幸的记载。

实在的恋爱绝不是游戏，也绝不是堕落的人生所能体验出其价值的，它具有引人向上的鞭策力，它也具有伟大无私的至上情操，它更是美丽的象征。

《恋爱不是游戏》庐隐

Though people love by instinct, yet all cannot understand it correctly. More often than not, love is but carnal desire in ***disguise*** and is treated as a mere game. That is why we so often hear tragic stories of love.

True love is not a game. Nor can its true value be appreciated by the morally degenerate. True love spurs one on to higher attainment. It embodies the supreme quality of selflessness, and is, above all, symbolic of beauty. [15]

"Love Is Not a Game" Lu Yin

"伪"之意为"诈"、"假装"，动词。译文中转换为名词，在于对原文内容的分析。原文中，"性欲**伪**充恋爱"，也可以理解为"恋爱是改头换面的性欲"。根据理解之意，"恋爱"是句中主语，"是"为系词，其余部分是表语。"改头换面"之意含在"伪"意之中，用作定语，因此，需转换其词性，才可与 in 构成介词短语，以 in **disguise** 的形式作为定语，以符合英语的语言规范。

休：会意字，由"人"傍着"木"会意[9]。

1. 名岂文章著，　How is it that I'm famous for my compositions?
官因老病**休**。　***Out of office***, old and sick…. [2]
《旅夜书怀》　"Night Thoughts on a Journey"
（唐）杜甫　（The Tang Dynasty）Du Fu

2. 多少事，　I've much to say, yet ***pause*** as soon as I begin.
欲说还**休**。　Recently I've grown thin,
新来瘦，　Not that I'm sick with wine,
非干病酒，　Not that for autumn sad I pine. [1]
不是悲秋。
《凤凰台上忆吹箫》　Tune: Playing Flute Recalled on Phoenix Terrace
（宋）李清照　（The Song Dynasty）Li Qingzhao

例 1 "休"之译文"**Out of office**"为意译。"office"之意除"办公室"外，还具有"官"的含义：一般来讲，坐办公室的大多是文职人员，所以往往含有当官的意思。

众：会意字，三人为众。

蛾儿雪柳黄金缕，　In gold-thread dress, with moth or willow ornaments,
笑语盈盈暗香去。　Giggling, they melt into the throng with trails of scents.
众里寻他千百度，　But in the ***crowd*** once and again
蓦然回首，　I look for her in vain.

那人却在，	When all at once I turn my head,
灯火阑珊处。	I find her there where lantern light is dimly shed.
《青玉案·元夕》	Tune: Green Jade Cup, "Lantern Festival"
（宋）辛弃疾	(The Song Dynasty) Xin Qiji

信：会意字。"人言为信"，"信"由"人"字和"言"字构成，表示人说的话有信用。

1. 露重飞难进，	Your progress through the heavy dew is slow;
风多響易沉。	Your voice the loud wind drowns:
无人**信**高洁，	When none ***believe*** in high integrity,
为谁表予心。	Who else could sing my soul?
《在狱咏蝉》	"To the Cicada, Composed in Prison"
（唐）骆宾王	(The Tang Dynasty) Luo Binwang

2. 大道之行，天下为公，选贤与能，讲**信**修睦。

《大道之行也》（春秋）孔子

The grand ideal, as realized in the remote antiquity, consists in creating a commonwealth for all, in which the sage and able are elected for office, ***faith*** is promoted and harmony between men fostered. [12]

" The Grand Ideal" (The Spring and Autumn Period) Confucius

例1"信"之意"相信"，动词，故译为"**believe**"。**例2**之"信"意"信义"，名词，因此其译文取"**faith**"。**例2**之原文与译文体现出主、客体思维方式的不同：原文的主动语态"讲信"在译文中则以被动语态的形式出现"…faith is promoted…"。

仰、俯、信、俯仰

仰：会意字，由"人"、由"卬"会意[9]。人昂着头，脸向上，即为"仰"。

是日也，天朗气清，惠风和畅。***仰***观宇宙之大，***俯***察品类之盛，所以游目骋怀，是以极视听之娱，***信***可乐也。……

及其所之既倦，情随事迁。感慨系之已。向之所欣，***俯仰***之间，已为陈迹，犹不能不以之兴怀；况修短随化，终期于尽。

《兰亭集序》（东晋）王羲之

That day the sky was serene, the air bracing and the wind benign. Looking ***up***, we perceived the immensity of the universe and, looking ***down***, we observed the great multiplicity of nature's species, thus broadening our view, giving the reins to our minds, and feasting our eyes and ears to the full. It was ***indeed*** a great happiness. …

But when they are tired of what they pursue as their feels change with circumstances, then they are filled with melancholy. The things which they used to court with a gay heart become stale ***in an instant***, but not without stirring up their sentiments. Besides, their spans of life, be they long or short, are decided by Providence and converge eventually to a common finish. [12]

"Preface to the Lanting Collecting"

(The Eastern Jin Dynasty) Wang Xizhi

原文中的"***仰***、***俯***"为动词，由于这里此二字都与"看"之意相关（观、察），为符合译语表达习惯，修饰译文中的"looking"，则需转换为副词"**up**"和"**down**"。"***信***"为副词，直译为"**indeed**"。"***俯仰***"本意为"低头和抬头"，泛指一举一动，比喻很短的时间，故译为"**in an instant**"。

讠

"***讠***"即"言"。用"讠"组合的字与说话有关。例字中除"***言***、***话***"外，其余为形声字：左形右声。

评

梅雪争春未肯降，
骚人搁笔费***评***章。
梅须逊雪三分白，
雪却输梅一段香。
《雪梅》
（宋）卢梅坡

Winter plums and snow vie for spring tints with each other,
Poets find it hard to be ***judges*** in this matter.
Although the former is not so white as the latter,
Yet the latter is not so fragrant as the former. [17]

"White Plum and Snow"

(The Song Dynasty) Lu Meipo

讽

昔楚襄王从宋玉、景差于兰台之宫，有风飒然而至，王披襟挡之，曰："快哉此风！寡人所与庶人共者也？"宋玉曰："此独大王之雄风耳，庶人安得共之！"玉之言盖有***讽***焉。

《黄州快哉亭记》（宋）苏辙

Once King Xiang of Chu stayed in the palace of Lantai in the company of Song Yu and Jingchai, a gust of wind came rustling over and the King spread his cloak against it, saying, "How bracing the wind is! Is this shared by us and the common people?" Song Yu replied, "This is the masculine wind of Your Majesty. How can it be enjoyed by the vulgar herd?" Song's remark had a hint of ***satire***. [12]

"The Huangzhou Ecstasy Arbor" (The Song Dynasty) Su Zhe

详、议

天下之事，闻者不如见者知之为**详**，见者不如居者知之为尽。吾侪未造乎道之堂奥，自藩篱之外而妄**议**之，可乎?

《书巢记》（宋）陆游

Talking of things in this world, those who have heard of something, say a room, cannot be so ***much informed*** about it than those who have seen it, and the latter, in a lesser degree, than those who have lived in it. If I and my like have not grasped the essentials of a thing and ***argue*** irrelevantly over it outside the hedge, will it do?[12]

"The Nest Built of Books" (The Song Dynasty) Lu You

译文"**argue**"（to give reasons why you think that sth is right/wrong, true/not true, etc.）含有原文中"议"之意:"评议；评说"。

诚

臣亮言：先帝创业未半，而中道崩殂。今天下三分，益州疲弊，此**诚**危急存亡之秋也。然侍卫之臣不懈于内，忠志之士忘身于外者，盖追先帝之殊遇，预报之于陛下也。诚宜开张圣听，以光先帝遗德，恢弘志士之气；不宜妄自菲薄，以塞忠谏之路也。

《前出师表》（汉）诸葛亮

Your humble subject Zhuge Liang has these to say: The late Emperor had by far not yet attained his objective of restoring the Han Dynasty before he deceased halfway in his career. Now the country is divided into three camps, and Yizhou has exhausted its resources. It is ***indeed*** a critical moment when survival is at stake. However, the royal guards keep vigilant at court while the loyal soldiers with high aim fight selflessly on the battlefields, because they bear in mind the late Emperor's special grace, wishing to repay it to Your Majesty. It would be most judicious that you give more open-minded hearing to your counselors, so as to aggrandize his legacy of noble virtues and heighten the army men's morale. In the meantime, it would be inadvisable to strain your modesty or make inapt remarks, thus blocking faithful remonstrances.[12]

"Memorial to the Emperor Before the Northern Expedition"
(The Han Dynasty) Zhuge Liang

询、说

博***询***众庶，则才能者进矣；不有忌讳，则***说***直之路开矣；不迩小人，则谗谀者自远矣；不拘文迂俗，则守职者辨治矣；不责人以细过，则能吏之志得以尽其效矣。

《兴贤》（宋）王安石

Inquire among the masses and talents will be found; if there are no taboos, the passages for ***honest*** advice will be open; if there is no pampering of snobs or sycophants, then they will not approach; if there is no literary restrictions and conventional scruples, then people on duty will have lucid judgment in fulfilling their responsibilities; if there are no punishments for lapses, then able officials will be able to give their full play. [8]

"Advocacy of Talents" (The Song Dynasty) Wang Anshi

话：会意字，由"言"、由"舌"会意。

开轩面场圃，	Opening the window we face a threshing ground and a vegetable garden,
把酒**话**桑麻。	Then we ***talk*** about farming o'er cups of wine. [13]
《过故人庄》	"Visiting an Old Friend's Village"
（唐）孟浩然	(The Tang Dynasty) Meng Haoran

诵、话：话，会意字。

有贵人游僧舍，酒甜，**诵**唐人诗云："因过竹院逢僧**话**，又得浮生半日闲。"僧闻而笑之。贵人问僧何笑？僧曰："尊官得半日闲，老僧却忙了三日。"

《谭概》（明）冯梦龙

A high official paid a visit to a monastery. The monk in charge, having been notified of this previously, had made meticulous preparations for this occasion. After several drinks, the official ***recited*** a Tang poem:

Passing by the monastery I drop in to ***have a chat*** *with the monk*;

Out of this busy life a moment of idleness I enjoy.

The monk laughed. When asked why he laughed, he replied, "Your Worship has enjoyed a moment of idleness, but I've been busy for three days." [14]

"Tan Gai" (The Ming Dynasty) Feng Menglong

言：象形兼形声（形声为下形上声）。

杨子之邻人亡羊。即率其党，又请杨子之竖追之。……

既反。问："获羊乎?"曰："亡之矣。"……

杨子戚然变容，不言者移时，不笑者竟日。

门人怪之，请曰："羊，贱畜，又非夫子之有，而损**言**笑者何哉？"

《列子》（战国）列子

One of Yang Zi's neighbors, who lost a sheep, sent all his men out to find it, and asked Yang Zi's servant to join in the search.

When his servant returned, Yang Zi asked him: "Well, did you find the sheep?"

He answered that they had not. …

At that Yang looked very thoughtful. He was silent for a long time, and did not smile all day.

His pupils were surprised.

"A sheep is a trifle," they said, "and this wasn't even yours. Why should you stop ***talking*** and smiling?"[14]

"Lie Zi" (The Warring States Period) Lie Zi

刂（刀）

用"**刀**"组合的字，多与刀或用刀的行为及结果有关。例字中除"**制**、**剥**、**删**"外，其他为形声字：右形左声。

割：从"害"声。古代"害"又同"曷"。

将军金甲夜不脱，	As all the warriors do, generals, too, spend the whole night with their iron armors on,
半夜军行戈相拨，	Only the sound of the spears striking the lances is heard at midnight when the troops march along,
风头如刀面如**割**。	And the men's faces are ***cut*** by the knife-like wind biting.[13]

《走马川行奉送封大夫出师西征》

"Song of Zouma River for Seeing Off Senior Feng on His Expedition to the West"

（唐）岑参　　(The Tang Dynasty) Cen Shen

剑（劍）

1. 醉里挑灯看**剑**，	Drunken, I lit my lamp to see my ***glaive***;
梦回吹角连营。	Awake, I heard the horns from tents to tents.
八百里分麾下炙，	Under the flags, beef grilled
五十弦翻塞外声，	Was eaten by our warriors brave
沙场秋点兵。	And martial airs were played by fifty instruments:
	'T was an autumn manoeuvre in the field.[1]

《破阵子 · 为陈同甫赋壮词以寄》

Tune: Dance of the Cavalry, "Written for Chen Liang"

（宋）辛弃疾 (The Song Dynasty) Xin Qiji

2. 十年书***剑***长吁， I sigh after ten years with books and ***sword***.
一曲琵琶按许。 The lutist's song is a promise without word.
月明江上别湓浦， I leave the river town when the moon shines bright,
愁听兰舟夜雨。 Afraid to hear rain in orchid boat at night.[5]

《醉高歌 · 感怀》 Tune: Drinking Song, "Reflection"

（元）姚燧 (The Yuan Dynasty) Yao Sui

此两例之“剑”均为直译。根据其所在诗句，**例 1**“挑灯看***剑***”之剑既然值得作者挑灯来看，一般来讲，此剑可能非同寻常，其译文取“**glaive**”[（古）剑，阔剑]，此其一；其二在于对押韵的考虑：glaive→brave。**例 2** 即指一般之剑，故译为“**sword**”。

剜、剔

剜苔***剔***藓露节角， We'll ***scoop*** out the moss and lichen on the stone drums so that the strokes of the characters will be clearly found,
安置妥帖平不颇。 And we'll place them securely and evenly on the ground.[13]

《石鼓歌》 "Song of Stone Drums"

（唐）韩愈 (The Tang Dynasty) Han Yu

刚

1. 君子宜净拭冷眼，慎勿轻动***刚***肠。

《菜根谭》（明）洪应明

It is better for an accomplished man to observe the world with cool detachment and show his ***uprightness*** with deliberation.[6]

"The Roots of Wisdom" (The Ming Dynasty) Hong Yingming

2. 居盈满者，如水之将溢未溢，切忌再加一滴；处危急者，如木之将折未折，切忌再加一搦。

“过满则溢　过***刚***即折”《菜根谭》（明）洪应明

A man at the height of power and splendor is like a vat fully filled with water which is about to spill. Do not add another drop in it. A man in a desperate situation is like a piece of heavily weighted wood which is about to snap. Do not put pressure on it any more.[6]

"Overfullness begets spillage and over '***rigidness***' induces fracture."
"The Roots of Wisdom"
(The Ming Dynasty) Hong Yingming

此两例之"***刚***"为形容词，其意："硬；坚强"（跟"柔"相对）。作为译文句中的宾语，皆需通过词形变化（词尾+ness）转变为名词。**例 1** 中"***刚***肠"之"肠"指"心思、情怀"，往往借指人的性情，译文选取"**uprightness**"［upright：(of a person) behaving in a moral and honest way］意指人的正直。**例 2** 中"刚"之译文"**rigidness**"（rigid：stiff and difficult to move or bend）即原文之"刚"意。

制：会意字，由"刀"、由"未"会意[9]。"未"（'制'的左半部）代表六月，这时树木老成，有滋味，可以裁断。

薄暮空潭曲，	At dusk I come to a meandering, limpid and deep pool, where,
安禅***制***毒龙。	In order to ***tame*** the vicious dragon in their minds, the monks are lost in Buddhist meditation there.[13]
《过香积寺》	"Visiting the Xiangji Temple"
（唐）王维	(The Tang Dynasty) Wang Wei

剥：会意字，由"刀"、由"录"会意。"录"表示"刻"、"割"[9]。

大儿锄豆溪东，	East of the brook their eldest son is hoeing weeds;
中儿正织鸡笼；	Their second son now makes a cage for hens he feeds.
最喜小儿无赖，	I like their youngest son who, having nothing done,
溪头卧***剥***莲蓬。	Lies by the brook ***podding*** lotus seeds one by one.[1]
《清平乐 · 村居》	Tune: Pure Serene Music, "Rural Life"
（宋）辛弃疾	(The Song Dynasty) Xin Qiji

"***剥***"在原文中为动词，译文中通过词形变化（词尾+ing）转换为现在分词"**podding**"，表示伴随情况，即分析型思维方式的体现。

删：会意字，由"刀"、由"册"会意。"册"表示简牍[9]。用刀刮去简牍上的字，即"删"。

有以文人画士孤僻之隐，明告鬻梅者：斫其正，养其旁条；***删***其密，夭其雅枝；锄其直，遏其生气，以求重价，而江南之梅皆病也。

《病梅馆记》（清）龚自珍

Someone succeeded in making clear to plum florists the secret eccentricity of the literati and painters, urging them to prune erect sprigs, fostering lateral branched, to ***do away with*** dense parts, cutting off tender slips and, in addition to eliminate straight stems, choking their sap and vitality, so as to seek a high price. As a consequence, all the plum trees in Jiangsu and Zhejiang have become sick. [12]

"The Sick Plum Chamber" (The Qing Dynasty) Gong Zizhen

阝

由"***阝***"组合的字一般与比较高平的土地、没有石头的山有关。例字中除"***阳***、***阴***、***陷***"外，其他为形声字：左形右声。

阶

玉***阶***空伫立，	On marble ***steps*** she waits in vain
宿鸟归飞急。	But to see birds fly back again. [1]
《菩萨蛮》	Tune: Buddhist Dancers
（唐）李白	(The Tang Dynasty) Li Bai

陆（陸）

由冉溪西南水行十里，山水之可取者五，莫若钴鉧潭。由溪口而西，***陆***行，可取者八九，莫若西山。由朝阳岩东南水行，至芜江，可取者三，莫若袁家渴。皆永中幽丽奇处也。

《永州八记》（唐）柳宗元

Within ten miles or so down the southwest waterway of the Ran Stream, of the five scenic attractions, Tarn Gumu stands head and shoulders above all. Down the west ***land*** route from the mouth of the stream, of the eight or nine scenic attractions, the Western Hill stands out from the rest. Down the southeast waterway from the Sun Cliff to the Wu River, of three scenic attractions, the Tributary of the Yuans is the best. However, these are all the most secluded, beautiful and anomalous scenic spots in the State of Yong. [8]

"Eight Journals on the State of Yong" (The Tang Dynasty) Liu Zongyuan

隔

1. 重冈已***隔***红尘断，	Hill on hill ***keeps apart*** the vanity fair
村楼更年丰。	From this village of bumper year.

移居就要，	I move house to come near
窗中远岫	The window-unframed distant hill
舍后长松。	And the pine-trees behind the windowsill. [5]

《人月圆 · 卜居外家东园（1）》

Tune: Man and Moon, "Moving to My Mother's East Garden"

（元）元好问　　(The Yuan Dynasty) Yuan Haowen

2. 满城烟水月微茫，	The dimming moon o'er mist-veiled town and water looms.
人依兰舟唱。	The beauty in orchid boat sings her dream.
常记相逢若耶上，	I oft remember our meeting on silk-washing stream.
隔三湘，	Now ***severed*** by three rivers long,
碧云望断空惆怅。	In vain through clouds into the azure sky I gaze. [5]

《小桃红 · 采莲女》　　Tune: Red Peach Blossoms, "The Lotus Gatherer"

（元）杨果　　(The Yuan Dynasty) Yang Guo

3. 从小丘西行百二十步，**隔**篁竹，闻水声，如鸣环佩，心乐之。

《至小丘西小石潭记》（唐）柳宗元

A walk of some one hundred and twenty paces west of the knoll took us to a bamboo grove, ***across*** which we heard the sound of water ringing like silver pendants. [12]

"The Small Tarn West of the Knoll" (The Tang Dynasty) Liu Zongyuan

例 2 之"隔"在原文中是主动形式，但含有潜在被动之意。译文中则将此被动以过去分词（severed）的形式体现出来，此乃汉英不同的思维方式使然。

例 3 中"隔"的词性从原文中的动词转换为译文中的介词"**across**"，乃译文句子结构的要求。

陇

空碛无边，	The boundless desert looked desolate,
万里阳关道路。	Long, long the road to Southern Gate.
马萧萧，	Your horse was heard to neigh,
人去去，	You were seen on your way,
陇云愁。	E'even ***border*** clouds felt sad. [1]

《酒泉子》　　Tune: Fountain of Wine

（唐）孙光宪　　(The Tang Dynasty) Sun Guangxian

"陇"意：（1）指"陇山"，在陕西、甘肃交界的地方；（2）为甘肃的别称。此外，本词的曲牌为“酒泉子”（酒泉属甘肃省），暗含“甘肃”之意。词中“***陇***云愁”之“陇”的译文“**border**”之意为“边界；边疆；边界地区”，基本上涵盖了上述的几个含义，用得较为贴切。

阳、阴：会意字。从“日”、“月”可会意阳与阴。

泰山之***阳***，汶水西流；其***阴***，济水东流。阳谷皆入汶，阴谷皆入济。当其南北分者，古长城也。最高日观峰，在长城南十五里。

《登泰山记》（清）姚鼐

On the ***south side*** of Mount Tai flows westward the River Wen, while on its ***north side*** flows eastward the River Ji. The streams south of the mountain all pour into the former and those north of the mountain all pour into the latter. The dividing line between the north and the south is the Great Wall of ancient times and the highest peak Riguan is situated fifteen *li* south if it.[12]

"Ascent to Mount Tai" (Qing Dynasty) Yao Nai

此例中的“阳”与“阴”分别被意译为“**south side**”和“**north side**”，盖因考虑其位于泰山之南还是之北。

陷：会意字，由“阝”、由“臽”会意[9]。臽：小陷阱。“臽”也表声。

楚有鬻矛与盾者。誉之曰：“吾盾之坚，物莫能陷也。”又誉其矛曰：“吾矛之利，于物无不***陷***也。”

或曰：“以子之矛，***陷***子之盾，何如？”

其人弗能应也。

《韩非子》（战国）韩非

In the state of Chu lived a man who sold shields and spears.

"My shields are so strong," he boasted, "that nothing can pierce them. My spears are so sharp there is noting they cannot ***pierce***."

"What if one of your spears ***strikes*** one of your shields?"

The man had no answer to that.[14]

"Han Fei Zi" (The Warring States Period) Han Fei

例中使用“**pierce**”和“**strike**”来分别对应前后两个“陷”字取决于“矛”和“盾”的作用。

三、三画

彳

“***彳***”构组的字，和行走、道路、脚的动作、趋向有关。例字中除“***徒***、

御”外，其他为形声字：左形右声。

径

杏花开候不曾晴，	Since apricots blooms, the weather drear
败尽游人兴。	Has disappointed the sight-seer.
红雪飞来满芳**径**。	Blooms fall like red snow over the fragrant ***way***.
问春莺，	I ask the oriole where is spring;
春莺无语风方定。	It answers not and the wind dies away. [5]
《小桃红·杂咏》	Tune: Red Peach Blossoms, "Mid-Spring"
（元）盍西村	(The Yuan Dynasty) He Xicun

徜徉

子瞻杖策载酒，乘渔舟，乱流而南。山中有二三子，好客而喜游。闻子瞻至，幅巾迎笑，相携**徜徉**而上。穷山之深，力极而息，扫叶席草，酾酒相劳。意适忘返，往往留宿于山上。

《武昌九曲亭记》（宋）苏辙

Zizhan takes a fishing boat, loads his wine, and carries his walking stick with him to cross the river to the south bank. Knowing that Zizhan has arrived, some scholars from the mountain, who are quite hospitable and also fond of sightseeing, come out to welcome him, smiles on their faces, and kerchiefs around their foreheads. Clasping each other's hands, ***in a carefree mood***, they scale the mountain and penetrate to the deepest possible area until they are exhausted. They then clear a spot and sit down on the grass to drink to each other. Very often they are so immersed in self-indulgence that they forget to return. So they stay there overnight. [8]

"The Pavilion on the Winding Mountain Ranges in Wuchang"

(The Song Dynasty) Su Zhe

例中“**徜徉**”为动词，其意“闲游；安闲自在地步行”。在译文中转换为介词短语“**in a carefree mood**”作为句中谓语动词“scale”的状语，以符合译语的语言规范。

彼

闻古之人有舜者，其为人也，仁义人也。求其所以为舜者，责于己曰：“**彼**，人也；予，人也，彼能是，而我乃不能是！”早夜以思，就其如舜者。

《原毁》（唐）韩愈

Hearing of Shun, an ancient who was kind and righteous, they would seek the reason of his being such and say, "***He*** was a man, and am I. But I cannot do what he could!" And they thought day and night, trying to do away with what was at variance with a man like Shun and to achieve what was in accord with his character. [12]

"On the Origin of Detraction" (The Tang Dynasty) Han Yu

徒：会意字，由“彳”、由“走”会意。

少壮不努力，　And one who mis-spends his youth
老大***徒***伤悲。　In old age will grieve ***in vain***. [4]
《长歌行》　"A Song in Slow Time"
（汉）　(The Han Dynasty)

徐、御：御，会意字，由“彳”、由“卸”会意。徐锴《段注》：“卸，解马车也。彳，行也。或行或御，皆御马者之职也。”[9]

清风***徐***来，水波不兴。举酒属客，诵明月之诗，歌窈窕之章。少焉，月出于东山之上，徘徊于斗牛之间。白露横江，水光接天。纵一苇之所如，凌万顷之茫然。浩浩乎如冯虚***御***风，而不知其所止，飘飘乎如遗世独立，羽化而登仙。

《前赤壁赋》（宋）苏轼

A fresh breeze was ***gently*** blowing our way and the waves were utterly calm. I raised my winecup and toasted my guests, joining them in chanting ***Ode to the Bright Moon*** and ***Song of Sylphs***. A little later, the moon rose above the eastern hills, loitering between the mansions of the Dipper and the Ox. A broad stretch of dewy white lay across the river. The sheen of the waters merged with the hues of the sky. The boat, once set adrift, traversed an immense expanse of water. What an ecstasy! It was as if we were ***harnessing*** the wind, riding through the ethereal vacant space, not knowing when to come to a halt, while the divine joy was as if we were forsaking the world and becoming winged deities, ascending to the land of immortals. [12]

"Boating at the Red Cliff" (The Song Dynasty) Su Shi

原文中“徐”为形容词。“清风***徐***来”之“来”的译文为“blow”，为符合译语语言规范，“徐”则需转换为副词“**gently**”。“***御***风”之“御”意“驾驭”，原文中其本身即含有“进行”之意。译文则采用了“be+现在分词”的形式（**harnessing**）来表达“进行”，体现出综合与分析思维方式的不同。

宀

“宀”意为交相覆盖的深邃的屋子。用“宀”组合的字与房屋有关。例字中除"**安**、**宝**、**容**"外，其他为形声字，上形下声。

家：此处的"豕"从"豭"（jia）音。

1. 烽火连三月，　With turmoil of battle three months on end,
   家书抵万金。　A letter from ***home*** is worth a fortune in gold. [2]
   《春望》　"Spring Perspective"
   （唐）杜甫　（The Tang Dynasty）Du Fu

2. 从今四海为**家**日，　Today the whole country is one ***family***,
   故垒萧萧芦荻秋。　Yet on the old military ruins the autumn reeds still sigh sadly. [13]
   《西塞山怀古》　" Meditating on an Ancient Event at Mount West Fort"
   （唐）刘禹锡　（The Tang Dynasty）Liu Yuxi

3. 烟笼寒水月笼沙，　The cold water of Qinhuai River is shrouded by mist and the sands on its banks are bathed in moonlight,
   夜泊秦淮近酒**家**。　I moor my boat on the Qinhuai River and near a ***tavern*** at night. [13]
   《泊秦淮》　" Mooring My Boat on the Qinhuai River"
   （唐）杜牧　（The Tang Dynasty）Du Mu

4. 四十年来**家**国，　A ***reign*** of forty years
   三千里地山河；　O'er a land of three thousand li,
   凤阁龙楼连霄汉，　My royal palaces touching the celestial spheres,
   玉树琼枝作烟萝。　My shady forest looking like a hazy sea.
   几曾识干戈？　What did I know of shields and spears?
   《破阵子》　Tune：Dance of the Cavalry
   （南唐）李煜　（The Nontang Dynasty）Li Yu

5. 旧时王谢堂前燕，　The swallows that nested in the halls of the nobles Wang and Xie in the old days,
   飞入寻常百姓**家**。　And now flying into the common people's ***hallways***. [13]
   《乌衣巷》　"The Wuyi Alley"
   （唐）刘禹锡　（The Tang Dynasty）Liu Yuxi

语境不同，译文各异。**例 1**"**家**书"之"家"乃指书信所发之处，选"**home**"（the house or flat/apartment that you live in，especially with your family），

着意于“住宅”（作为建筑物的“家”）。**例 2**“如今四海为**家**日”赞美了天下一统的兴旺局面，此“家”意“一家”，译文取“**family**”（a group consisting of one or two parents, their children and close relations）着意于“家庭”。**例 3**“酒**家**”之“家”并非一般概念之“家”，与“酒”搭配，其意为“酒馆”：**tavern**。**例 4** 作者为南唐后主。南唐建国于 937 年，亡于 976 年，享国共 39 年。“四十年来**家**国”之“家”即“国家”之“家”，四十来年为南唐的统治时期，此处“家”的译文选取“**reign**”（the period during which a king, queen, emperor, etc. rules）符合原文之意。**例 5**“堂前燕”飞入“百姓**家**”之“家”与“堂”相对应，故译文选取“**hallways**”。

客

1. 林泉隐居谁到此？	Who'd come to my hermitage amid the trees?
有**客**清风至。	My only ***guest*** is the fresh breeze.
会做山中相，	Living by the fountain,
不管人间事。	I'm minister in the mountain.
争什么半张名利纸？	I do not care for worldly affair.
	Why should I strive to enter the vanity fair?[5]
《清江引·野兴》	Tune: Song of Clear River, "Rural Pleasure"
（元）马致远	(The Yuan Dynasty) Ma Zhiyuan

2. **客**舍并州已十霜，	Ten frosts have come and gone since as a ***stranger*** I first came to Bingzhou,
归心日夜忆咸阳。	Morning, noon, and night my heart's yearned only for Xianyang. [2]
《旅次朔方》	"Heading North Again"
（唐）刘皂	(The Tang Dynasty) Liu Zao

3. 帘外雨潺潺，	The curtain cannot keep out the patter of rain,
春意阑珊。	Springtime is on the wane.
罗衾不耐五更寒。	In the deep of the night my quilt is not cold-proof.
梦里不知身是**客**，	Forgetting I am ***under hospitable roof***,
一晌贪欢。	Still in my dream I seek for pleasures vain.
《浪淘沙》	Tune: Ripples Sifting Sand
（南唐）李煜	(The Nontang Dynasty) Li Yu

4. **客**里看春多草草，	But ***roam alone*** and cannot relish spring,

总被诗愁分了。　Distracted by the sad songs I must sing.[1]

《清平乐》　Tune：Pure Serene Music

（宋）张炎　（The Song Dynasty）Zhang Yan

5. 少孤为**客**早，　Orphaned in boyhood，I ***wandered*** early in a sad state，

多难识君迟。　Disaster-ridden，I got to know you very late.[13]

《送李端》　"Seeing Li Duan Off"

（唐）卢纶　（The Tang Dynasty）Lu Lun

以上5例中"**客**"，除**例1**外，其余皆为意译。**例2**"**客**舍并州已十霜"之意为"外出寄居在并州已十年"。这里"客"即非本地之人，据此意，译为"**stranger**"。**例3**之"客"的译文在于作者李煜之身世：身为宋之俘虏，从曾经贵为一呼万应的皇上沦为阶下囚遭到软禁，此"客"含"身在他人屋檐下"之意，故译为"**under hospitable roof**"。**例4**两句诗所表达的是"流落异乡总是以写诗诉说愁苦，哪有心思细细欣赏春天的光景"。据此"客"的译文为"**roam alone**"（to walk or travel around an area without any definite aim or direction），含意"旅人之情，游子之思，无心细赏，随意走走"。**例5**"少孤为**客**早"之意为"少年丧亲，过早地漂泊异土"。译文"**wandered**"（to walk slowly around or to a place，often without particular sense or direction），体现出身为异乡之客的"漂泊"之感。

富："畐"取"畐（fu）"音。

丹青不知老将至，　You are too devoted to painting to notice your old age approaching，

富贵于我如浮云。　And you regard the ***riches*** and honors as the clouds in the sky floating.[13]

《丹青引赠曹将军霸》　"Song of the Paintings to General Cao Ba"

（唐）杜甫　（The Tang Dynasty）Du Fu

例字"**富**"为形容词。为符合译文语言规范，其词性在译文中转换为名词。

宫：从"躳（gong）"声。

地犹鄹氏邑，　The place is still the Zou people's place，

宅即鲁王**宫**。　The house is still Prince Lu's ***palace***.[13]

《经路祭孔子而叹之》

"Passing the State Lu and Offering a Sacrifice to and Sighing o'er Confucius"

（唐）李隆基　（The Tang Dynasty）Li Longji

宵

巧笑东邻女伴,	My neighbor' s daughter and her friends are sweet,
采桑徑里逢迎。	Mulberry leaves to gather now they meet.
疑怪昨**宵**春梦好,	Last ***night***, she wonders, why such happy dreams?
原是今朝斗草赢,	They foretell that she wins the game of grass, it seems.
笑从双脸生。	A sparkling smile upon her fair face beams. [1]

《破阵子》 Tune: Dance of the Cavalry

(宋) 晏殊 (The Song Dynasty) Yan Shu

寄

有弟皆分散,	I have younger brothers, who scattered here and there,
无家问死生。	So to ask about their life or death I have no where.
寄书长不达,	Often my letters can' t reach my brothers to whom I ***send***,
况乃未休兵。	Moreover the civil war hasn' t come to an end. [13]

《月夜忆舍弟》 "Thinking of My Younger Brothers on a Moonlit Night"

(唐) 杜甫 (The Tang Dynasty) Du Fu

安: 会意字, 由"女"在"宀"下会意。桂馥《义证》引《六书故》"室家之内, 女所安也。"[9]

马上相逢无纸笔,	Meeting you on the horseback I have no paper nor brush to write,
凭君传语报**平安**。	So I can but ask you to give my kinsfolk a message that I' m ***all right***. [13]

《逢入京使》 "Coming Across a Messenger Going to Chang' an"

(唐) 岑参 (The Tang Dynasty) Cen Shen

宝: 会意字, 由"宀"、由"玉"会意[9]。

濯冠沐浴告祭酒,	I washed my hat , took a bath and told the person of the Imperial Academy in charge,
如此至**宝**存岂多?	Saying "Could the number of such priceless ***treasure*** be large?"[13]

《石鼓歌》 "Song of the Stone Drums"

(唐) 韩愈 (The Tang Dynasty) Han Yu

容：会意字，由“宀”、由“谷”会意[9]。

清能有**容**，仁能善断，明不伤察，言不过矫，是谓蜜饯不甜，海味不咸，才是懿德。

《菜根谭》（明）洪应明

To be pure and upright in morality, and yet ***magnanimous*** in bearing; to be kind-hearted and righteous in behavior, and yet acute in judgment; to be clear-sighted in observation, and yet not excessive in demand; to be forthright in character, and yet not aggressive in action—all these are excellent qualities that are esteemed as the doctrine of the mean, saying that the candied fruit should not taste too sweet and seafood not too salty.[6]

"The Roots of Wisdom" (The Ming Dynasty) Hong Yingming

“清能有**容**”的意思是“清廉而有包容一切的雅量”。例字“容”为动词，意“容纳，宽容”。考虑到译文句子的结构，“容”转换为形容词“**magnanimous**”，作系动词“be”的表语。

艹

用“艹”组合的字与草木植物有关。例字中，除“**蕊**、**苗**”外，余者皆为形声字：上形下声。

落

无可奈何花***落***去，	Deeply I sigh for the ***fallen*** flowers in vain;
似曾相识燕归来，	Vaguely I seem to know the swallows come again.
小园香径独徘徊。	Loitering on the garden path, I alone remain.[1]
《浣溪沙》	Tune: Sand of Silk-washing Stream
（宋）晏殊	(The Song Dynasty) Yan Shu

原文中“落”为动词，译文中作定语修饰“flowers”，则需转换为形容词“**fallen**”。

芳

花褪残红青杏小。	Red flowers fade, green apricots still small
燕子飞时，	When swallows pass
绿水人家绕。	Over blue water which surrounds the garden wall.
枝上柳绵吹又少。	Most willow catkins have been blown away, alas!
天涯何处无***芳***草。	But there is no place where grows not the ***sweet*** green grass.[1]

《蝶恋花》　　Tune：Butterflies Lingering over Flowers
（宋）苏轼　　（The Song Dynasty）Su Shi

苔

池上碧**苔**三四点，　We hear, amid the leaves, the orioles sing;
叶底黄鹂一两声，　Besides the pool we see the green ***moss*** spread.
日长飞絮轻。　The willow catkins fly as the day's lengthening. [1]
《破阵子》　　Tune：Dance of the Cavalry
（宋）晏殊　　（The Song Dynasty）Yan Shu

芦

不知何处吹**芦**管，　I know not in what place a ***reed*** pipe is played on,
一夜征人尽望乡。　Which makes the warriors homesick all night long. [13]
《夜上受降城闻笛》　"Ascending the Wall of the Surrender-Accepting Town at Night and Hearing the Sound of Reed Pipe"
（唐）李益　　（The Tang Dynasty）Li Yi

茅

茅亭宿花影，　In the ***thatched*** arbor rests the flower shadow,
药院滋苔纹。　In the medicinal herbs courtyard patches of green moss grow. [13]
《宿王昌龄隐居》　" Staying Overnight in Wang Changling's Hermitage"
（唐）常建　　（The Tang Dynasty）Chang Jian

例字"茅"为名词，在译文中作修饰"亭"的定语，故转换为形容词。客体型思维同时也体现在"**thatched**"的使用上。

荷

干**荷**叶，色苍苍。　***Lotus*** leaves go dry;
老柄风摇荡。　Their green color fades
减了清香，越添黄。On the long stem of age.
都因昨夜一场霜，　Now, they stand and sway.
寂寞在秋江上。　Their fragrance dwindles,
And a brownish tint grows.
Woe, all due to the frost last night
On the lonely river of autumn. [10]

《干荷叶》 "Dried Lotus Leaves"
（元）刘秉忠 (The Yuan Dynasty) Liu Bingzhong

蘋

1. 淑气催黄鸟， The spring warmth makes the orioles sing,
晴光转绿**蘋**。 The warm sunshine makes the clover ***fern*** turn green. [13]
《和晋陵陆丞早春游望》
"In Reply to the Poem Looking Around at the Scenery of Early Spring by County Magistrate Lu in Jingling"
（唐）杜审言 (The Tang Dynasty) Du Shenyan

2. 谁见汀洲上， Who sees on this shoal I stay,
相思愁白**蘋** And sadly fix my eyes on the white ***duckweed*** thinking of You far away. [13]
《饯别王十一南游》
"Giving a Farewell Dinner to Wang the 11th Going on a Tour of the South"
（唐）刘长卿 (The Tang Dynasty) Liu Changqing

蓬

1. 花径不曾缘客扫， The paths amid the flowers are not swept for guests ever,
蓬门今始为君开。 My ***grass*** door for the first time is opened for you today. [13]
《客至》 "The Arrival of a Guest"
（唐）杜甫 (The Tang Dynasty) Du Fu

2. 吊影分为千里雁， Each of my brothers flies like a solitary wild goose that has left the flock,
辞根散作九秋**蓬**。 And also like the ***grasses*** that after leaving their roots in the autumn fly about. [13]

"自河南经乱，关内阻饥，兄弟离散，各在一处。因望月有感，聊书所怀。……"

（唐）白居易

"Since the war chaos in Henan, the transportation in the Central Shanxi has been blocked, the people there have suffered from famine and my brothers and sisters have scattered here and there. Looking up the bright moon, feel sad. So I write this poem to my brothers and sisters..."

(The Tang Dynasty) Bai Juyi

3. 士生于世，使其中不自得，将何往而非病？使其中坦然，不以物伤性，将何适而非快？今张君不以谪为患，窃会计之余功，而自放山水之间，此其中宜有过人者。将**蓬**户瓮牖，无所不快，而况乎濯长江之清流，挹西山之白云，穷耳目之胜以自适也哉！

《黄州快哉亭记》（宋）苏辙

If a man born into this world does not feel contentment with what he has, he would find worries wherever he goes. But if he has ease of mind and does not allow things material to interfere with his nature, then there is no place where he will not feel happy. Now Zhang thinks little of his relegation and uses the spare time after his business hours to abandon himself to the scenic beauty, he must indeed have something unusual about him. Given such a quality, one can live in a ***shabby*** house and still find happiness in everything imaginable, to say nothing of laving his feet in the limpid water of the Yangtze and drawing the white clouds over the western mountain, enjoying to the full the sensuous pleasure from nature![12]

"The Huangzhou Ecstasy Arbor" (The Song Dynasty) Su Zhe

原文中之“蓬”为名词。**例 1** 之“蓬”在译文中作定语，英语中作定语的名词一般为单数形式，故其译文为单数“**grass**”。**例 2** 之“蓬”乃“九秋**蓬**”：秋天有九十天，所以称九秋。这里，把兄弟姐妹的离散比作秋天的蓬草被风吹散。因是九秋之蓬，其译文选取其复数形式“**grasses**”。**例 3**“**蓬**户瓮牖”往往指贫苦人家的简陋住房，并非特指以茅草覆盖之屋。译文“**shabby**”即体现此“蓬”之意。

蔓

齐安无名山，而江之南武昌诸山，陂陁**蔓**延，涧谷深密，中有浮图精舍，西曰西山，东曰寒溪。依山临壑，隐蔽松枥，萧然绝谷，车马之流不至。

《武昌九曲亭记》（宋）苏辙

While Qi'an boasts no famous mountains, the mountains in Wuchang, on the south side of the Yangtze River, are undulating and far-***crawling***, complete with deep and tranquil ravines and gullies. Embosomed in these mountains are Buddhist temples with Buddhist pagodas. The one on the west is called the West Hill Temple, and the other on the east is named the Chilly Stream Temple. They were both perched with their backs against mountains and their fronts towards valleys, ensconced in pine and oak woods—aloof from the mundane world and beyond the reach of vehicles or horses.[8]

"The Pavilion on the Winding Mountain Ranges in Wuchang"

(The Song Dynasty) Su Zhe

蕊：会意字，由“艹”、由“惢”会意。

风乍起，	The breeze begins to blow
吹皱一池春水。	And it ruffles a pool of spring water below.
闲引鸳鸯芳径里，	Crushing pink apricot ***petals*** in hand, I play
手挼红杏**蕊**。	With a pair of lovebirds on the fragrant pathway. [1]
《谒金门》	Tune: Paying Homage at the Golden Gate
（南唐）冯延巳	(The Nontang Dynasty) Feng Yanyi

苗：会意字，由“艹”、由“田”会意[9]。

宋人有闵其苗之不长而揠之者。

茫茫然归，谓其人曰：“今日病矣！予助**苗**长矣。”

其子趋而往视之，苗则槁矣。

— 天下之不助苗长者寡矣：以为无益而舍之者，不耘苗者也；助而长之，揠苗者也。非徒无益，而又害之。

《孟子》

A man in the state of Song felt the shoots in his fields were not growing fast enough. So he pulled them all up, then went home quite exhausted.

"I'm tired out today," he told his family. "I've been helping the ***young shoots*** to grow."

His son ran out to the fields to have a look, and found all their ***seedlings*** were dead.

Most people would like to help young shoots to grow, but some think all efforts useless and make no attempt, not even weeding the fields; others try to help the ***shoots*** grow by pulling them up. This, of course, is worse than useless. [14]

"Mencius"

辶

用“辶”组合的字往往与行走有关。“辶”意为忽行忽止。例字（词）均为形声字（词）：外形内声。

通

1. 身无彩凤双飞翼，	Though we have no wings of phoenix by which we can fly together as we please,

心有灵犀一点**通**。　Yet our hearts are closely ***linked*** in common beat.[13]

《无题》　"A Poem Without a Title"

（唐）李商隐　(The Tang Dynasty) Li Shangyin

2. 饥则附，饱则翱，燠则趋，寒则弃，人情**通**患也。

《菜根谭》（明）洪应明

It always follows that when people are hungry and frustrated they tend to go and live as dependents on others, but as soon as they have adequate food and clothing they will slip away from their benefactors to distant places. And also it follows that when people meet the rich and powerful they tend to fawn on them. But as soon as they become declining they will fling off at once. All these are the ***common*** failings of human nature.[6]

"The Roots of Wisdom" (The Ming Dynasty) Hong Yingming

例 1 中之"灵犀"即犀牛。据说，犀牛角中有一条白纹，直通大脑，感应十分灵敏，所以称犀牛为灵犀。"一点通"：一线通。故"心有灵犀一点**通**"之"通"含两心相通，如同被感应灵敏的一线所联，其译文"**linked**"符合原文之意思。原文中主动语态与译文中被动语态的使用体现出了主体与客体型思维的不同。**例 2** 之"通"为"普通、共同、一般"之意，"**common**"即其意。

近

1. 花**近**高楼伤客心，　The flowers ***near*** the tower sadden my heart,
   万方多难此登临。　Because I climb up this tower when disasters are tearing our country apart.[13]

《登楼》　"Ascending a Tower"

（唐）杜甫　(The Tang Dynasty) Du Fu

2. 移舟泊烟渚，　Mooring the boat among the mists—
   日暮客愁新。　Day wanes
   野旷天低树，　A wanderer's ache persists.
   江清月**近**人。　In the vast wilds the sky descends to touch the trees
   　As brightening waters ***bear*** the moon ***to*** me.[2]

《宿建德江》　"Spending the Night on the Jiande River"

（唐）孟浩然　(The Tang Dynasty) Meng Haoran

例 1 之"近"为动词，但译文诗句中以"伤"（sadden）为谓语，为符合语言规范，"近"之词性需转换为介词，构成介词短语"**near** the tower"作为定语用来修饰充当句子主语的"花"flowers"。**例 2** 之"近"（**bear** … **to**…）为意译。

远

1. 长江一帆**远**，　On the Yangtze River your lonely boat sails ***farther*** and farther and out of my sight,

落日五湖春。　At sunset you'll see the spring scenery of the five lakes all right. [13]

《饯别王十一南游》

"Giving a Farewell Dinner to Wang the 11th Going on a Tour of the South"

（唐）刘长卿　(The Tang Dynasty) Liu Changqing

2. 高树晓还密，　At dawn still thick and dense are the tall trees,

远山晴更多。　Under sunshine more of the ***distant*** mountains one sees. [13]

《早秋》　"Early Autumn"

（唐）许浑　(The Tang Dynasty) Xu Hun

3. 孤帆**远**影碧空尽，　His solitary sail ***in the distance*** gradually disappears in the blue sky,

唯见长江天际流。　So that I can only see the Yangtze River to the horizon running by. [13]

《送孟浩然之广陵》　"Seeing off Meng Haoran Going to Guangling"

（唐）李白　(The Tang Dynasty) Li Bai

以上 3 例"远"之译文的选取在于译语句子结构及其所充当的成分。**例 1** 之"远"在句中用作状语，译文副词"**farther**"。**例 2** 在句中作定语，译为形容词"**distant**"。**例 3** 在句中用作状语，其译文选取介词短语"**in the distance**"。

迟

闲鹭栖常早，　The leisurely egret oft go back to their nests earlier,

秋花落更**迟**。　The autumn flowers here wither and fall much ***later***. [13]

《谷口书斋寄杨补阙》　"To Official Yang from My Study at Gukou"

（唐）钱起　(The Tang Dynasty) Qian Qi

遥

路**遥**遥，水迢迢，　Life is short, ***long*** is the road, drawing you

功名尽在长安道，　Towards the capital, Chang'an, and the court

今日少年明日老。 As you are young now, but tomorrow old.
山，依旧好， The Empire is on the way,
人，憔悴了。 But you, on the wane.[10]

《山羊坡 · 叹世》 Tune: Sheep on the Slope, "The World Changes"
（元）陈草庵 (The Yuan Dynasty) Chen Caoan

遂

一仕官将之官，其厚友送之，嘱曰："公居官无他难，只要耐烦。"仕者唯唯。

已而再嘱，三嘱，犹唯唯，及于四五，其人忿然怒曰："君以我为呆子乎？只此二字，奈何言之数四？"

厚友曰："我才多说两次，尔**遂**发恼，辄为能耐烦者乎？"

《雪涛小书》（明）江盈科

A man was going to take up an official post. A close friend came to see him off. "One thing you must remember when you become an official," he said, "is that you must always be patient."

The man replied that he would. His friend then repeated his advice three times, and three times the man nodded in assent. When for the fourth time his friend repeated his counsel, the man became angry and said, "Do you take me for an idiot? Why do you repeat such a simple thing over and over again?"

His friend sighed. "It is not easy to be patient, see!" he said. "I have only said that a few times, and here you are ***already*** impatient."[14]

"Stories by Xue Tao" (The Ming Dynasty) Jiang Yingke

"遂"的意思是"于是、就"，表示动作相继发生，或交待上一动作的结果。其译文"already"（ prior to a specified or implied past, present, or future time）中表达出此意。

逍遥

海上风雨至， When from the sea comes the breeze with a drizzle,
逍遥池阁凉。 The pavilion and the pool in the prefecture yard become ***pleasantly*** cool.[13]

《郡斋雨中与诸文士燕集》 "Entertaining the Scholars in the Hall of My Prefecture Office When It's Raining Outside"
（唐）韦应物 (The Tang Dynasty) Wei Yingwu

遏

遥襟甫暢，逸兴遄飞。爽籁发而清风生，纤歌凝而白云**遏**。

《滕王阁序》（唐）王勃

Glancing into the distance, one feels his mind broadened and elevated with a flight of lofty fancy. The melodious piping sounds give rise to a refreshing breeze. The delicate songs, as if frozen, make the white clouds ***stop*** to drift. [12]

"The Tower of Prince Teng" (The Tang Dynasty) Wang Bo

扌

用"**扌**"构组的字，字义与"手"、"手"的动作、用"手"做的事有关。例字皆为形声字：左形右声。

扣

扣门无犬吠，　No dogs bark when I ***knock*** at the gate,
欲去问西家。　Then I go to his neighbor in the west. [13]
《寻陆鸿渐不遇》　"Visiting Lu Hongjian Without Meeting Him"
（唐）僧皎然　(The Tang Dynasty) Seng Jiaoran

摧

安能**摧**眉折腰事权贵，　Why should I—with ***lowered*** eyes, on bent knee—serve the high and mighty?
使我不得开心颜。　Such things can never make my heart rejoice! [2]
《梦游天姥吟留别》
"Dream Journey to the Heavenly Mother Mountain: A Song of Parting"
（唐）李白　(The Tang Dynasty) Li Bai

此处"**摧**"的翻译在于其上下文语境。"眉"不可"摧"，但可以用"眉高眼低"或"低眉顺眼"来表明人的表情或神色。用"**lower**"来对应"摧"，表达出作者不肯低眉弯腰去地侍奉权贵的傲气和不屈。

抬

怒发冲冠，　Wrath sets on end my hair,
凭栏处、　I lean on railings where
潇潇雨歇。　I see the drizzling rain has ceased.
抬望眼，　***Raising*** my eyes

仰天长啸，	Towards the skies
壮怀激烈。	I leave long sighs,
	My wrath not yet appeased.
三十年功名尘与土，	To dust is gone the fame achieved in thirty years;
八千里路云和月。	Like cloud-veiled moon the thousand-mile land disappears.
莫等闲、	Should youthful heads in vain turn gray,
白了少年头，	We would regret for aye. [1]
空悲切。	
《满江红》	Tune: The River All Red
（宋）岳飞	(The Song Dynasty) Yue Fei

动词“抬”的原文与译文体现出思维方式的不同。汉语“抬”在诗词中无词形变化，“抬、仰、啸”三个动作的安排在于其语意逻辑及发生的次序。译文则是通过语法形式来体现动作的先后，即“抬”构成的分词短语“**raising** my eyes, towards the skies”。

捲

1. 北风***捲***地白草折，	As overnight, the spring wind can bring
胡天八月即飞雪。	A hundred thousand pear trees into bloom—
忽如一夜春风来，	In only the eighth month,
千树万树梨花开。	The north wind ***swept across*** the plain,
	Tore down the white plumed grass, And filled the Tartar sky with swirling snow. [2]
《白雪歌送武判官归京》	“Song of the White Snow: Seeing Magistrate Wu Off upon His Return to the Capital”
（唐）岑参	(The Tang Dynasty) Cen Shen

2. 东篱把酒黄昏后，	After dusk I drink wine by East Hedge in bloom,
有暗香盈袖。	My sleeves filled with fragrance and gloom.
莫道不消魂，	Say not my soul
帘***捲***西风，	Is not consumed! Should the west wind up ***roll***
人比黄花瘦！	The curtain of my bower,
	'T would show a thinner face than yellow flower. [1]
《醉花阴・九日》	Tune: Tipsy in the Flower's Shade, “The Double Ninth Festival”
（宋）李清照	(Song Dynasty) Li Qingzhao

以上两例之“捲”为动词。**例 1**“捲”的意思是“一种强大的力量把东西撮起或裹住”。“北风捲地”即北风席卷大地，译文“**swept across**”（to move suddenly and/or with force over an area or in a particular direction）即表达此意。**例 2**“捲”之意为“把东西弯转裹成圆筒形”，故译为“**roll**”（to make sth into the shape of a ball or tube）。

抱

1. 蜀僧***抱***绿绮， The Shu monk, ***holding*** in his arms a, zither green,
西下峨眉峰。 Walks down the west side of the Emei Mountain.[13]
《听蜀僧濬弹琴》 “Listening to Shu Monk Jun Playing the Zither”
（唐）李白 (The Tang Dynasty) Li Bai

2. 驾一叶之扁舟，举匏樽以相属。寄蜉蝣于天地，渺沧海之一粟，哀吾生之须臾，羡长江之无穷，挟飞仙以遨游，***抱***明月而长终。

《前赤壁赋》（宋）苏轼

We row a boat, toast each other, depositing our ephemeral life in the universe, our being as infinitely small as a grain in the ocean. Lamenting our fleeting existence and envying the everlasting Yangtze River, I wish I could travel with fairies in heaven and ***hold*** the bright moon in my arms through eternity.[12]

“Boating at the Red Cliff ” (The Song Dynasty) Su Shi

例 1 之“抱”为动词，诗句中的“抱”与“下”为蜀僧的两个动作。为符合译语语言规范，译文中“抱”转换为现在分词“**holding**”构成非限制性定语。只保留“下”作为谓语动词。

攫

昔齐人有欲金者。清旦，衣冠而之市，适鬻金者之所，因***攫***金而去。

吏捕得之，问曰：“人皆在焉，子***攫***人之金何?”对曰：“取金之时，不见人，徒见金。”

《列子》（战国）列子

There was a man in the state of Qi who wanted some gold. One morning he dressed himself smartly and went to the market. Arriving at the gold-dealer’s stall, he ***seized*** a piece of gold and made off.

The officer who caught him asked him: “ Why did you ***steal*** gold in front of so many people?”

"When I took the gold," he answered, "I saw nobody. All I saw was the gold."[14]

"Lie Zi" (The Warring States Period) Lie Zi

"攫"之意为"抓；夺"。**例 1** 的译文"**seized**"为直译。**例 2** 则是根据对上下文的理解，采用意译的方法："偷"属于违法行为，所以才会招致官吏的捉捕，第二个"攫"意译为"**steal**"更能表达原文所含之意。

擒

山谷间，常数十为群。里人以酒并槽设于路侧，织草为屐，更相连接。猩猩见酒及屐，知里人设张，则知张者祖先姓字，乃呼名云："奴欲张我！"舍而去。后自再三，相谓曰："试共尝酒。"及饮其味，逮乎醉。因取屐着之而蹶。乃为人***擒***，无遗者。

《谭概》（明）冯梦龙

In the valleys in the south there are savage baboons which always go in groups. The local people, knowing their ways, place wine dregs by the roadside, and a string of straw sandals across the road. On seeing the wine and sandals, the baboons set up a loud clamour and turn tail. But they have already caught the scent of the wine. Cautiously, they begin to edge back, then scampering away and retracing their steps. Finally they decide to try a few mouthfuls. They drink the wine and get drunk, put on the sandals and trip and fall. Then the people come up and ***catch*** them.[14]

"Tan Gai" (The Ming Dynasty) Feng Menglong

氵

"氵"同"水"。用"氵"组合的字中，一般都与水有关。例字中，除"***泪***、***洒***、***水***"外，其余为形声字：左形右声。

沾

海内存知己，　Close friends remain close friends wherever they roam;
天涯若比邻。　Even at the earth's end, you would seem next door.
无为在歧路，　Before this crossroad let's not act as little children,
儿女共***沾***巾。　***Drenching*** our handkerchiefs with tears.[2]

《杜少府之任蜀州》　"Seeing Magistrate Du Off to His Post in Sichuan"
（唐）王勃　(The Tang Dynasty) Wang Bo

为符合译语语言规范，原文中的动词"沾"在译文中改为现在分词

"**Drenching**"，作定语，其意：to make sb/sth completely wet，即"沾"之含意。

湧

细草微风岸，　Slender reeds，faint breeze along the banks.
危樯独夜舟。　High-masted boat，alone in the night.
星垂平野阔，　Stars descend，rimming the endless land.
月***湧***大江流。　The moon ***emerges***，on the great river flowing. [2]

《旅夜书怀》　"Night Thoughts on a Journey"
（唐）杜甫　（The Tang Dynasty）Du Fu

澄

登临送目，　I climb a height
正故国晚秋，　And strain my sight.
天气初肃。　Of autumn late'tis the best time：
千里***澄***江似练，　The ancient capital looks sublime！
翠峰如簇。　The ***limpid*** River，belt-like，flows a thousands miles；
　Emerald peaks on peaks tower in grandiose styles. [1]

《桂枝香 · 金陵怀古》
Tune：Fragrance of Laurel Branch，"Memories of the Past at Jinling"
（宋）王安石　（The Song Dynasty）Wang Anshi

沟

忆昔午桥桥上饮，　I still remember drinking on the Bridge of Noon
坐中多是豪英。　With bright wits of the day.
长***沟***流月去无声。　The silent moon
杏花疏影里，　On endless ***river*** rolled away.
吹笛到天明。　In shadows sparse of apricot flowers
　We played our flutes till morning hours. [1]

《临江仙 · 夜登小阁忆洛中旧游》
Tune：Immortal at the River，"Mounting a Tower at Night and Recalling the Old Friends Visiting Luoyang Together"
（宋）陈与义　（The Song Dynasty）Chen Yuyi

此处"沟"为意译。"忆昔午桥桥上饮"之"桥"意味着"河"的存在。"河"即词中之"沟"，译为"**river**"，符合原文之意。

酒

乍暖还寒时候， 最难将息。	How hard is it To keep me fit In this lingering cold! Hardly warmed up.
三杯两盏淡***酒***， 怎敌他、 晚来风急？	By cup on cup Of ***wine*** so dry. Oh! How could I Endure at dusk the drift Of wind so swift? [1]

《声声慢》 Tune: Slow, Slow Tune

（宋）李清照 (The Song Dynasty) Li Qingzhao

滚

无边落木萧萧下，	The leaves far and near fall whirling and rustling,
不尽长江***滚***滚来。	The endless waters of the Yangtze River ***roll*** on crashing and splashing. [13]

《登高》 "Ascending a Height"

（唐）杜甫 (The Tang Dynasty) Du Fu

洲

1. 天边树若荠， The trees far away look like shepherd's purses small and low in height,

   江畔***洲***如月。 The riverside ***sandbar*** looks like a crescent moon white. [13]

   《秋登万山寄张五》

   "To Zhang the Fifth After Ascending Mountain Wan in Autumn"

   （唐）孟浩然 (The Tang Dynasty) Meng Haoran

2. 斜晖脉脉水悠悠， The slanting sun sheds a sympathetic ray,

   肠断白蘋***洲***。 The carefree river carries it away.

   My heart breaks at the sight

   Of the ***islet*** with duckweed white. [1]

   《梦江南》 Tune: Dreaming of the South

   （唐）温庭筠 (The Tang Dynasty) Wen Tingyun

"***洲***"的字义之一为"河流中由泥沙淤积而形成的陆地"。**例 1 "sandbar"** (a long mass of sand at the point where a river meets the sea that is formed by the movement of the water）含“江边”之意，与原文“江畔洲”之“洲”词义相符。**例2**之“洲”为“白蘋***洲***”。“蘋”为蕨类植物，生在浅水中。译文所取之“**islet**”意“a very small island（a piece of land that is completely surrounded by water）”，含被水环绕之意，与白蘋作为定语所修饰的“洲”词义相合。

潮

潮平两岸阔， The river is wide because the spring ***tide*** rises high,
风正一帆悬。 The wind is favorable, so the sail on my boat is hoisted high.[13]
《次北固山下》 "Mooring at the Foot of Mount Beigu"
（唐）王湾 （The Tang Dynasty）Wang Wan

溪

桃花尽日随流水， The peach flowers drift by on the stream all day,
洞在清***溪***何处边？ To the hillside hole near the clear ***stream***, where is the way?[13]
《桃花溪》 "The Peach Flower Stream"
（唐）张旭 （The Tang Dynasty）Zhang Xu

淤泥、濯、清涟

自李唐来，世人盛爱牡丹。予独爱莲之出***淤泥***而不染，***濯清涟***而不妖，中通外直，不蔓不枝，香远益清，亭亭净植，可远观而不可亵玩焉。

《爱莲说》（宋）周敦颐

Since Tang, under the rule by the Li family, people like peony a great deal. But my love is all for lotus, because of its growing up from the ***silt*** without being stained, and its ***laving*** in the ***rippling clean water***, having no seducing charms. It is hollow inside and straight outside, it has no ramifications whatsoever. Its fragrance becomes more refreshing as it wafts farther. Standing upright with its slender and shapely figure, it is to be admired at a distance, not to be fiddled with in a frivolous manner.[12]

"On My Love Lotus"（The Song Dynasty）Zhou Dunyi

此例中“***淤泥***”直译为“**silt**”。“***濯清涟***”三字译文的选取在于其所在句子的整体结构。“濯”为动词，意“洗”。原文中“濯”与前面的“出”并列。译文之“出”为“growing”，“濯”的翻译就要转换词类：成为动名词“**laving**”，与前面的“growing”并列。“清”在这里直译为“**clean**”。“涟”之意为“风吹水面所形成的波纹”。“濯清涟”与“出淤泥”相并列。“出淤泥”之译文为“its growing up from the silt”，要与其结构对应，“濯清涟”之“涟”需改为作定语的现在分词“**rippling**”，与清“clean”一起修饰“water”，才可构成介词短语“in the rippling clean water”，与“from the silt”对应。

泪：会意字，由“水”、由“目”会意。

多情却似总无情，　Passion so deep appears as none:
惟觉樽前笑不成。　Before these farewell cups, unable even to smile.
蜡烛有心还惜别，　The candle too takes pity on our parting,
替人垂***泪***到天明。　Shedding ***tears*** until the coming of the dawn. [2]
《赠别二首》　" Bidding Farewell"
（唐）杜牧　(The Tang Dynasty) Du Mu

潇洒、清：“洒”：假借字。原音为“xi”，借用为“sa”扫的“洒”。

膝上琴横，　With zither on my knees,
哀愁动离情。　I'm moved to think of my far-off dear.
指下风声，　My fingers play ***with ease***
潇洒弄***清***音。　On zither strings a music ***clear***.
锁窗前月色朗，　Before my window screen the moon is bright;
雕栏外夜气***清***。　Beyond the balustrade ***fresh*** is the night.
指法轻，　My touches light
助起骚人兴。　Would make the poets verve freer.
听！　O heart!
玉漏断，　From water clock there comes no sound;
人初静。　Silence begins to reign all around. [5]
《碧玉箫》　Tune: Green Jade Flute
（元）关汉卿　(The Yuan Dynasty) Guan Hanqing

原文中“潇洒”为形容词，因“弄清音”之“弄”作为句中谓语，故“萧洒”在此译为介词短语“**with ease**”，作为状语修饰“play”（弄）。“清音”之“清”（1）指声音清晰，取“**clear**”之“easy to hear”。（2）根据上文“哀愁动离情”，此“清”中还含有“凄清”之意。此含意也借用“clear”暗示出来：free from entanglement (complicated relationship with another person)。“夜气清”之“清”即“清新、清爽”之意，“**fresh**”即表此“清”。

水：象形字。

1. 昔闻洞庭**水**，　Long have I heard of Dongting ***lake***:
今上岳阳楼。　Now I ascend the tower at Yueyang.

吴楚东南坼，	Her waters divided Wu from Chu in the southeast,
乾坤日夜浮。	The universe of sun and moon upon their surface. [2]
《登岳阳楼》	"Climbing Yueyang Tower"
（唐）杜甫	(The Tang Dynasty) Du Fu

2. 胭脂泪，	Your rouged tears like crimson rain
留人醉。	Intoxicated my heart.
几时重？	When shall we meet again?
自是人生长恨**水**长东。	As ***water*** eastward flows, so shall we part. [1]
《乌夜啼》	Tune: Crows Crying at Night
（南唐）李煜	(The Nontang Dynasty) Li Yu

例 1 之"洞庭**水**"即"洞庭湖"，故"水"这里译为"**lake**"。

纟

用"**纟**"组合的字，与"丝、麻、颜色"有关。例字中除"**缀**"外，余者皆为形声字，其中，"**紫**"为下形上声，其他为左形右声。

缝

慈母手中线，	The threads in the tender mother's hand,
游子身上衣。	Makes clothes for her son who is going to a far-off land.
临行密密**缝**，	Stitch close to stitch she ***sews*** before he leaves home-town,
意恐迟迟归。	Lest his return will be delayed long.
谁言寸草心，	Who says the little grass can in a way,
报得三春晖？	Such warm sunshine of the three months of spring repay? [13]
《游子吟》	"Song of the Son Who Is Going to a Far-off Land"
（唐）孟郊	(The Tang Dynasty) Meng Jiao

绕

驿寄梅花，	Mume blossoms sent by friends
鱼传尺素，	And letters brought by post,
砌成此恨无重数。	Nostalgic thoughts uncounted assail me oft in host.
郴江幸自**绕**郴山，	The local river flows ***around*** the local hill.
为谁流下潇湘去？	Should it flow to foreign lands and flow against its will? [1]
《踏莎行·郴州旅舍》	Tune: Treading on Grass, "At an Inn of Chenzhou"
（宋）秦观	(The Song Dynasty) Qin Guan

原文中"**绕**郴山"之"绕"为动词。"郴江幸自**绕**郴山"之意为"郴江本来是围绕着郴州而流的"。译文中取动词"流"(flows)为"江"之谓语,"绕"在译文中之词性也随之发生变化,转换为介词"**around**"。

绿

可惜一溪风月,	My horse's hoofs may break, I'm afraid,
莫教踏碎琼瑶。	The breeze-rippled brook paved by moon light's white jade.
解鞍欹枕**绿**杨桥,	I tie fast my horse to a bough of ***green*** willow
杜宇一声春晓。	Near the bridge then I pillow
	My head on saddle and sleep till thecuckoo's songs awake
	A spring daybreak. [1]
《西江月》	Tune: The Moon over the West River
(宋)苏轼	(The Song Dynasty) Su Shi

缕

客有吹洞箫者,倚歌而和之。其声呜呜然,如怨如慕,如泣如诉;余音袅袅,不绝如**缕**。

《前赤壁赋》(宋)苏轼

A *xiao* player among the guests accompanied the song, which produced a woeful tune, now like someone murmuring and languishing for love, now like someone sobbing and complaining. The lingering sound was as unbroken as ***silk***, …[12]

" Boating at the Red Cliff " (The Song Dynasty) Su Shi

线

浙江之潮,天下之伟观也。自既望以至十八日为最盛。方其远出海门,仅如银**线**,既而渐近,则玉城雪岭,际天而来,大声如雷霆,震撼激射,吞天沃日,势极雄豪。杨诚斋诗云:"海涌银为郭,江横系玉腰"者是也。

《观潮》(宋)周密

Tidal waves of the Qiantang River are a grandiose spectacle in the world. The climax comes between the sixteenth and the eighteenth of the lunar month. Emerging far from the estuary, they merely look like a silver ***thread***. But with their gradually approach they seem to be jade walls and snow-capped mountain ridges descending from heaven. They rumble like thunders, shake with tremors, spurt sprays and seem to be swallowing the sky and laving the sun, showing an overpowering momentum, as is precisely described by Yang Chengzhai's verses: "The sea pours out many towns of silver and a jade sash is tied across the river. "[12]

"Viewing Tidal Waves" (The Song Dynasty) Zhou Mi

纪纲

善医者，不视人之瘠肥，察其脉之病否而已矣；善计天下者，不视天下之安危，察其***纪纲***之理乱而已矣。天下者，人也；安危者，肥瘠也；纪纲者，脉也。脉不病，虽瘠不害；脉病而肥者，死矣。通于此说者，其知所以为天下乎！

《医说》（唐）韩愈

A good doctor does not treat a patient by looking at his weight, but by observing whether anything is wrong with his pulse. A good strategist does not administer a country by inspecting its safety, but by checking if ***political guidelines*** are properly followed. Administering a country is like treating a patient; a country's safety is like a patient's weight; political guidelines are like a human's pulse. If a patient's pulse is not diseased, then his thinness is not detrimental. However, if his pulse is diseased, although he is fat, he may die. Anyone who is conversant with this principle also knows the principle of administering a country![8]

"On the Treatment of Illness" (The Tang Dynasty) Han Yu

紫

十旬休暇，胜友如云；千里逢迎，高朋满座。腾蛟起凤，孟学士之词宗；**紫**电青霜，王将军之武库。

《滕王阁序》（唐）王勃

It being a vacation of ten days, good friends gather here in great number, and noble guests come all the way to meet, filling the tower hall. The writings of Meng, the erudite, are praised for capable of moving a dragon or a phoenix to rise. The arms of General Wang are believed to be as peerless as the swords, called "the ***purple*** lightening" and "the clear frost."[12]

"The Tower of Prince Teng" (The Tang Dynasty) Wang Bo

缀：会意字，由"纟"、由"叕"会意[9]。"叕"：连缀。

并州有人姓纥干，好剧。承间在外有狐魅，遂得一狐尾，**缀**着衣后。至妻旁，侧坐露之。其妻私心疑是狐魅，遂密持斧，欲斫之。其人叩头云："我不是魅。"妻不信。走遂至邻家，邻家又以刀杖逐之。其人惶惧告言："我戏剧，不意专欲杀我。"此亦妖由人兴矣。

《太平广记选》（宋）李昉等

In Bing Prefecture there was a man who took pleasure in playing practical jokes. Thinking that he could take advantage of people's belief in the fox's ability to bewitch and change shapes, he procured a fox tail while he was out of town. He ***pinned*** the tail inside the back of his coat in such a way that when he sat down the tip of it would be dangling out. Thus he went home to his wife.

His wife spotted his tail and suspected he was a fox vampire in her husband's guise. She returned to the room with a hidden ax, and swung it down on him. Dodging and bowing, he proclaimed that he was no fox, but his wife couldn't be convinced. He fled to a neighbor's. They, too, drove him out with swords and sticks. Scared out of his wits, he confessed his silly trick and said he never expected his jokes could almost cause him his life.

Aren't evil spirits created by man himself?[3]

"The Selections from Records of the Taiping Era"
(The Song Dynasty) Li Fang *et al.*

彡

象形，表示毛发、彩饰、笔画、花纹。例字中除“**影**、**形**、**须**、**彰**”外，其他为形声字：右形左声。

彩

众矜夸，	All maidens vie
是交加。	In swinging high.
彩云飞上日边霞。	Like ***rainbow*** clouds near to the sun they fly,
体态轻盈那闲雅，	With body light and spirit bright,
精神羞落树头花。	Their grace would make the blooming trees feel shy.[5]
《感皇恩 · 采茶歌》	Tune: Gratitude to the Emperor, "Tea-Picking Song"
（元）无名氏	(The Yuan Dynasty) Anonymous

此例之“彩”为意译。“rainbow”有七种颜色，“如虹”意含颜色丰富，这里与“彩”意相合。

修：右为“彡”，左为“攸”。

赖天之灵、宗庙之福，**修**我戈矛，从王于师，以为前驱，雪九庙之耻，复高祖之业，所谓誓不与贼俱生，所谓鞠躬尽力，死而后已，亦义也。

《指南录后序》（宋）文天祥

With the help of the gods of Heaven and Earth, and the blessings of the ancestral temples, I will ***polish*** my weapons and, following the army of my Sovereign, march in the vanguard, so as to erase the disgrace of our dynasty and restore the great empire created by the First Emperor. It is what is called "Sworn never to coexist with enemies" and what is called "Do one's utmost with all humbleness till one's death." This is also righteousness![12]

"Epilogue to the Zhinan Collection"
(The Song Dynasty) Wen Tianxiang

影

高枝已约风为友，	Friendly with the wind, the upward branches grow;
密叶能留雪作花。	Thick leaves turn to flowers flakes of snow.
昨夜嫦娥更潇洒，	Last night, Chang'e, more amiable than ever before,
又携疏**影**过窗纱。	Carried again their light ***shade*** past the gauze window.[17]
《竹》	"Bamboo"
（宋）陈与义	(The Song Dynasty) Chen Yuyi

影、形：影，会意字，由"景"、由"彡"会意；形，象形字。

一在天之涯，一在地之角，生而**影**不予吾**形**相依，死而魂不与吾梦相接，吾实为之，其又何由！彼苍者天，曷其有极！

《祭十二郎文》（唐）韩愈

Now, one of us two is in the depth of heaven, another is at a corner of the earth. While living, your ***shadow*** did not follow my ***body***. Being dead, your soul has never come into my dream. Oh, Heaven! Could my sorrow know its bounds?[12]

"Lament for My Twelfth Nephew" (The Tang Dynasty) Han Yu

例1之"影"着意于"影子"(used when you are referring to things that remind you of a particular person, thing or time)，故译为"**shade**"。**例2**"影"之意为"影儿"(the dark shape made when a light shines on a person or an object)，据此，其译文选取"**shadow**"。

须：会意字，由"页（含义为'头'）"、由"彡"会意。

唐傅黄中为越州诸暨县令。有部人饮大醉，夜中山行，临崖而睡。忽有虎临其上而嗅之，虎**须**入醉人鼻中，遂喷嚏声震。虎遂惊跃，便落崖，腰胯不遂，为人所得。

《太平广记选》（宋）李昉等

Fu Huangzhong, magistrate of Zhuji County in the Tang Dynasty, recounted a true story to one of his former subordinates.

The man was quite drunk after a party, but he insisted on walking home alone through the night. Following a familiar mountain path, he dropped asleep on the brink of a precipice.

A tiger came sniffling at the smell of man. Its ***whiskers*** somehow poked into the man's nostrils, setting off such a violent sneeze that the big cat jumped with a start and fell off the cliff. It sprained its waist and was caught by the drunkard.

"The Selections from Records of the Taiping Era"
(The Song Dynasty) Li Fang *et al.*

彰：会意字，由"彡"、由"章"会意。"章"也表声[9]。

怨因德**彰**，故使人德我，不若德怨之两忘；仇因恩立，故使人知恩，不若恩仇之俱泯。

《菜根谭》（明）洪应明

The ***rising*** of men's resentment is the result of partial benevolences. So when you show your benevolence it is better to let others forget both gratitude and resentment than to expect gratitude from them. And the being of men's enmity is the product of different bounties. So when you bestow bounties on others it is better to let both bounties and enmities be buried in oblivion than to make them aware of your bounties.[6]

"The Roots of Wisdom" (The Ming Dynasty) Hong Yingming

此例之"彰"为意译。"怨因德彰"即"一切怨恨都会因善行而更加明显"。译文取"**rising**"，含有"彰"之意。

忄

"**忄**"同"心"。例字中除"**恒**"外，其余为形声字：左形右声。

忧

先天下之**忧**而**忧**，后天下之乐而乐。

《岳阳楼记》（宋）范仲淹

Worry before all others have ***worried***; rejoice after all others have rejoiced.[12]

"Yueyang Tower" (The Song Dynasty) Fan Zhongyan

原文"先天下之**忧**而**忧**"中的第一个"忧"为名词，第二个为动词。"先"字的使用体现出综合型思维通过词汇手段来表达次序；分析型思维则通过时间状语从句以及从句中所使用的时态（现在完成时）来体现，即译文"**worried**"。

惆怅、悟

归去来兮，田园将芜胡不归！既自以心为行役，奚**惆怅**而独悲？**悟**以往之不谏，知来者之可追。实迷途之未远，觉今是而昨非。

《归去来兮辞》（东晋）陶渊明

Go home! My homestead is being desolated, why not go home? Since I myself had my mind enthralled by my body, why should I be so sad and ***forlorn***? I ***conceive*** that the past is irredeemable, yet in the future things may still be retrievable. I did not go far astray. I feel today I am doing what is right, though what I did yesterday as all wrong. [12]

"Sentiments on My Homecoming"

(The Eastern Jin Dynasty) Tao Yuanming

惧、忧、懈、慎、惧

君人者，诚能见可欲，则思知足以自戒，将有作则思知止以安人，念高危则思谦冲而自牧，**惧**满盈则思江河下百川，乐盘游则思三驱以为度，**忧懈**怠则思**慎**始而敬终，虑壅蔽则思虚心以纳下，**惧**谗邪则思正身以黜恶，恩所加则思无因喜以谬赏，罚所及则思无因怒以滥刑。

《谏太宗十思疏》（唐）魏征

A sovereign, it is earnestly hoped that you will surely act in this manner: If you have seen something desirable, think of continence and be content with what you already possess. If you undertake a project, think of ending it in due time so as to give the people relief. If you are uneasy about your perilously elevated position, think of exercising modesty and self-discipline. If you ***fear*** complacency, think of imitating the sea, which places itself lower in altitude than rivers. If you take to hunting, think of leaving an escape to the hounded game as a token of your gracious moderation. If you are ***apprehensive*** of ***indolence*** and remissness, think of being ***prudent*** in starting an undertaking and being serious in bringing it to an end. If you worry about impostures, think of being open-minded to receive the opinions of your subjects. If you ***dread*** the influence of vicious traducers, think of rectifying yourself and ridding yourself of knavish persons. When you wish to vouchsafe your favors, think of avoiding undeserved rewards, which might owe to your partiality. When you want to inflict upon someone punishment, think of refraining from the abusive use of tortures which might be caused by your anger. [12]

"Ten Points of Deliberation Recommended to Emperor Taizong"

(The Tang Dynasty) Wei Zheng

例中两个"惧"的译文为直译。第一个"惧"即可指轻微的害怕也可以指极度的恐惧："**惧**满盈则思江河下百川"之"惧"的对象是自身的心理状态，可控性较大，害怕程度会低一些，故译文选取"**fear**"。第二个"惧"表示因害怕某种伤害或不幸而产生的极度恐惧的心情："**惧**谗邪则思正身以黜恶"之"惧"的对象是外部因素，可控性较差，故此"惧"之程度较之第一个为甚，译文选取“**dread**”与原文意思更为贴切。原文中的“忧”为动词，“懈”为形容词，其所在句子的结构为主、系、表，为符合译语语言规范，故分别转换为形容词“**apprehensive**”和名词“**indolence**”。“慎”之译文“**prudent**”为直译。

恒、惴、慄：恒，会意字。由“心”、由“舟”会意。小篆体“恒”的右边“二”之间的“日”是一个“舟”字，由“舟”在天地之间往返会意。思念之心靠舟运转，是“恒”的意思[9]。

自余为僇人，居是州，**恒惴慄**。时隙也，则施施而行，漫漫而游。日与其徒上高山，入深林，穷回溪，幽泉怪石，无远不到。

《永州八记》（唐）柳宗元

After I was declared a sinner, I was relocated to this state and lived in ***constant fear*** and ***worry***. I spent most of my spare time wandering around, every day, with my men, engaged in climbing hills, hiking in forests, and traveling along meandering streams. Where there was a secluded spring or an unusual rock, there we went, regardless of distance. [8]

"Eight Travel Journals on the State of Yong"

(The Tang Dynasty) Liu Zongyuan

此例中“惴”与“慄”在原文中皆为动词。其译文“**fear**”和“**worry**”的选取在于其所在之句型结构，故其词性转换为名词，用作介词“in”的宾语。

犭

用“犭”（犬）组合的字，与“狗”或别种兽类有关。例字皆为形声字：左形右声。

猿

巫峡啼**猿**数行泪，	You may shed lines of tears while hearing near the Wu Gorge the ***gibbons***' cry,
衡阳归雁几封书。	You may send letters when the wild geese from Hengyang back to the north fly. [13]

《送李少府贬峡中王少府贬长沙》

"Farewell to Vice-Prefect Li Demoted to Xiazhong and Vice-Prefect Wang Demoted to Changsha"

（唐）高适　　(The Tang Dynasty) Gao Shi

狐

虎求百兽而食之，得**狐**。

狐曰："子无敢食我也！天帝使我长百兽；今子食我，是逆天命也。予以我为不信，我为子先行，子随我后，观百兽见我而敢不走乎！"

虎以为然，故遂与之行。兽见之皆走。

虎不知兽畏己而走也，以为畏狐也。

《战国策》（汉）刘向

While hunting for prey, the tiger caught a ***fox***.

"You can't eat me," said the fox. The Emperor of Heaven has appointed me king of the beasts. If you eat me, you'll be disobeying his orders. If you don't believe me, follow me. You'll soon see whether other animals run away at the sight of me or not."

Agreeing to this, the tiger accompanied; and when all the beasts saw them coming they dashed away. Not realizing that they were afraid of him, the tiger thought they were afraid of the fox.[14]

"Warring States Anecdotes" (The Han Dynasty Liu Xiang)

狮

华山道士明思远，勤修道策。三十余年，常教人金水分形之法，并闭气存思，师者甚众。

永泰中，华州虎暴。思远告人曰："虎不足畏。但闭气存思，令十指头各出一**狮**子。但使向前，虎即去。"

思远兼与人同行，欲暮，于谷口行逢虎。其伴惊惧散去，唯思远端然，闭气存思。俄然为虎所食。其徒明日于谷口相寻，但见松萝与双履耳。

《太平广记选》（宋）李昉等

For more than 30 years Ming Siyuan, a Taoist priest on Mount Hua, had been practicing the magic arts of Tao. He delighted in giving lectures on alchemy and meditation, and his disciples were many.

In Yongtai reign, Mount Hua was infested with tigers. Ming assured his audience that there was nothing to fear. If only one knew how to regulate his breathing and concentrate these thoughts, he would be able to produce a ***lion*** from each fingertip and drive the herd forth with his will power. That alone would frighten away that man-eater.

At sunset one day, he and a group of his disciples came face to face with a tiger at the mouth of a ravine. His followers took to their heels. While he held his ground and plunged into meditation.

His disciples ventured to return the next morning. All they found was his torn shoes in the bushes.

"The Selections from Records of the Taiping Era"
(The Song Dynasty) Li Fang *et al.*

狙

宋有**狙**公者，爱狙，养之成群，能解狙之意；狙亦得公之心。

损其家口，充狙之欲。俄而匮焉，将限其食。恐众狙之不驯己也，先诳之曰：“与若茅，朝三而暮四，足乎？”

众狙皆起而怒。

俄而曰：“朝四而暮三，足乎在？”

众狙皆伏而喜。

《列子》（战国）列子

A ***monkey***-trainer in the state of Song was fond of monkeys and kept a great many of them. He was able to understand them and they him. Indeed, he used to save some of his family's food for them. But a time came when there was not much food left at home, and he wanted to cut down the monkey's rations. He feared however, they might not agree to this, and decided to deceive them.

"I'll give you three chestnuts each morning and four each evening," he said, "Will that be enough?"

All the monkeys rose up to express their anger.

"Well, what about four in the morning and three in the evening?" he asked.

Then the monkeys squatted down again, feeling quite satisfied. [14]

"Lie Zi" (The Warring States Period) Lie Zi

猛

至莫夜月明，独与迈乘小舟至绝壁下。大石侧立千尺，如**猛**兽奇鬼，森然欲搏人。

《石钟山记》（宋）苏轼

That night, with a bright noon in the sky, I went boating with ***Mai*** close to the foot of the precipice. A cliff, standing as high as a thousand ***chi*** in its profile, looked like a ***ferocious*** beast or a fantastic demon hurling itself upon its prey in a most formidable manner. [12]

"The Stone Bell Hill" (The Song Dynasty) Su Shi

独（獨）

人心一真，便霜可飞，城可陨，金石可镂。若伪妄之人，形骸徒具，真宰已亡，对人则面目可憎，**独**居则形影自愧。

《菜根谭》（明）洪应明

Complete sincerity of a man could let frostworks fall in June, make walls collapse by wail and get metal and stone affected. But for a treacherous, hypocritical man, it seems that his soul has already departed and only his body remains. Such a man will disgust people with his repulsive looks while walking in the street and will feel ashamed of himself for his own body and shadow when getting ***alone***. [6]

"The Roots of Wisdom" (The Ming Dynasty) Hong Yingming

狠

炎凉之态，富贵更甚于贫贱；妒忌之心，骨肉尤**狠**于外人。此处若不当以冷肠，御以平气，鲜不日坐烦恼障中矣。

《菜根谭》（明）洪应明

Inconstancy of human relationships is more common among the rich and noble than among the poor and humble. Psychology of jealousy is more ***biting*** between kinsfolk than between strangers. Under such circumstances, if people do not go with cool-headed approach nor restrain themselves with ease, few of them could be free from everyday vexation. [6]

"The Roots of Wisdom" (The Ming Dynasty) Hong Yingming

这里“狠”为意译。从原文可知，此“狠”非指动物咬/吃人之凶狠，译文选用“**biting**”［(of remarks) cruel and critical］即表示语言上所带给人的伤害。

饣（食）

“饣”（食）本意为聚集的米。由“饣”（食）组合的字往往与食物有关。例字皆为形声字，左形右声。

馁（餒）

有人相信我不写文章就不能够生活。两个月以前，一个同情我的上海朋友寄稿到《广州民国日报》，说了许多关于我的生活的话。他也说我一天不写文章第二天就没有饭吃。这是不确实的。这次旅行就给我证明：即使我不再写一个字，朋友们也不肯让我冻**馁**。

《朋友》巴金

Some people believe that, without writing, I should lose my livelihood. One of my sympathizers, in an article published two months ago in the ***Guangzhou Republic Daily*** supplement, gives a full account of the conditions of my life. He also says that I would have nothing to live on once I should lay down my pen. That is not true at all. It has already been proved by my recent travels that my friends would never let me suffer from cold and ***hunger*** even if I should go without writing a single word. [15]

"Friends" Ba Jin

饱

秋天，无论在什么地方的秋天，总是好的；可是呀，北国的秋，却特别地来得清，来得静，来得悲凉。我的不远千里，要从杭州赶上青岛，更要从青岛赶上北平来的理由，也不过想**饱**尝一尝这“秋”，这故都的秋味。

《故都的秋》郁达夫

Autumn, wherever it is, always has something to recommend itself. In China, however, it is particularly limpid, serene and melancholy. To enjoy its atmosphere ***to the full*** in the onetime capital, I have, therefore, made light of traveling a long distance from Hangzhou to Qingdao, and thence to Peiping. [15]

"Autumn in Peiping" Yu Dafu

馍

南国之秋，当然也是有它的特异的地方的，比如廿四桥的明月，钱塘江的秋潮，普陀山的凉雾，荔枝湾的残荷等等，可是色彩不浓，回味不永。比起北国的秋来，正像黄酒之于白干，稀饭之于**馍**馍，鲈鱼之于大蟹，黄犬之于骆驼。

《故都的秋》郁达夫

Autumn in the South also has its unique features, such as the moon-lit Ershisi Bridge, the flowing sea tide at the Qiantangjiang River, the mist-shrouded Putuo Mountain and lotuses at the Lizhiwan Bay. But they all lack strong colour and lingering flavour. Southern autumn is to Northern autumn what yellow rice wine is to ***kaoliang*** wine, congee to ***steamed buns***, perches to crabs, yellow dogs to camels. [15]

"Autumn in Peiping" Yu Dafu

馋

鸵鸟蹒跚地走着，一身的肉真**馋**人，它之生似乎是为了供人食用。她没有防卫的手段，敌人来了就跑，跑得特别快。当跑不脱的紧急时刻，将头钻进沙堆，它看不见敌人了，以为已安全，人笑这是鸵鸟心态。是鸵鸟学会了阿Q，还是Q学了鸵鸟，无从考证，也不必考证了。

《鸵鸟·孔雀·老鹰》吴冠中

The ostrich hobbles with its ***tantalizing*** fleshy body. The bird seems destined to be human food. It has no self-defence means. In the face of an enemy, it just runs away, and that very quickly. At the critical moment when it is hard pressed, it buries its head in the sand, thinking itself safe simply because it can't see the enemy. People, therefore, refer to it in ridicule as ostrichism. It is impossible and also unnecessary to find out if Ah Q is the teacher of the ostrich or vice versa. [15]

"Ostrich · Peacock · Eagle" Wu Guanzhong

饲

驼铃声声，在广袤的戈壁上空回荡。

那是经人**饲**驯的专门载着旅客走戈壁的"沙漠之舟"呀，可不是野骆驼。

《过戈壁》哲中

The jingling bells of my camel echoed through the boundless Gobi.

It was not a wild camel, but a camel known as the "ship of the desert" that had been ***raised*** and trained specifically to carry travelers across the Gobi. [15]

"Crossing the Gobi Desert" Zhe Zhong

"饲"在原文中无词形变化，其被动含义通过词汇手段"经人"二字表达出来；译文则是通过词形变化来体现被动，故"饲"在这里被译为"**raised**"。

饥

杜鹃是不营巢的，也不孵卵哺雏。到了生育季节，产卵在莺巢中，让莺替它孵卵哺雏。雏鹃比雏莺大，到将长成时，甚且比母莺还大。鹃雏孵化出来之后，每将莺雏挤出巢外，任它啼**饥**号寒而死，它自己独霸着母莺的哺育。莺受鹃欺而不自知，辛辛苦苦地哺育着比自己还大的鹃雏：真是一件令人不平、令人流泪的情景。

《杜鹃》郭沫若

Cuckoo doesn't build her own nest, nor does she hatch or feed her young. During the breeding season, she deposits her eggs in the nests of orioles for them to hatch and rear. A baby cuckoo is bigger in size than a baby oriol, and, when full grown, bigger even than the mother oriol. After she is hatched, she often pushes the baby oriol out of the nest, leaving the poor chick to cry and die of ***hunger*** and cold so that she may have the mother oriol's care all to herself. The mother bird, however, being treated unfairly without her knowledge, continues laboriously to feed the baby cuckoo who is bigger than herself. The tragic spectacle is such as to arouse great indignation and draw tears of sympathy! [15]

"The Cuckoo" Guo Moruo

饿

我以为，如果你的东西确是好的，直接说它好，没有什么不对。老王卖瓜，只要卖的是好瓜，为什么不能自卖自夸？

老兄，老王是靠卖瓜吃饭的，叫他也学我们书生扭扭捏捏，对自己的瓜谦虚一番，生意还用做么？他保证**饿**死大吉。

《欣赏自己》英培安

I don't think it's wrong for you to freely praise yourself if you're really worthy of praise. As we know, there is an old Chinese saying disparaging a melon peddler, named Lao Wang, who keeps praising his own goods. Well, why can't he praise his melons if they are really sweet and juicy?

Friends, Lao Wang sells melons for a living. How could he carry on business if he, by imitating the affectations of us intellectuals, were to show false modesty about his melons? He would sure enough die of ***starvation***.[15]

"On Self-Appreciation" Ying Pei'an

馆、饱、饭、饿

车子驶到卡德路，我就下来了。怀着一颗兴奋的心，跑去找光光。她和元真正穷的没发过日子，见我去时很高兴，猜想我一定拿到了钱，连忙向我瓜分。我立刻给了她们两元，其余的两元多，就花在请她们吃饭的小**馆**子里，等到回去，又只剩几毛钱了。但我并不难受，我觉得吃了一顿**饱饭**，至少可以挨**饿**三天。

《饥饿》谢冰莹

After I got off the streetcar at the Carter Road stop, I hurried excitedly to call on Guang Guang. Being hard up, she and Yuan Zhen were immensely pleased to see me, guessing I must have brought some money with me to share with them. I quickly gave them two dollars and spent the remaining two dollars and something treating them to dinner at a small ***eatery***. I returned home with only a few cents left. But I didn't care, because I knew I had had a ***full meal*** to last me three days without feeling ***hungry***.[15]

"Hunger" Xie Bingying

四、四画

牜（牛）

"牛"本意为"大的畜牲"，用"**牜**（牛）"组合的字往往与牲畜相关。例字中除"**牛、牢**"外，其他为形声字：左形右声。

物

你如果有时情绪烦躁，心情抑郁，我劝你到小巷里负手行吟一阵，你一定会豁然开朗，怡然自得，**物**我两忘。

《巷》柯灵

When you are fidgety or depressed, go to the lane and wander around reciting or composing poems with your hands crossed behind your back. You will then suddenly fall into a bright mood and enjoy inner peace, forgetting both yourself and ***the external world***.[15]

"The Lane" Ke Ling

此例中"**物**"为意译。根据对上下文的理解，"**物**我两忘"的"我"指自己、自身，含"内"之意。"物"与"我"相对，故其所指并非某种物质，而是与"内"相对的"外"即"**the external world**"。

犊、牛：象形字。

"渐"的作用，就是用每步相差极微缓的方法来隐蔽时间的过去与事物的变迁的痕迹，使人误认为其恒久不变。这真是造物主骗人的一大诡计。这有一件比喻的故事：某农夫每天朝晨抱了**犊**而跳过一沟，到田里去工作，夕暮又抱了它跳过沟回家。每日如此，未尝间断。过了一年，犊已渐大，渐重，差不多变成大**牛**，但农夫全不察觉，仍是抱了它跳沟。有一天他因事停止工作，次日再就不能抱了这牛而跳沟了。造物的骗人，使人流连于其每日每时的生的欢喜而不觉察其变迁与辛苦，就是用这个方法的，人们每日在抱了日重一日的牛而跳沟，不准停止。自己误以为是不变的，其实每日在增加其劳苦！

《渐》丰子恺

Through bit-by-bit change, "gradualness" conceals from notice the lapse of time and the change of things, so that people are misled into believing that everything remains the same eternally. What a trick the Creator is playing on humans! Here is a story by way of illustration. There was a farmer who would jump over a ditch holding a ***calf*** in his arms on his way to work in the fields every morning and also on his way back home every evening. A year later, this calf had grown bigger and heavier, almost like a ***cow***, but the farmer, insensible to its increasing weight, continued the same old daily routine. One day, however, he didn't go to work for some reason. And starting from the next day, he was no longer able to carry his calf in his arms in jumping over the ditch. The Creator used the same trick to make you so obsessed with life that you become oblivious to its changeableness and hardships. You are kept jumping over the ditch nonstop day after day with the growing calf in your arms. While you suppose wrongly that life is immutable, you are in fact putting heavier burdens on yourself from day to day. [15]

"Gradualness" Feng Zikai

牢：会意字。由宀、由牛会意。"宀"意为交相覆盖的深邃的屋子。

在这个中学时期中，本来是我的黄金时代，谁知我的活泼快乐的童年，竟销灭于这如**牢**狱似的学校生活中，至今想来，对于当时那种专门以压迫手段的学校教育，犹觉不寒而栗了。

《中学时代生活的回忆》庐隐

My high school days would have been my golden age had it not been for the ***prison***-like life. Today, I still cannot help shuddering at the thought of the erstwhile coercion-oriented school education. [15]

"Recollections of My High School Days" Lu Yin

五、五画

钅（金）

由"钅"（金）组合的字与金属有关。例字皆为形声字：左形右声。

钟

古木无人径，　Among the old trees no path is seen anywhere,
深山何处**钟**。　In the deep mountain the sound of the temple ***bell*** comes from somewhere. [13]

《过香积寺》　"Visiting the Xiangji Temple"
（唐）王维　（The Tang Dynasty）Wang Wei

钩

无言独上西楼，　Silent, I climb the Western Tower alone
月如**钩**。　And see the ***hook***-like moon.
寂寞梧桐深院锁清秋。　Parasol-trees lonesome and drear
　Lock in the courtyard autumn clear.

剪不断，　Cut , it won't sever;
理还乱，　Be ruled, 'twill never.
是离愁。　What sorrow 'tis to part! [1]
别是一番滋味在心头。　It's an unspeakable taste in the heart. [1]
《相见欢》　Tune: Joy at Meeting
（南唐）李煜　（The Nontang Dynasty）Li Yu

锁（鎖：其右半部音 suo）

翠立数峰寒，	Peak on peak stands like emerald;
碧**锁**暮云间。	Cloud on cloud ***locks*** the evening cold.
媚景春前赏，	Gaze on the charming vernal plain
晴岚雨后看。	And sun-lit hills after the rain!
开颜，	O brighten up
玉盏金波满。	And fill to the brim with golden wine the jade cup!
狼山，	Deep in the hill,
人生相会难。	It's hard for us to meet, so let's enjoy our fill![5]
《得胜令》	Tune: Triumphant Song
（元）庾天赐	(The Yuan Dynasty) Yu Tianci

锐

何日请缨提**锐**旅？	When can I get the order
一鞭直渡清河洛。	To lead my warriors ***brave***,
	Whipping my steed, to cross the river wave
	And clear the border?[1]

《满江红·登黄鹤楼有感》

Tune: The River All Red, "On Mounting Yellow Crane Tower"

（宋）岳飞 (The Song Dynasty) Yue Fei

镕

钓晚霞寒波濯锦，	The rainbow cloud steeped in cold waves looks like brocades;
看秋潮夜海**镕**金。	The autumn moon like ***molten*** gold on the sea fades.[5]

《满庭芳·渔父词》

Tune: Courtyard Full of Fragrance, "Song of a Fishman"

（元）乔吉 (The Yuan Dynasty) Qiao Ji

原文中"***镕***"为主动形式，译文中用过去分词"**molten**"表达出其潜在的被动含义。

镜

心虚则性见，不息心则求见性，如拨波觅月；意净则心清，不了意而求明心，如索**镜**增尘。

《菜根谭》（明）洪应明

When internal distracting thoughts are banished, the true nature will emerge of itself. If one tries to seek the true nature by not banishing the distracting thoughts, it is like seeking the moon in a pool. When the mind is purified, the heart will then become clear. If one tries to keep a clear heart by not purifying his mind, it is like strewing more dust onto a misty ***mirror***. [6]

"The Roots of Wisdom" (The Ming Dynasty) Hong Yingming

鏦鏦錚錚

欧阳子方夜读书，闻有声自西南来者，悚然而听之，曰："异哉!"初淅沥以萧飒，忽奔腾而澎湃，如波涛夜惊，风雨骤至。其触于物也，***鏦鏦錚錚***，金铁皆鸣；又如赴敌之兵，衔枚疾走，不闻号令，但闻人马之声。予谓童子："此何声也？汝出视之。"童子曰："星月皎洁，明河在天。四无人声，声在树间。"

《秋声赋》（宋）欧阳修

I was just beginning my night reading when a sound was heard coming from the southwest and I listened to it with awe and astonishment, saying, "How strange!" For it was first like something rustling and soughing, then like boisterous waves raised by a sudden night tempest, dashing, pounding and booming. The moment it touched a thing, it brought forth a ***clanking*** metallic ring, or it struck me as the sound of troops going to the front, having gags in their mouths, with muffled words of command, leaving audible only the treading of men and horses. I asked my page, "What sound is it? You just go and have a look." He however replied, "The moon and the stars are bright and the Milky Way is in the sky. No sound is heard around here, it is in the trees." [12]

"The Sound of Autumn" (The Song Dynasty) Ouyang Xiu

铲

铲刈秽草，伐去恶木，烈火而焚之。嘉木立，美竹露，奇石显。

《永州八记》（唐）柳宗元

We ***mowed*** the noisome weeds and cut the rotted trees and then set them on fire. Soon sturdy trees, graceful bamboos and anomalous rocks all stood out. [8]

"Eight Travel Journals on the State of Yong"
(The Tang Dynasty) Liu Zongyuan

锋

观夫高祖之所以胜、项籍之所以败者，在能忍与不能忍之间而已矣。项籍唯不能忍，是以百战百胜而轻用其**锋**；高祖忍之，养其全**锋**而待其敝，此子房之教也。

《留侯论》（宋）苏轼

As indicated by the victory of Emperor Liu Bang and the defeat of King Xiang Ji, forbearance or no forbearance made a world of difference. King Xiang Ji, being impatient, and encouraged by one victory after another, made light of using his apparently invincible ***force***. Emperor Liu Bang, on the other hand, overcame his impatience and kept the full ***vigor*** of his army, waiting for the King's spending himself. And this strategy was taught by the Marquis. [12]

"On the Marquis of Liu" (The Song Dynasty) Su Shi

语篇中所指的"**锋**"是军队，而非刀剑之锋。第一个"用其**锋**"之"锋"，指武力，译为"**force**"（violent physical action to obtain or achieve sth）。第二个"养其全**锋**"之"锋"的含义从"养精蓄锐"之"养"字体现出来，故译为"***vigor***"（energy, force or enthusiasm）。

铺

东边路西边路南边路，	East, west and south, everywhere you see the path,
五里铺七里铺十里**铺**。	Five, seven and ten miles, every step you get to the ***stop***. [10]

《塞鸿秋·山行警》

Tune: Autumn Swan on Frontier, "Along the Mountain Path"

（元）无名氏　　(The Yuan Dynasty) Anonymous

"**铺**"是古时驿站或兵站。两行诗中，并列了六种具象（三路、三铺），行路人之"倦"与"盼"即凸现而出，无需任何赘词冗语。译文中，出于英语遣词造句的语法要求，更是由于严密的抽象逻辑思维表达形式的需要，根据英语的句法结构，增添了动词、冠词、连词和介词，将原句中的具象组合改换成两个完整的逻辑语句，不仅句式工整，词义贴切对应，语句流畅通顺，而且最大限度地保留了原诗的具象。

疒

由"**疒**"组成的字大都与疾病有关。例字皆为形声字：外形内声。

病

亲朋无一字，	Not a word from family or friends.
老**病**有孤舟。	Old and ***sick***, on a solitary boat,

戎马关山北，	As the war rages on in the northern mountain passes.
凭轩涕泗流。	Leaning from the balustrade, I cannot control my tears. [2]
《登岳阳楼》	"Climbing Yueyang Tower"
（唐）杜甫	（The Tang Dynasty） Du Fu

疴

烦**疴**近消散，	My gloomy mood and minor ***illness*** are no more,
嘉宾复满堂。	Furthermore the honored guests crowd the hall. [13]
《郡斋雨中与诸文士燕集》	"Entertaining the Scholars in the Hall of My Prefecture Office When It's Raining Outside"
（唐）韦应物	（The Tang Dynasty） Wei Yingwu

痕

纱窗日落渐黄昏，	The sunlight on the window is gone and dusk gradually nears,
金屋无人见泪**痕**。	In her gilded room no one sees the ***stains*** of the maid's tears.
寂寞空庭春欲晚，	The courtyard is deserted and spring is almost gone,
梨花满地不开门。	The pear flowers have covered the ground but she has no heart to open the door to look on. [13]
《春怨》	"A Palace Maid's Resentment on a Spring Day"
（唐）刘方平	（The Tang Dynasty） Liu Fangping

瘴

江静潮初落，	The river's calm because the tide has just edded,
林昏**瘴**不开。	The woods are dim because the ***miasma*** hasn't dispersed. [13]
《题大庾岭北驿》	"A Poem Written at the North Side of the Dayu Ridge"
（唐）宋之问	（The Song Dynasty） Song Zhiwen

瘦

1. 枯藤老树昏鸦，	Over old trees wreathed with rotten vines fly crows;
小桥流水人家，	Under a small bridge beside a cot a stream flows;
古道西风**瘦**马。	On ancient road in western breeze a ***lean*** horse goes.
夕阳西下，	Westwards declines the setting sun.
断肠人在天涯。	Far, far from home is the heart-broken one. [5]
《天净沙 · 秋思》	Tune: Sunny Sand, "Autumn Thoughts"
（元）马致远	（The Yuan Dynasty） Ma Zhiyuan

2. 东风花外小红楼，　The east wind can't bring flower to her small red bower;
南浦山横眉黛愁。　The mountains bar the sky like eyebrows in green dye.
春寒不管花枝**瘦**，　The cold spring cares not of the ***slender*** blooming tree,
无情水自流。　The heartless water flows away, carefree. [5]
《水仙子》　Tune: Song of Daffodils
（元）倪瓒　(The Yuan Dynasty) Ni Zan

两例“**瘦**”的译文取决于其所修饰的词。“**瘦**马”之“瘦”意指马膘之不肥，故译文选取“**lean**”（without much flesh）。“花枝**瘦**”之“瘦”在于表现花枝的“细”及“柔弱”，译文选取“**slender**”（thin or narrow）与原文之意思相符。

痤、痔

有医竘者，秦之良医也。为宣王割**痤**，为惠王疗**痔**，皆愈。
张子之背肿，命竘治之，谓竘曰：“背非吾背也，任子制焉。”治之遂愈。
竘诚善治疾也，张子委制焉。

《尸子》（战国）尸子

Dr. Ju was a famous physician of the state of Qin. He had cut a ***tumor*** for Emperor Xuanwang and healed ***haemorrhoids*** for Emperor Huiwang.

A certain Mr. Zhang who was afflicted with a sore back asked the physician to treat it.

"I will not regard it as my back any longer. Do whatever you think fit with it!" he said.

Given a free hand, the physician cured his patient in no time.

There is no doubt that Dr. Ju was well versed in his craft, but the fact that Zhang put himself entirely in the doctor's hands also accounts for his prompt recovery. [14]

"Shi Zi" (The Warring States Period) Shi Zi

疲

天下之事，常发于至微，而终为大患；始以为不足治，而终至于不可为。当其易也，惜旦夕之力，忽之而不顾；及其即成也，积岁月，**疲**思虑，而仅克之，……盖众人之所可知者，众人之所能治也，其势虽危，而未足深畏。唯萌于不必忧之地，而寓于不可见之初，众人笑而忽之者，此则君子之所畏也。

《指喻》（明）方孝孺

Things in the world often occur in the most insignificant form and grow to be great troubles. What is considered at the outset undeserving of care proves at last irremediable. What can be easily remedied is ignored on account of one's grudging a moment's effort. Once it is far advanced, it can only be overcome at the cost of ***carking*** cares over months or years. ...Those known and manifest to everybody can be remedied by all and, no matter in how perilous a condition, they are not to be much feared. Only things at the budding stage where no worries are needed, and in the initial state where no indications are evident, thus liable to be taken lightly and ignored, are really to be dreaded by sensible people. [12]

"The Parable of a Thumb Disease" (The Ming Dynasty) Fang Xiaoru

疾、病：疾，矢声。矢，上古属脂部。疾属质部。

盖尝试论之：天下之势，譬如一身。王公贵人所以养其身者，岂不至哉？而其平居常苦于多**疾**。至于农夫小民，终岁勤苦而未尝告**病**。此其故何也？

《教战守策》（宋）苏轼

It would be appropriate to try this analogy: The world may be likened to a human body. Are not the members of the nobility doing their utmost to preserve their health? But in their daily life they are often plagued with many ***illnesses***, whereas the vulgar farmers are seldom afflicted with ***ailments*** in spite of their hard labor during the whole year. How to explain it? [12]

"On Military Training" (The Song Dynasty) Su Shi

例中"疾"与"病"为直译。"苦于多**疾**"之"疾"指的是任何疾病或不适，故译文取"**illnesses**"(sickness)。根据对原文的理解，这里"告**病**"之"病"一般指小恙，故将其译为"**ailments**"(an illness that is not very serious)。

衤

用"**衤**"（衣）组合的字与衣服、衣料等有关。例字中除"**初**"外，其余为形声字，其中，"**裳**、**袋**"为下形上声，其他为左形右声。

裳

幽映每白日，	On every sunny day through the willows shines the sun bright,
清辉照衣**裳**。	Upon his ***clothes*** shedding its clear and brilliant light. [13]
《阙题》	"A Poem Without a Title"
（唐）刘昚虚	(The Tang Dynasty) Liu Shenxu

袋

昔有愚人入京选，皮**袋**被贼盗去。

其人曰："贼偷我袋，终将不得我物用。"

或问其故，答曰："钥匙尚在我衣带上，彼将何物开之？"

《朝野佥载》（唐）张鷟

There was once a fool who, on coming to the capital for the civil examination, discovered that he had lost his leather ***bag***.

"Though a thief has stolen my bag," he said calmly, "he won't be able to touch the contents."

Asked why, he said, "I still have the key, so what is he going to open the bag with?"[14]

"Chao Ye Xian Zai" (The Tang Dynasty) Zhang Zhuo

褪

人倚梨花病酒，	Drunk, I lean on pear trees in blossoms bright,
月明杨柳维舟。	But willow twigs cannot tie the boat with moonlight.
试上层楼，	I try to go upstairs to gaze far, far away,
绿满江南，	But find the Southern River-shore with green overspread
红***褪***春愁。	And vernal grief ***fading*** in ***fallen*** red.[5]
《折桂令 · 次韵》	Tune: Plucking Laurel Branch, "Rhyming with a Friend"
（元）张可久	(The Yuan Dynasty) Zhang Kejiu

"褪"在原文中为动词。"绿满江南"，说明已进入夏季。"红***褪***春愁"既指春愁之消退，也指夏季之"绿肥红瘦"。随着季节的更替，"春愁"逐渐消失，"褪春愁"之"褪"的译文选取"**fade**"（to disappear gradually）即此"褪"之意。为符合译语语言规范，"fade"转换为现在分词（fading），与其逻辑主语"vernal grief"一起构成"find"的复合宾语"红褪"可以理解为暮春时节，花渐凋谢，此"褪"之译文"**fall**"（to drop down from a higher level to a lower level）之意含"落"花之"落"，即诗中所含之意。在诗句中转换为形容词，修饰"red"。

袖

天寒翠***袖***薄，	The weather becomes cold and her ***clothes*** are thin,
日暮倚修竹。	Yet she still leans against the tall bamboos when the sun's setting.[13]
《佳人》	"A Beauty"
（唐）杜甫	(The Tang Dynasty) Du Fu

此处"袖"译为"**clothes**"乃取其上位词，即"袖"之意的外延。"袖"为衣服的一部分，"***袖***薄"之意乃所穿衣服单薄。

襟

相送情无限，	I see you off with affection boundless,
沾**襟**比散丝。	***The front part of my garment*** is wet with my tears like the drizzle endless. [13]

《赋得暮雨送李曹》

"A Poem with the Given Title Evening Rain in Farewell to Mr. Li"

（唐）韦应物 （The Tang Dynasty） Wei Yingwu

裙

钿头银篦击节碎，	Beating time they oft shattered pearl-decorated silver-combs and so on,
血色罗**裙**翻酒污。	In applauding my performance wine was oft spilt to stain many a ***gown***. [13]

《琵琶行》 "Song of a Female Pipa-Player"

（唐）白居易 （The Tang Dynasty） Bai Juyi

补

天薄我以福，吾厚德以迓之；天劳我以形，吾逸吾心以**补**之；天厄我以遇，吾亨吾道以通之。天且奈我何哉？

《菜根谭》（明）洪应明

Should the fate make my fortune inadequate, I would increase the store of my virtue to replenish it. Should the fate make my body exhausted in labor, I would relax my mind to ***remedy*** it. Should the fate make my life unfavorable, I would enhance my moral principles to smooth it. That way, what then, can the fate do to me?[6]

"The Roots of Wisdom" （The Ming Dynasty） Hong Yingming

初：会意字，由“刀”、由“衣”会意：开始裁衣。

1. 薄雾浓云愁永昼，	In thin mist and thick cloud of incense, sad I stay.
瑞脑销金兽。	The animal-shaped censer I see all day.
佳节又重阳，	The double Ninth Festival comes again.
玉枕纱橱，	Still alone I remain
半夜凉**初**透。	In the curtain of gauze, on a pillow of jade,
	Which the midnight chill ***begins*** to invade. [1]

《醉花阴 · 九月》

Tune: Tipsy in the Flower's Shade, "The Double Ninth Festival"

（宋）李清照　　　　（The Song Dynasty）Li Qingzhao

2. 江畔何人***初***见月，　When did the moon ***first*** shine on men?
江月何年***初***照人？　Who ***first*** saw the moon from the riverside?[2]
《春江花月夜》　　“Spring, the River, Flowers, the Moon: Night”
（唐）张若虚　　（The Tang Dynasty）Zhang Ruoxu

3. 孤山寺北贾亭西，　North of Gushan Temple, west of the Jia Pavilion,
水面***初***平云脚低。　Cloud mists hug the ***newly*** brimming banks.[2]
《钱塘湖春行》　　“A Spring Outing by Qiantang Lake”
（唐）白居易　　（The Tang Dynasty）Bai Juyi

4. 少年智则国智，少年富则国富；少年强则国强，少年独立则国独立；少年自由则国自由，少年进步则国进步；少年胜于欧洲则国胜于欧洲，少年雄于地球则国雄于地球。红日***初***升，其道大光。

《少年中国说》梁启超

If the youth are wise, so will be their country. If the youth are rich, so will be their country. If the youth are strong, so will be their country. If the youth are independent, so will be their country. If the youth are free, so will be their country. If the youth are progressive, so will be their country. If the youth are superior to Europe, so will be their country. If the youth stand majestically on the globe, so will their country.[12]

The red sun is ***just*** rising, the way ahead is bathed in its brilliant rays.

“A Youthful China” Liang Qichao

例 1“凉***初***透”之意为“开始感觉到凉意”。译文“**begins**”即“开始”。**例 2** 之“初”含有“最初”之意，译为“**first**”（at the beginning）。**例 3** 之“初”含意“刚刚”，故译为“**newly**”（recently）。**例 4**“初”之意为“此时，眼下”，“**just**”（at this/that moment; now）即含此意。

罒（网）

用“罒”（网）组合的字，往往与“网”状物及其用途相关。例字中，除“**罪**”外，其余皆为形声字：上形下声。

署

有趣的是 1949 年 10 月新中国成立，政务院有个管出版事业的直属机构叫出版总**署**，胡愈老任署长，周建老和我任副署长，二十多年前在商务编译所共事的老朋友又聚在一起了。

《我和我的商务印书馆》叶圣陶

Interestingly enough, when the General ***Administration*** of Publication was established following the birth of New China to take charge of publication directly under the Government Administration Council, Hu Yuzhi was appointed as its director and Zhou Jianren and I as its deputy director. So the three old friends who had been colleagues over 20 years before at the Editing and Translating Department of The Commercial Press met again. [15]

"The Commercial Press and I" Ye Shengtao

罩

1. 我们的兄弟，爱斯基摩人用冰块建筑的房子，像个白玉的钟**罩**一般，是没有什么窗子的。过去的鄂伦春兄弟们住的“神仙柱”，因为没有屋顶，在屋里，到晚上可以看到头上的月亮和星光，也就无须开窗子了。

《黎明的眼睛》端木蕻良

Our Eskimo brothers' houses, built of large blocks of frozen snow and shaped like white-jade clock ***covers***, have no windows at all. Our Oroqen brothers used to live in roofless houses with no need for windows because they could in the evening enjoy the moon and stars overhead indoors. [15]

"The Window" Duanmu Hongliang

2. 我们开车北行，一路上经过塔尖如梦的牛津，城楼似幻的勒德洛（Ludlow），古桥野渡的蔡斯特（Chester），雨云始终**罩**在车顶，雨点在车窗上也未干过。

《西欧的夏天》余光中

We drove up north through Oxford with its dreamy spires, Ludlow with its illusory old castles and Chester with its ancient bridge and solitary ferry crossing. Rain clouds continued to ***hang*** over our car and raindrops remained intact on its windows. [15]

"Summer in Western Europe" Yu Guangzhong

例 2 之“**罩**”为动词，意译。“雨云始终**罩**在车顶”，此“云”只能是如同罩子一般悬浮在车顶的上方，而非真正罩在其上，译文取“**hang**（be suspended）”。

骂

1. 我联想到母亲死的时候。母亲死以后，父亲怎样打我，又娶一个新母亲来。这个母亲很客气，不打我，就是**骂**，也是指着桌子或椅子来骂我。客气是越客气了，但是冷淡了，疏远了，生人一样。

《祖父死了的时候》萧红

Then I remembered how, after mother's death, father had remarried and often beat me. My new mother was seemingly polite and never beat me. Even when she ***cursed*** me, she would do it in a roundabout way by referring to something else, say, a chair or table. Polite as she was, we were strangers yet.[15]

"When Grandpa Died" Xiao Hong

3. 他常常说："凡事只要差不多，就好了。何必太精明呢？"

他小时候，他妈叫他去买红糖，他买了白糖回来。他妈**骂**他，他摇摇头说："红糖白糖不是差不多吗？"

《差不多先生》胡适

He often says, "Whatever we do, it's OK to be just about right. What's the use of being précise and accurate?"

One day, when he was a child, his mother sent him out to buy her some brown sugar, but he returned with some white sugar instead. As his mother ***scolded*** him about it, he shook his head and said, "Brown sugar or white sugar, aren't they about the same?"[15]

"Mr. About-the-Same" Hu Shi

此两例"**骂**"之译文的不同在于其施动者。**例 1** 的作者受到其继母的"骂"，其译文使用"**curse**"（to say rude things to sb）表达出了这位继母对作者的"不喜欢"。**例 2** 是一位母亲对自己做错事孩子的"骂"。其译文使用"**scold**"（to speak angrily to sb, especially to a child, because he has done sth wrong），表达出这位母亲因孩子做错事所表现出的那种口头上唠唠叨叨的指责。不同的译文充分体现出原文所中所蕴含的不同情感。

置

这贮藏室于是成了我一生中唯一的书房，也许称之为小作坊更为贴切。狭长逼仄的一小间，北窗下靠墙**置**一旧书桌，进门处兀立两只叠起来的玻璃书柜，都是原先住户废弃的家具。除了窗下书桌前可容纳我的一把旧藤椅，就没有多余的空间了。

《书房》何为

The storeroom was the only study I've ever had in my life. Perhaps it could be aptly called a workshop. It was long, narrow and small. An old desk ***stood*** against a wall under the northern window. Two piled-up glass bookcases rose erect near the entrance. They were the furniture abandoned by a former resident. There was no room for anything else besides my old cane chair placed before the desk under the window. [15]

"My Study" He Wei

此"置"之译文"**stand**"(to put sth/sb in an upright position somewhere)体现出书桌的放置状态。

罪:会意字,由网、非会意[9](非法捕鱼)。

别了,我爱的中国,我全心爱着的中国!

我不忍离了中国而去,更不忍在这大时代中放弃每人应做的工作而去,抛弃了许多亲爱的勇士们在后面,他们是正用他们的血建造着新的中国,正在以纯挚的热诚,争斗着,奋击着。我这样不负责任的离开了中国,我真是一个**罪**人!

《离别》郑振铎

Farewell, China, my beloved homeland!

I cannot find it in my heart to leave China, much less during these stormy times when I have to abandon my bounden duty and leave behind so many dear brave fighters—men who are building a new China with their own blood and struggling and battling in all earnest. To quit China at this moment means to dodge my responsibility and that makes me feel very ***guilty*** indeed! [15]

"Parting Sorrows" Zheng Zhenduo

六、十画

髟

由"***髟***"组成的字往往与须、发相关。例字皆为形声字:上形下声。

鬓

1. 瘦马驮诗天一涯,　I roam on a lean horse laden with verse I write;
   倦鸟呼愁村数家。　Tired birds over desolate villages in sight.
   扑头飞柳花,　Overhead willow down in flight
   与人添**鬓**华。　Adds to my ***forehead hair*** white. [5]

   《凭阑人·金陵道中》

   Tune: Leaning on Balustrade, "On My Way to Jinling "

   (元)乔吉　(The Yuan Dynasty) Qiao Ji

2. 从他绿**鬓**斑,　Let my black ***hair*** turn grey!
   欹枕白石烂。　I'll pillow my head on white stone till its decay.

回头红日晚，　I turn my head: the setting sun reddens the sky;
满目青山矸。　Verdant hills look serene to the eye. [5]
《燕儿落》　Tune: Falling Swan
（元）庾天赐　(The Yuan Dynasty) Yu Tianci

髻

1. 系行舟谁遣卿卿？　Who sends you, my fair songstress, to my boat?
爱林下风姿，　I love you come like breeze into the wood with ease.
云外歌声。　Beyond the cloud your songs float.
宝**髻**堆云，　I see your cloudlike ***hair***
冰弦散雨，　And hear your icy strings spread rain in the air,
总是才情。　In which I find a genius mind. [5]
《蟾宫曲·赠乐府珠帘秀》
Tune: Song of Moon Palace, "Written for My fair Songstress While Dunks"
（元）卢挚　(The Yuan Dynasty) Lu Zhi

2. 予九岁憩书斋，汝梳双**髻**，批单缣来，温《缁衣》一章。适先生奓户入，闻两童子音郎朗然，不觉莞尔，连呼则则。

《祭妹文》（清）袁枚

One day when I was only nine, I was taking a rest in my study when you came in with your double ***chignons*** and in your sateen robe. Then we reviewed the passage of Ziyi in the *Book* of *Odes*. At that moment our tutor opened the door and heard us two children reading aloud; he could not help smiling and uttering some praises. [12]

"Lament for My Younger Sister" (The Qing Dynasty) Yuan Mei

"髻"：在头顶或脑后盘成各种形状的头发。译文中两例"髻"的不同在于其所盘之形状。

鬑

为人洁白皙，　His skin is so fair
鬑鬑颇有须；　And he wears a ***long*** beard.
盈盈公府步，　He moves in the yamen
冉冉府中趋。　With steps slow and stately;
坐中数千人，　He sits among thousands
皆言夫婿殊。　Who owns him their best. [4]
《陌上桑》　"By the Roadside Mulberry"
（汉）　(The Han Dynasty)

髭鬚

追往事，	Recalling days gone by,
叹今吾，	I sigh over my plight:
春风不染白**髭鬚**。	The vernal wind can't change my ***hair*** to black from white.
却将万字平戎策，	Since thwarted is my plan for gaining the lost land,
换得东家种树书，	I'd learn from gentle neighbors how to plant fruit trees by hand. [1]
《鹧鸪天》	Tune: The Partridge Sky
（宋）辛弃疾	(The Song Dynasty) Xin Qiji

"髭"为嘴边的胡子；"鬚（须）"原来指长在下巴上的胡子，后来泛指胡须。根据上下文"追往事，叹今吾，春风不染白髭鬚"可以看出，作者已处暮年，须发皆白，即使春风也不能将其染黑。"**hair**"即可指头发，也含"毛发"之意，译文使用"hair"似更能表达出作者的本意。

髮

睨柱吞嬴，	Against the chieftain of the foe,
回旗走懿，	I would fight in weal and in woe.
千古冲冠**髮**。	Wrath sets my ***hair*** on end
伴人无寐，	And it will never die.
秦淮应是孤月。	Sleeping at night, you would only have for friend The lonely moon on the River Qinhuai. [1]

《念奴娇·驿中言别友人》

Tune: Charm of a Maiden Singer, "Farewell to a Friend at Post House"

（宋）文天祥　　(The Song Dynasty) Wen Tianxiang

髯

先外祖长身白**髯**，喜饮酒；酒酣，辄大声吟所作诗，令吾母指其疵。

《鸣机夜课图记》（清）蒋士铨

My maternal grandfather was tall and grew a long white ***beard***, much given to wine. When intoxicated, he would read aloud the poems he had written and ask Mother to pick holes in them. [12]

"The Picture of Nocturnal Weaving and Reading" (The Qing Dynasty) Jiang Shiquan

练　　习

写出下列划线词的构成及其在文中的词意，将斜体字译出，并简要说明所使用的方法。

1. 莫嫌旧日云中守，　Oh, my emperor, never cold-shoulder him, a Wei Shang of yore,
   犹堪一战取**功**勋。　He still can fight and achieve ________ after all.[13]
   《老将行》　"Song of an Old General"
   （唐）王维　(The Tang Dynasty) Wang Wei

2. **男**儿事长征，　________ joined the forces of the expedition long,
   少小幽燕客。　So he came to the northern frontier when young.[13]
   《古意》　"The Frontier Guard"
   （唐）李颀　(The Tang Dynasty) Li Qi

3. 谦虚的工作者常易**取**得热情的支持，浮夸的工作者则常受到冷淡的对待。

《杂感集》黄药眠

Modesty will ________ warm support; boastfulness will be cold shouldered.[15]

"Random Thoughts" (Excerpt) Huang Yaomian

4. 我应该感谢母亲，她教给我与困难作斗争的经验，我在家庭生活中已经饱尝艰苦，这使我在三十多年的军事生活和革命生活中，再没有感到困难和被困难吓倒。母亲**又**给我一个健康的身体和一个劳动的习惯，使我从来没有感到过劳累。

《母亲的回忆》朱德

I owe mother a debt of gratitude because she taught me how to cope with the numerous difficulties that I ran into at home so that later during my over 30 years of military and revolutionary life I have never bowed down to my difficulty. She ________ bequeathed me a strong constitution as well as a strong inclination for labour so that I have been able to work untiringly.[15]

"Loving Memories of Mother" Zhu De

5. **山**随平原尽，　The ________ end where begins the plain,
   江入大荒流。　The Yangtze River runs on the boundless champaign.[13]
   《渡荆门送别》　"Farewell to Sichuan at Mountain Jingmen"
   （唐）李白　(The Tang Dynasty) Li Bai

6. **明**月出天山，　From behind Mount Tian rises the moon ________,
苍茫云海间。　Then it goes through a sea of clouds white.
长风几万里，　The mighty wind blows by from ten thousand li away,
吹度玉门关。　And passes through the Yumen Pass on its way. [13]
《关山月》　"The Moon Over the Passas and the Mountains"
（唐）李白　(The Tang Dynasty) Li Bai

7. 深秋帘幕千家雨，　In deep autumn, a thousand shuttered households in the rain.
落日**楼**台一笛风。　Upon the ________ at sunset, a single flute against the wind. [2]
《题宣州开元寺水阁》　"Composed at the Water Pavilion of Kaiyuan Temple"
（唐）杜牧　(The Tang Dynasty) Du Mu

8. 泛浮**槎**，　I pass my life
寄生涯，　On floating ________
长江万里秋风驾。　Steered by the autumn breeze on the river with pleasure. [5]
《拨不断 · 闲乐》　Tune: Unbroken String, " Leisure and Pleasure"
（元）吴弘道　(The Yuan Dynasty) Wu Hongdao

9. 抽刀断水水更流，　I draw my sword to cut the running water and still it flows,
举杯消**愁**愁更愁。　I drink wine to drown my ________ and still it grows. [13]
《宣州谢朓楼饯别校书叔云》　" Giving a Farewell Dinner to Uncle Yun, a Book Collator, on Xie Tiao Tower in Xuanzhou"
（唐）李白　(The Tang Dynasty) Li Bai

10. 征帆去棹残阳里，　In the declining sun sails come and go;
背西风、　In west wind wineshop flags fly high and low.
酒旗斜矗。　The painted ________
彩**舟**云淡，　In clouds afloat,
星河鹭起，　Like stars in Milky Way white egrets fly.
画图难足。　What a picture before the eye! [1]
《桂枝香 · 金陵怀古》
Tune: Fragrance of Laurel Branch, "Memories of the Past Jinling"
（宋）王安石　(The Song Dynasty) Wang Anshi

11. 碧绿是代表和平，代表一种静美。一个人，哪怕他的脾气有如虎狼那么凶暴，我相信如果常住在海滨，一定会变得和**羔羊**一般驯良；同时，那些心怀狭隘的人，如果常与海做朋友，我相信如果他也会改变成豪爽，痛快的性格。

《海恋》谢冰莹

There is no denying the mightiness of the sea. I love her not only because she has the beautifulness and many intriguing objects hidden deep underneath her, but also because she is broad and liberal enough to turn the foul into the pure. The numerous small rivers that she accommodates may be of a black or yellow colour, but once they flow into her bosom, they instantly take on the green colour signifying peace and tranquility. A person with a terrifying hot temper will become, I believe as meek as a ________ after a long stay by the seashore. Likewise, I believe a narrow-minded person will become tolerant and open-hearted if he often keeps company with the sea. [15]

"I Love the Sea" Xie Bingying

12. 若是在鄙野的乡间，这时令满耳是虫声了。……它们高、低、宏、细、徐、作、歇，仿佛经过乐师的**精心**训练，所以这样无可批评，踌躇满志，其实他们每一个都是神妙的乐师；众妙毕集，各舒灵趣，哪有不成人间绝响的呢。

《没有秋虫的地方》叶圣陶

At a time like this, if I were in the lowly countryside, I would hear insects all around me.... Their performance, with a voice high or low, sonorous or piping, quick or slow, sustained or suspended, is flawless and skiful, as if they had undergone ________ training under a music master. In fact, each and every one of them is a consummate music master all by itself. As a constellation of fine artists, they each give full play to their unique talent. No wonder their performance has reached the peak of artistic perfection. [15]

" A Place Without Autumn Insects" Ye Shengtao

13. 昨夜梦见萧珊，她拉住我的手，说："你怎么成了这个样子?"我安慰她："我不要紧。"她哭起来，我心里难过，就**醒**了。

《再忆萧珊》巴金

Last night I met Xiao Shan again in a dream. She held me by the hand and asked, "What's up, dear? You're a wreck." "I'm all right," I answered consolingly. Then she wept. And I ________ up with grief in my heart. [15]

"More Memories of Xiao Shan" Ba Jin

14. 大概**趣**味云云，是指年长之后自动做学问之时而言，在年轻时候为学问打根底之际恐怕不能过分重视趣味。学问没有根底，趣味也很难滋生。任公先生的学问之所以那样的博大精深，涉笔成趣，左右逢源，不能不说的一大部分得力于他的学问根底之打得坚固。

《学问与趣味》梁实秋

Generally speaking, the so-called ________ begins to exist only when one is mature enough to engage in independent studies. It is improper, I am afraid, for young people to overstress the importance of interest while they are still in the period of leaning the basics of knowledge. Interest will never develop where no solid foundation has been laid for learning. There is no denying the fact that Mr. Liang owed his wide erudition and unusual literary talent, for the most part, to his good grasp of foundation knowledge. [15]

"Learning and Personal Inclination" Liang Shiqiu

15. 云销雨**霁**，彩彻区明。

《滕王阁序》（唐）王勃

The rainbow vanishes and the rain ________, and prismatic colours penetrate the bands of cumulus. [12]

"The Tower of Prince Teng" (The Tang Dynasty) Wang Bo

16. 浩荡离愁白日斜，
吟**鞭**东指即天涯。

My parting grief is boundless when the sun sinks low;
Eastward I point my ________ and far away I'll go. [22]

《已亥杂诗之五》（清）龚自珍

"Miscellanies of the Year 1839 (V)" (The Qing Dynasty) Gong Zizhen

17. 落红不是无情物，
化作春泥更**护**花。

The fallen blossoms are not an unfeeling thing;
Though turned to mud, they'd ________ flowers' growth next spring. [22]

《已亥杂诗之五》（清）龚自珍

"Miscellanies of the Year 1839 (V)" (The Qing Dynasty) Gong Zizhen

18. 顾瞻望宫阙，
俯仰御飞轩。
据**鞍**长叹息，
泪下如流泉。

I look back on the palace high;
My cab runs up and down the mountain.
Leaning on ________, long I sigh;
My tears stream down like flowing fountain. [21]

《扶风歌》（西晋）刘琨

"Riding the Wind" (The Western Jin Dynasty) Liu Kun

19. 散晴雪杨花清昼，
又一场心事悠悠。

Willow down wafts like snow on sunny day,
My heart is gone with it far, far away.

翠丝长不系雕鞍，　The willow twigs, though long, cannot retain
碧云寒空**掩**珠楼。　His parting steed; green clouds ________ the bower in vain.[5]

《集贤宾·咏柳忆别》
Tune: Meeting of Good Friends, "Parting underWillows Recalled"
（元）乔吉　(The Yuan Dynasty) Qiao Ji

20. 野**鹿**眠山草。　________ are lying peacefully in the grass,
山猿戏野花。　And monkeys are playing with flowers.[10]
《雁儿落兼得胜令·归隐》
Tune: From Falling Swan to Triumphant Song, "Retreating"
（元）张养好　(The Yuan Dynasty) Zhang Yanghao

21. 写字作画是雅事，亦是俗事。大丈夫不能立功天地，滋养生民，而以区区笔**墨**供人玩好，非俗事而何？

《潍县署中与舍弟墨第五书》（节录）（清）郑燮

Calligraphy and painting are considered fine arts, but are also vulgar occupations. Is it not a vulgar thing for a man who cannot do some service to the country and improve the life of the people to occupy himself with pen and ________ for the amusement of other people?

"Fifth Letter to Brother Mo, from the Magistrate's Residence at Weihsien"
(The Qing Dynasty) Zheng Xie

22. 严关百尺界天西，　The hundred-foot-high Great Wall bars the western sky;
万里征人驻马**蹄**。　Having journeyed for miles and miles, I stop my ______.
飞阁遥连秦树直，　The endless battlements join proud trees far and nigh;
缭垣斜压陇云低。　The surrounding walls weigh on clouds flying with speed.[22]

《出嘉峪关感赋》　"The Westernmost Stronghold"
（清）林则徐　(The Qing Dynasty) Lin Zexu

23. 花见我，　I see the bloom,
我见花，　The bloom sees me,
花应憔瘦。　Languid and lean she'd also be..
　I and the moon,
月对咱，　The moon and I,

咱对月，	Looking in my face, she'd feel shy.
月更害羞。	I ask the ________ soon,
与**天**说，	It won't reply,
说与天，	For like me it's slso in deep gloom. [5]
天也还愁。	
《水仙子·相思》	Tune: Song of Daffodils, "Lovesickness"
（元）刘庭信	(The Yuan Dynasty) Liu Tingxin

24. 花艺可以邀蝶，累石可以邀云，栽松可以邀风，贮水可以邀萍，筑台可以邀月，种蕉可以邀雨，植柳可以邀蝉。

《幽梦影》（节录）（清）张潮

Planting flowers invites the butterflies, and in the same way rocks invite ________, the pine invites winds, a water pond invites duckweed, a terrace may be said to invite the moon, bananas invite the rains and willows invite cicadas. [19]

"Quiet Dream Shadows" (The Qing Dynasty) Zhang Chao

25. 暮云收尽意清寒，	Evening clouds withdrawn, pure cold air floods the sky;
银汉无声转玉盘。	The River of Stars mute, a jade plate turns on high.
此生此夜不长好，	How oft can we enjoy a fine mid-autumn night?
明月明年**何**处看。	______ shall we view next year a silver moon so bright? [17]
《阳关曲·中秋月》	Tune: Song of the Sunny Pass, "The Mid-Autumn Moon"
（宋）苏轼	(The Song Dynasty) Su Shi

26. 禁里疏钟官舍晚，	The sound of the bell from the palace lingers at the off-work hour,
省中啼鸟**吏**人稀。	The birds in the left court are twittering and the ______ there are fewer. [13]
《赠郭给事》	"To High-Ranking Official Guo"
（唐）王维	(The Tang Dynasty) Wang Wei

27. 社坛烟淡散林鸦。	The incense on the altar fades
把酒观多稼。	And crows disperse into the glades.
霹雳弦声斗高下，	Wine cup in hand and bumper harvest in view,
	I hear strings rumbling low and high,
笑喧哗，	Mingle with cheerful cry.

壤歌亭外山如**画**。 Beyond Labor Pavilion hills look like ________ fair.[5]

《平湖乐 · 尧庙秋社》 Tune: Joy of Calm Lake, "Autumn festival at EmperorYao's Temple"

（元）王恽 (The Yuan Dynasty) Wang Yun

28. **画**屋风轻， Though the wind is light in the ________ hall,
翠被寒增， My green quilt is still cold.
也温不过早来袜儿冷。 How can it warm up my stockings at all?[5]

《高平煞》 Tune: High Level Epilogue

（元）曾瑞 (The Yuan Dynasty) Zeng Rui

29. 前日归时花正红， Peach blossoms were thriving when I returned the other day,
今夜宿时**枝**半空。 But half the ________ stand bare when I retire tonight.[17]

《夜惜禁中桃花因怀钱员外》 "Pity on the Fall of Peach Blossoms at Night"

（唐）白居易 (The Tang Dynasty) Bai Juyi

30. 海棠不惜胭脂色， The Chinese crabapple, sparing no carmine of her own,
独立蒙蒙细雨**中**。 Stands alone ________ misty drizzle in display.[17]

《春寒》 "Spring Chill"

（宋）陈与义 (The Song Dynasty) Chen Yuyi

31. 万物并育而不相害，道并行而不相悖。小德**川**流，大德敦化。

《中庸》（战国）子思

All things get nourished without impairing one another; all ways function without going against each other. Small virtues run forever like ________ currents, while great virtues keep purifying and enriching all.[23]

"Doctrine of the Mean" (The Warring States period) Zi Si

32. 读其书，见其人，精神且**千**万倍，若彼形骸外矣，又何如我书乎？

《焚书》（节录）（明）李贽

When you read my books, you shall see my mind and spirit even a ________ times more clearly than even if I were daily with you.[19]

"Exhortations" (The Ming Dynasty) Li Zhi

33. 子曰："中庸其至矣乎！民鲜能**久**矣！"

《中庸》（战国）子思

Confucius said, "Pefect is the doctrine of the mean as a great virtue! But it hasn't been found in the people ________!"[23]

"Doctrine of the Mean" (The Warring States period) Zi Si

34. 从来善养生者，莫过于孔子。何以知之？知之于“寝不尸，居不容”二语。使其好饰观瞻务，修边幅，时时求肖君子，处处欲为圣人，则其寝也，居也，不求尸而自尸，不求容而自容；则五官四体，不复有舒展之刻。岂有泥塑木雕之形，而能**久**长于世者哉？

《随时即景就事行乐之法》（节录）（清）李渔

No one knows the art of living better than Confucius. I know this from the statement that he "did not sleep like a corpse (with straight legs) and did not sit like a statue." If the Master had been completely absorbed in keeping decorum, intent on appearing like a gentleman at all hours and being seen as a sage at all times, then he would have had to lie down like a corpse and sit like a statue. His four limbs and his internal system would never have been able to relax. How cold such a stiff wooden statue expect to live a ________ life?

"The Arts of Sleeping, Walking, Sitting and Standing"

(The Qing Dynasty) Li Yu

35. 诗余戏笔不知狂，	Painting for pleasure after writing verses
岂是**丹**青费较量。	One brushes on the ________ and blues at random;
聚叶泼成千点墨，	A thousand ink-dots form the leaves,
攒花染出几痕霜。	Traces of frost stain the clustering flowers; …
《画菊》	"Painting the Chrysanthemums"
（清）曹雪芹	(The Qing Dynasty) Cao Xueqin

36. 谢公扶病，	What matters if the minister was ill,
羊昙挥泪，	And his friend shed tear on tear!
一醉都休。	What can I do but drink my fill?
古今几度：	How many splendid houses of olden days appear
生存华屋，	Fallen to ruins in the ________![5]
零落山**丘**。	
《人月圆 · 卜居外家东园》	Tune: Man and Moon, "Moving to My Mother's East Garden"
（元）元好问	(The Yuan Dynasty) Yuan Haowen

37. 独坐幽篁里，	Sitting in the bamboo grove alone,

弹琴复长啸。	I ________ the zither and long croon.
深林人不知，	Deep in the grove, no one sees me
明月来相照。	And high above is shining the moon. [17]
《竹里馆》	"In a Bamboo Grove"
（唐）王维	(The Tang Dynasty) Wang Wei

38. 关城树色**催**寒近，	The turning leaves of frontier trees will ________ the winter near,
御苑砧声向晚多。	And louder still at dusk will sound the palace washing blocks. [2]
《送魏万之京》	"Seeing Wei Wan Off to the Capital"
（唐）李颀	(The Tang Dynasty) Li Qi

39. 青山隐隐**水**迢迢，	Green mountains dim, and ________ wide;
秋尽江南草未凋。	Unwithered yet by autumn's end, the grasses in the south.
二十四桥明月夜，	Along Bridge Twenty Four bright moonlit nights,
玉人何处教吹箫。	Does jadelike beauty still provide instruction on the flu-te? [2]
《寄扬州韩绰判官》	"To Han Chuo, Magistrate of Yangzhou"
（唐）杜牧	(The Tang Dynasty) Du Mu

40. 一人偶扑地，方爬地复**跌**。乃曰："啐！早知还有此一跌，便不走起来也罢。"

《笑林广记选》（清）游戏主人

Someone stumbled on the floor by chance. As soon as he got up, he again. He regretted, "Blast! If I had known there would be a second fall, I would not have gotten up the first time." [18]

"A Collection of Classic Chinese Jokes" (The Qing Dynasty) You Xi Zhu Ren

41. 细草穿沙雪半销，	Tender grass spouts cover the sands when half of snow is gone,
吴宫烟冷水迢迢。	The mist is cold at the Wu Palace and water flows gently on.
梅花竹里无人见，	From the wintersweet hidden somewhere in the bamboo grove,
一夜吹香过**石**桥。	Wafts of fragrance float past the ________ bridge

all night long. [17]

《除夜自石桥归苕溪》 "Returning from Shihu to Tiaoxi on New Year Eve"
（宋）姜夔 (The Song Dynasty) Jiang Kui

42. **孤**松停翠盖， Like a canopy, a ________ pine towers.
托根临广路。 It struck root on the wayside and there it stood—
不以险自防， Exposed—unaware of the danger ahead.
遂为明所误。 Torch-makers saw in it good resinous wood. [17]
《孤松》 " A Lonely Pine"
（唐）柳宗元 (The Tang Dynasty) Liu Zongyuan

43. 一声声， Pitter-patter, pitter-patter,
一更更， One watch after another.
窗外芭蕉窗里**灯**， Outside banana groves, inside ________ flickering;
此时无限情。 What a medley of felling! [17]
《长相思 · 雨》 Tune: External Longing, "Rain"
（宋）万俟咏 (The Song Dynasty) Wan Siyong

44. 当年**万**里觅封侯， Alone I went ________ miles long, long ago
匹马戍梁州。 To serve the army well at the frontier.
关河梦断何处， The fortress town in dreams I could not go,
尘黯旧貂裘。 Dusty and outworn my sable-coat of cavalier. [1]
《诉衷情》 Tune: Telling of Innermost Feelings
（宋）陆游 (The Song Dynasty) Lu You

45. **万**树寒无色， ________ trees in winter show no beauty of spring,
南枝独有花。 Only plum branches spreading southward are blooming.
香阁流水处， With babbling rivers and steams flows their sweet smell,
影落野人家。 And around a cottage their slender figures dwell. [17]
《早梅》 "Winter Plum Tree Blooming Early"
（明）道源 (The Ming Dynasty) Dao Yuan

46. 醉翁之意不在**酒**，在乎山水之间也。

"醉翁亭记"（宋）欧阳修

The Drunken Greybeard does not aim at ________, but at the splendid scenery. [12]

"The Arbor of the Drunken Greybeard"

(The Song Dynasty) Ouyang Xiu

47. 千古兴亡多少事，　It has seen dynasties fall and rise
悠悠，　As time flies
不尽长江**滚**滚流。　Or as the endless River ________ before my eyes.[1]
《南乡子·登京口北固亭有怀》　Tune: Song of a Southern Country, "Reflection on Ascending the Tower on the Northern Hill at Jingkou"
（宋）辛弃疾　(The Song Dynasty) Xin Qiji

48. 乡**泪**客中尽，　Wandering far away from home my homesick ______ run dry,
孤帆天际看。　Now a lonely traveler, I, gaze at the remote sky with a sigh.[13]
《早寒有怀》　"Thoughts on the Early Cold Weather"
（唐）孟浩然　(The Tang Dynasty) Meng Haoran

49. 清溪一叶舟，　On the clear stream she rows a leaf-like boat,
芙蓉两岸秋。　Lotus blooms spread autumn hue to the shore.
采菱谁家女？　Who is gathering lotus seed, at dusk afloat?
歌声起暮鸥。　She startles gulls with her folklore.
乱云**愁**，　From gloomy clouds ________ is shed,
满头风雨，　Wind and rain overspread,
戴荷叶归去休。　She goes back with a lotus leaf over her head.[5]
《后庭花·秋思》　Tune: Backward Flowers, "Autumn Thoughts"
（元）赵孟頫　(The Yuan Dynasty) Zhao Mengfu

50. 光阴寸隙流如电，　Time flies away as fast as flashing light,
风霜两鬓白如**练**。　Like frosted ________ the hair on our forehead turns white.[5]
《塞鸿秋》　Tune: Autumn Swan on Frontier
（元）薛昂夫　(The Yuan Dynasty) Xue Angfu

参 考 答 案

一、划线字的构成及其在文中的词意

1. 守：会意字，由宀、由寸会意，表示衙门里的事。“寸”表示法度。其意：古代官名。

2. 幽：会意字，从山中有“幺幺”（幽暗）会意。其意：古州名，大致在今河北北部和辽宁南部。

3. 谦：形声字，左形右声。　其意：恭敬别人。

4. 艰（艱）：形声字，左形右声（艮声）。　其意：困难。

5. 江：形声字，左形右声。　其意：水名。

6. 苍：形声字，上形下声。　其意：草的颜色（青色）。

7. 笛：形声字，上形下声。　其意：七孔竹管乐器。

8. 寄：形声字，上形下声。　其意：托付。

9. 刀：象形字。其意：用以切、割、砍、削的工具。

10. 残：形声字，左形右声。　其意：不完整的，剩余的。

11. 平：会意字，由亏，由八会意。“八”表示分均。　其意：安定。

12. 徐：形声字，左形右声。　其意：缓慢。其本意为安舒地行走。

13. 昨：形声字，左形右声。　其意：时间，泛指过去。这里指昨天。

14. 底：形声字，外形内声。　其意：底子；物体的最下部分。

15. 彻（徹）：会意字，由彳、由攴、由育会意。　其意：穿通。

16. 吟：形声字，左形右声。　其意：声调抑扬的吟咏。

17. 情：形声字，左形右声。　其意：人有所欲求的属于阴的心气。

18. 叹（嘆）：形声字，左形右声。　其意：深深的叹息。

19. 悠：形声字，下形上声。　其意：忧思。

20. 鹿：象形字。　其意：兽名。

21. 俗：形声字，左形右声。　其意：庸俗。

22. 缭：形声字，左形右声。　其意：缠绕。

23. 害：会意字，由宀、由口会意，是说伤害之言，从家中发起。　其意：发生。本意为“伤”。

24. 植：形声字，左形右声。　其意：栽种。

25. 银：形声字，左形右声。　其意：白色的金属。

26. 晚：形声字，左形右声。　其意：日落。

27. 烟：形声字，左形右声。　其意：火燃烧时产生的气状物。

28. 被：形声字，左形右声。 其意：被子。
29. 花：形声字，上形下声。 其意：可供欣赏的植物。
30. 棠：形声字，下形上声。 其意：杜梨。
31. 物：形声字，左形右声。 其意：万物。
32. 骸：形声字，左形右声。 其意：胫骨。
33. 鲜：形声字，左形右声，鱻（shan）省声。 其意：少。
34. 幅：形声字，左形右声。 其意：布帛的宽度。
35. 狂：形声字，左形右声。 其意：无拘束，纵情地。
36. 谢：形声字，左形右声。 其意：姓。
37. 篁：形声字，上形下声。 其意：竹田。
38. 苑：形声字，上形下声。 其意：用来养禽兽的地方。
39. 箫：形声字，上形下声。 其意：长短度等的竹管乐器。
40. 跌：形声字，左形右声。 其意：摔。
41. 销：形声字，左形右声。 其意：熔化金属。
42. 路：形声字，左形右声。 其意：道路。
43. 蕉：形声字，上形下声。 其意：指某些有像芭蕉那样的大叶子的植物。
44. 裘：形声字，下形上声。 其意：皮衣。
45. 落：形声字，上形下声。 其意：树叶脱落。
46. 翁：形声字，下形上声。 其意：年老的男子。其本意是"鸟颈上的毛"。
47. 多：会意字，由重叠的夕子构成。夕的意思是相抽引而无穷尽，所以叫多。
48. 际（際）：形声字，左形右声。 其意：靠边的或分界的地方。
49. 采：会意字，由木、有爪会意。 其意：摘取。
50. 练：形声字，左形右声。 其意：白绢。

二、参考译文

1. great deeds 2. He 3. win 4. also 5. mountains 6. bright 7. tower 8. raft 9. sorrow 10. boat 11. lamb 12. thorough 13. woke 14. interest 15. no longer falls 16. whip 17. nurture 18. saddle 19. veil 20. Deer 21. ink 22. steed 23. sky 24. clouds 25. Where 26. officials 27. pictures 28. painted 29. branches 30. in 31. river 32. thousand 33. for a long time 34. long 35. reds 36. hill 37. play 38. urge 39. waters 40. stumbled 41. stone 42. lonely 43. lamp 44. a thousand 45. other 46. wine 47. rolls 48. tears 49. grief 50. silk

参考文献

[1] 唐宋词一百首［M］. 许渊冲 选译．北京：中国对外翻译出版公司、商务印书馆（香港）有限公司，1990.

[2] 唐诗一百首［M］. 张廷琛，魏博思，选译．北京：中国对外翻译出版公司、商务印书馆（香港）有限公司，1991.

[3]（宋）李昉等编，太平广记选［M］. 张光前，英译．北京：外文出版社，2001.

[4] 乐府［M］. 杨希，今译，杨宪益、戴乃迭，英译．北京：外文出版社，2001.

[5] 元曲三百首［M］. 许渊冲，译．北京：中国对外翻译出版公司，2009.

[6]（明）洪应明，菜根谭［M］. 周文标，译．上海：上海人民出版社，2009.

[7] 楚辞选［M］. 杨宪益，戴乃迭，英译．北京：外文出版社，2010.

[8] 唐宋八大家散文精选［M］. 徐英才，译，上海：上海外语教育出版社，2011.

[9]（汉）许慎撰，思履，说文解字（上、下）［M］. 北京：中国华侨出版社，2013.

[10] 元曲百首［M］. 王宏印，选译．上海：上海外语教育出版社，2013.

[11] 李乐毅．汉字演变 500 例［M］. 北京：北京语言大学出版社，2014.

[12] 中国历代散文译萃（上、下）［M］. 谢百魁，译．北京：中国对外翻译出版公司，2014.

[13] 唐诗三百首［M］. 王福林，注译．南京：东南大学出版社，2015.

[14] 中国古代寓言选［M］. 杨宪益，戴乃迭，英译．北京：外文出版社，2016.

[15] 英译中国现代散文（1~4 册）［M］. 张培基译注．上海：上海外语教育出版社，2016.

[16] 陈梦然．中华经典故事精选［M］. 南昌：江西人民出版社，2016.

[17] 冯修文，李柯，等．中国古典诗词中的传统文化（英文版）［M］. 上海：上海交通大学出版社，2015.

[18] 笑林广记选汇［M］. 郑孝先、袁孝竞，选译．北京：外文出版社，2011.

[19] 明清小品．（林语堂英译诗文选上、中、下）［M］. 北京：外语教学与研究出版社，2015.

[20] 诸子百家．（林语堂英译诗文选），北京：外语教学与研究出版社，2015.

[21] 汉魏六朝诗选［M］. 许渊冲，译．北京：海豚出版社，2015.

[22] 元明清诗［M］. 许渊冲，译．北京：海豚出版社，2015.

[23] 大学、中庸（最新英文全译全注本）［M］. 吴国珍，译注．海峡出版发行集团，福建教育出版社，2015.

[24] 孟子（最新英文全译全注本）［M］. 吴国珍，译注．海峡出版发行集团，福建教育出版社，2015.

[25] 张培基，等．英汉翻译教程［M］. 上海：上海外语教育出版社，1980.

[26] 吕瑞昌，等．汉英翻译教程［M］. 西安：陕西人民出版社，1983.

[27] 包惠南．文化语境与语言翻译［M］. 北京：中国对外翻译出版公司，2001.

[28] 林佩汀．中英对译技巧［M］. 学习出版有限公司，1995.

[29] 郭建中．文化与翻译［M］. 北京：中国对外翻译出版公司，2000.

[30] 庄绎传．英汉翻译教程［M］. 北京：外语教学与研究出版社，1999.

[31] 胡壮麟．英语同义词近义词例解词典［M］. 北京：北京大学出版社，2003.

[32] 高凌．英语易混词语辨析词典［M］. 北京：商务印书馆国际有限公司，2003.